Discover
Las Vegas

Contents

Contents

Discover Las Vegas

This is Las Vegas

It's three in the morning when you spot an Elvis look-alike sauntering by arm-in-arm with a glittering showgirl. A bride in a miniskirted white dress shrieks 'Blackjack!' as a stoic blue-haired granny feeds nickels into a slot machine while tossing back a gin and tonic. It's a surreal, Technicolor-tinged fantasy straight out of the movies – and there's only one place you could be.

Vegas, baby: it's the ultimate escape.

This is the only place you can spend the night partying in ancient Rome, wake up in Egypt and brunch under the Eiffel Tower, watch an erupting volcano at sunset and get married in a pink Cadillac at midnight. Double down with the high rollers, browse couture or tacky souvenirs, sip a neon 3ft-high margarita or a frozen vodka martini from a bar made of ice – it's all here for the taking.

Time is irrelevant in Sin City.

There are no clocks inside casinos, just never-ending buffets, ever-flowing drinks and adrenaline-fueled gaming tables. Almost any desire can be instantly gratified, because the luxe casino resorts stand ready to cater to your every whim 24/7. Emptying your wallet never felt so damn good.

The landscape is a constantly shifting paradox, a volatile cocktail of dueling forces: sophistication and smut, risk and reward, boom and bust.

And that's all part of its charm. Head downtown to explore Vegas' nostalgic beginnings and its cultural renaissance of indie shops and cocktail bars where local culture thrives, then detour off the Strip to find intriguing museums that investigate Vegas' gangster, atomic-fueled past.

So, America's dirty little secret or dream factory?

Vegas is both – and remains a bastion of hangover-inducing weekends for people from all walks of life. You can reinvent yourself a hundred times over, or hide out with your lover in a hotel room for days. It doesn't matter if you play the penny slots or drop a bankroll every night – you'll leave town convinced you've had the time of your life.

> " Emptying your wallet never felt so damn good "

Showgirl outside Golden Gate (p185)

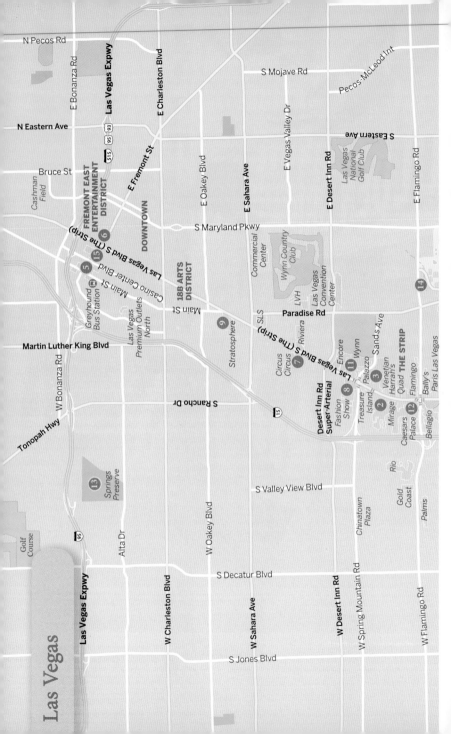

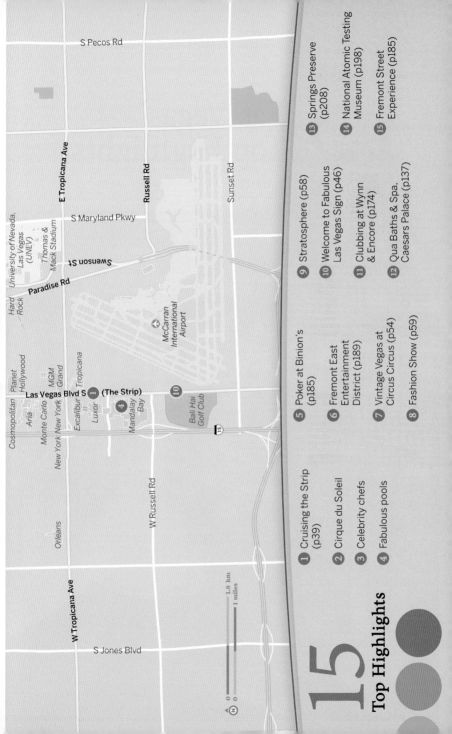

15
Top Highlights

Las Vegas Blvd S (The Strip)

McCarran International Airport

1 Cruising the Strip (p39)

2 Cirque du Soleil

3 Celebrity chefs

4 Fabulous pools

5 Poker at Binion's (p185)

6 Fremont East Entertainment District (p189)

7 Vintage Vegas at Circus Circus (p54)

8 Fashion Show (p59)

9 Stratosphere (p58)

10 Welcome to Fabulous Las Vegas Sign (p46)

11 Clubbing at Wynn & Encore (p174)

12 Qua Baths & Spa, Caesars Palace (p137)

13 Springs Preserve (p208)

14 National Atomic Testing Museum (p198)

15 Fremont Street Experience (p185)

15 Las Vegas' Top Highlights

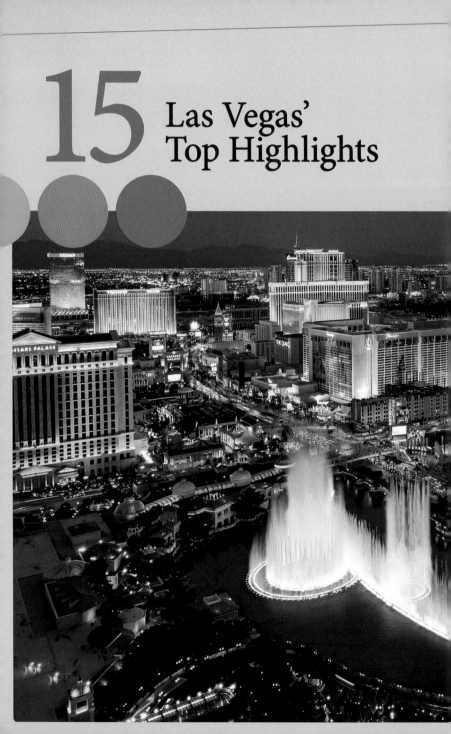

Cruising the Strip (p39)

Rolling into Vegas is a classic experience – play it right and you'll feel like you're moving through a movie set. If you're behind the wheel as a Sin City first-timer, arrive after dark. As you approach the city, pull over and admire the neon glow from afar. Then exit off the interstate and cruise the length of Las Vegas Blvd (aka the Strip), taking in the Luxor's glowing beacon, the soaring Eiffel Tower, the Bellagio's dancing fountains and the Mirage's exploding volcano.

SYLVAIN SONNET/GETTY IMAGES ©

② Cirque du Soleil

Cirque du Soleil is made for Las Vegas. The troupe's eight resident shows on the Strip are the hottest tickets in town. Whimsical costumes, aerial acrobatics and artful synchronized swimming create an electrifying, heart-pounding atmosphere. Splash out on the original aquatic spectacular *O* (p128) the martial-arts-inspired *Kà* (p91), the musically themed *Beatles LOVE* (p145) or *Michael Jackson ONE* (p68). For avant-garde circus antics, choose *Mystère* (p152) or *Zarkana* (p102). Cirque du Soleil's *Beatles LOVE*

Celebrity Chefs

Celebrity chefs still dominate the cuisine scene on the Strip, especially at the elegant Venetian and Palazzo. Heavy-hitting dining rooms at those sister resorts include Napa Valley wunderkind Thomas Keller's bistro, Bouchon; LA trendsetter Wolfgang Puck's Cut steakhouse; TV personality Emeril Lagasse's Table 10 and Delmonico Steakhouse; and a bounty of eateries by Italian culinary expert Mario Batali and winemaker Joe Bastianich, including Carnevino steakhouse, Otto Enoteca Pizzeria and casual B&B Burger and Beer. Only a few other Strip casino resorts can compete with such a star-studded line-up.

Tapas, Julian Serrano (p108)

The Best...
Replica Architecture

CAESARS PALACE
Vegas' own mini Colosseum with Roman statuary. (p131)

LUXOR
An Egyptian-esque pyramid and giant sphinx. (p71)

NEW YORK–NEW YORK
Modeling the Empire State Building and Statue of Liberty. (p77)

PARIS LAS VEGAS
Three words: Eiffel Tower Experience. (p116)

VENETIAN
Grand canals, a towering campanile and St Mark's Sq. (p155)

The Best...
Pool Parties

WET REPUBLIC
Bathing beauties, rockin'
DJs and pitchers of
mojitos. (p90)

ENCORE BEACH CLUB
Laze by white lilypads while
famous-name DJs spin
electronica. (p174)

REHAB
A-list celebs and rock stars
hang poolside on week-
ends at the Hard Rock.
(p204)

MARQUEE
Splash and groove on a
rooftop pool deck over-
looking the Strip. (p102)

VENUS
Adults-only topless pool
lounge with mod chaise
lounges and palm trees.
(p136)

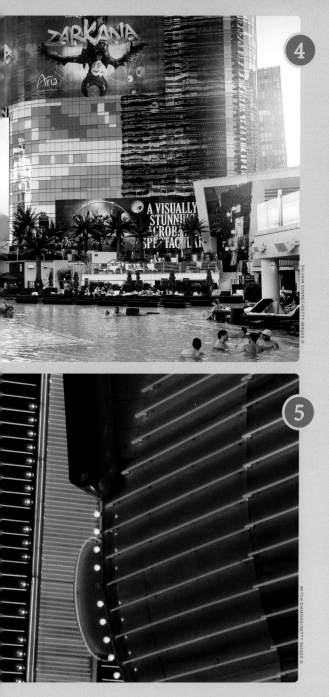

Fabulous pools

4

In the race for the best hotel swimming pool in Las Vegas, the complex at Mandalay Bay (p62) wins, hands down. 'M-Bay' features 2700 tons of imported southern Californian sand and 6ft-high artificial waves where surfing competitions happen in summer. Float on a 'lazy river,' hit the beachside casino or catch a summer concert under the stars. Other contenders include the MGM Grand's waterfalls with another lazy river (p86), the Hard Rock's swim-up blackjack (p204) and the Golden Nugget's shark-tank waterslide (p190). Swimming pool, Cosmopolitan (p99)

SYLVAIN SONNET/GETTY IMAGES ©

Poker at Binion's (p185)

5

Texas hold'em didn't come to Las Vegas until 1963 when Texan Felton 'Corky' McCorquodale introduced it at the long-departed California Club casino. It quickly became the game of choice among poker pros, because its structure allowed a good player to risk a relatively small amount of money to win potentially enormous pots. Where better to try your luck today than downtown on Fremont St at Binion's casino, where the World Series of Poker was born?

MITCH DIAMOND/GETTY IMAGES ©

Fremont East Entertainment District (p189)

Head downtown for a few cocktails at hip local watering holes. This buzzing nightlife enclave is anchored by the Beauty Bar, a converted '60s-era beauty salon where live bands rock; Griffin, a fireplace-lit bohemian dive; Downtown Cocktail Room, a speakeasy lounge; and Commonwealth, a double-decker Prohibition-style saloon with a rooftop patio. It's a magnet for the art crowd on First Fridays. Fremont St

SYLVAIN SONNET/GETTY IMAGES ©

MITCHELL FUNK/GETTY IMAGES ©

Vintage Vegas at Circus Circus (p54)

As if Vegas was ashamed of its sordid but fascinating history, old-school casinos are being demolished at a frenetic pace and the heyday of outrageous theme hotels is almost over. This is precisely why a trip to a hold-out like Circus Circus is so satisfying. One million vintage bulbs illuminate the entry to this campy casino with low-roller tables, a classic steakhouse, carnival and arcade games and free circus acts suspended high above the casino floor. Scout out more vintage Vegas gems downtown on Fremont St.

Fashion Show (p59)

The striking facade of this fashionista favorite is an eye-catcher – from far away, it looks as if a UFO has landed on Las Vegas Blvd. Inside, the shopping center's offerings are fairly standard chains and department stores, but with a Sin City twist. British import Topshop, for example, carries a Vegas-specific accessories collection, just in case you'd like to hit the casinos with an English-style fascinator in the form of a red sequined queen of hearts.

The Best...
Only-in-Vegas Shops

GAMBLERS GENERAL STORE
Poker chips, slot machines and gambling souvenirs galore. (p193)

RAINBOW FEATHER DYEING CO
Showgirl feather boas in every color of the rainbow. (p194)

BONANZA GIFT SHOP
Self-proclaimed 'largest gift shop in the world' is a kingdom of kitsch. (p59)

WILLIAMS COSTUME COMPANY
Elvis jumpsuits for hire year-round, not just for Halloween. (p195)

Stratosphere (p58)

Soaring at the north end of the Strip, this three-legged tower is the tallest of its kind in the USA. There's no better place to get a bird's-eye perspective on Las Vegas than from this glitzy neon metropolis springing up like a mirage in the middle of the Mojave Desert. Ride the country's fastest elevators up to the observation deck at sunset or for a cocktail in the slowly revolving lounge. Nighttime is best for the biggest scares on the tower's thrill rides, or do a SkyJump freefall into thin air.

The Best...
Hip Hotels

COSMOPOLITAN
Chic suites for moneyed hipsters. (p96)

ARIA
High contemporary design and public art. (p101)

DELANO
A South Beach twist at Mandalay Bay. (p65)

PALMS PLACE
Sophisticated condos at the Palms. (p215)

HARD ROCK
Made for rock 'n' roll royalty. (p204)

ALAN BAXTER/GETTY IMAGES ©

Welcome to Fabulous Las Vegas Sign (p46)

If the Luxor's striking beacon or the shape of the Eiffel Tower on the skyline weren't enough to warn you, this classic road sign – wishing you a warm 'Welcome to Fabulous Las Vegas Nevada' – confirms you have officially arrived. The iconic landmark, designed by Betty Willis in the 1950s, inspires frequent U-turns and obligatory photo ops. As you leave town with empty pockets and a possible hangover, the flip side of the same sign cheerfully reminds you to 'Come Back Soon.'

LEE PETTET/GETTY IMAGES ©

Clubbing at Wynn & Encore (p174)

Count on casino impresario Steve Wynn to dream up the next big thing on the Strip's nightlife scene. His eponymous resort is where gorgeous Tryst nightclub awaits with a waterfall – the mist cools you off after you've worked up a sweat on the dance floor. A glam crowd gathers behind the red-velvet ropes next door at Wynn's Encore resort, where XS reigns at the top of the Vegas club scene, followed closely by Surrender ultra lounge, both poolside party spots where jet-set DJs star.

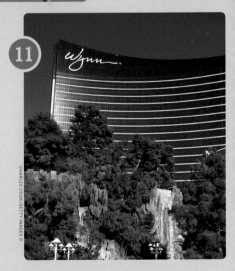

CHARLES COOK/GETTY IMAGES ©

MITCH DIAMOND/GETTY IMAGES ©

12

Qua Baths & Spa, Caesars Palace (p137)

Indulge in bodily bliss at a modern oasis with an ancient Roman twist. Qua Baths & Spa inside Caesars Palace has everything your body craves and more. Sweat out a hangover inside the cedar sauna. Take a dip in the Roman baths. Chill in the arctic room, where dry-ice snowflakes fall. Recline in the exotic tea lounge, just made for socializing. Over in the Men's Zone, guys can get an expert shave or have their muscles kneaded while watching the big game.

RICHARD CUMMINS/GETTY IMAGES ©

13

National Atomic Testing Museum (p198)

Recalling an era when the word atomic meant modernity and mystery, the Smithsonian-affiliated National Atomic Testing Museum is testament to the period in US history when the fantastical (and destructive) power of nuclear energy was tested just outside Las Vegas. It's almost possible to imagine 1950s gamblers and tourists picnicking on downtown casino rooftops while mushroom clouds rose on the horizon. Step down into the deafening Ground Zero Theater, which mimics a concrete test bunker.

Springs Preserve (p208)

Detour from the Strip for a breath of fresh air and a fix of ecoconscious design at the Springs Preserve. This educational museum complex is situated on the site where natural springs once fed *las vegas* (Spanish for 'the meadows'), and southern Paiutes and Old Spanish Trail traders set up camp. Family-oriented attractions include the Origen Museum, Nevada State Museum and Desert Living Center, plus hiking trails, wildlife viewing, botanic gardens, a healthy-living cafe and a weekly farmers market. Solar-powered parking lot, Springs Preserve

14

The Best...
Museums & Galleries

MOB MUSEUM
Trace the growth of organized crime in America. (p182)

ATOMIC TESTING MUSEUM
A throwback to Sin City's bomb-happy heyday. (p198)

ORIGEN MUSEUM
Dynamic natural and cultural history exhibits at the Springs Preserve. (p209)

BELLAGIO GALLERY OF FINE ART
Petite but sophisticated museum-quality art exhibits. (p125)

BURLESQUE HALL OF FAME
Play peek-a-boo with the art of the striptease. (p187)

The Best...
Free Shows

FOUNTAINS OF BELLAGIO
Dramatically dancing jets, as seen in *Ocean's Eleven*. (p124)

MIRAGE VOLCANO
The faux Polynesian eruption heard round the Strip. (p142)

CIRCUS CIRCUS
Trapeze acts and acrobats perform over the casino floor. (p54)

FREMONT STREET EXPERIENCE
A chaotic canopy of light and sound downtown after dark. (p185)

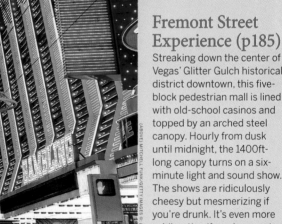

Fremont Street Experience (p185)

Streaking down the center of Vegas' Glitter Gulch historical district downtown, this five-block pedestrian mall is lined with old-school casinos and topped by an arched steel canopy. Hourly from dusk until midnight, the 1400ft-long canopy turns on a six-minute light and sound show. The shows are ridiculously cheesy but mesmerizing if you're drunk. It's even more exhilarating if you happen to be zooming by on the zipline cables attached to the 12-story Slotzilla, a slot-machine-themed platform at the mall's eastern end.

Top Days in
Las Vegas

Best of the Strip

If you only have 24 hours in Las Vegas, stay on the beaten path, stepping into Sin City's most classic casino megaresorts. Work your way north along the Strip, strolling through mini versions of New York and Venice and dining in a faux Parisian bistro.

DAY 1

① Mandalay Bay (p61)

The Strip starts here. Venture into the walk-through Shark Reef Aquarium, then ride the glass elevator to rooftop Mix Lounge for staggering views over Sin City.

MANDALAY BAY ❍ NEW YORK–NEW YORK
🚋 Catch the free tram north to Excalibur, then take the skybridge over Tropicana Ave.

② New York–New York (p77)

Walk the Brooklyn Bridge, gaze at the Statue of Liberty and ride the Coney Island–style roller coaster.

NEW YORK–NEW YORK ❍ PARIS LAS VEGAS
🚌 Ride the Deuce bus north to Paris Las Vegas.

③ Lunch at Paris Las Vegas (p113)

Stop for a *croque madame* and *pommes frites* at Mon Ami Gabi, then ascend to the top of the Strip's Eiffel Tower Experience.

PARIS LAS VEGAS ❍ BELLAGIO
🏃 Walk north to Flamingo Rd, then cross the skybridge over Las Vegas Blvd to Bellagio.

④ Bellagio (p121)

Admire the glass flowers on the lobby ceiling and visit the conservatory before catching the Fountains of Bellagio show.

BELLAGIO ❍ CAESARS PALACE
🏃 Take the skybridge north over Flamingo Rd.

⑤ Caesars Palace (p131)

Grab a boozy lemonade from the Spanish Steps, outdoors. After ogling statuary and ceiling frescoes in the colossal casino, strut through the luxe Forum Shops.

CAESARS PALACE ❍ MIRAGE
🏃 Walk north along the Strip to the Mirage.

⑥ Mirage (p139)

Gawk at the exploding volcano before being mesmerized by the 20,000-gallon aquarium in the hotel lobby and the casino's rainforest atrium.

MIRAGE ❍ VENETIAN & PALAZZO
🏃 Walk east over a skybridge to the Venetian.

⑦ Venetian & Palazzo (p155)

Soak up the charm of Vegas' Little Italy aboard a gondola. Afterward, treat yourself to gelato in bustling St Mark's Square.

Paris Las Vegas (p113)
SYLVAIN SONNET/GETTY IMAGES ©

Doing Downtown

So you prefer old-school casinos, vintage neon signs and dive bars to celebrity chefs and clubbing? No problem. Leave the Strip behind to explore Sin City's origins in historic 'Glitter Gulch' along Fremont St, then hang out with the locals in newly emerging downtown 'hoods.

❶ Fremont Street Experience (p185)

Revel in the low-roller carpet joints, free sound-and-light canopy shows and zip-liners whooshing overhead. Don't miss the restored neon signs inside the Neonopolis and outside on N 3rd St.

FREMONT ST ➡ MOB MUSEUM

🚶 Walk two blocks up N 3rd St to Stewart Ave.

❷ Mob Museum (p182)

Step inside a 1930s federal courthouse to learn about the ultimate cops-and-robbers showdown – law enforcement vs the American mafia – and how it shaped Sin City.

MOB MUSEUM ➡ NEON MUSEUM

🚌 Walk east to Las Vegas Blvd. Catch bus 113 north to the Neon Museum.

❸ Neon Museum (p184)

When old-school casinos get imploded, some fantastical signs go to this non-profit museum's 'neon boneyard.' Reserve guided tours in advance.

NEON MUSEUM ➡ ARTS FACTORY

🚌 From the opposite side of Las Vegas Blvd, catch bus 113 southbound. At downtown's Bonneville Transit Center, transfer to bus 206.

❹ Arts Factory (p187)

The vibrant hub of downtown's 18b Arts District is this gallery and workshop space, which comes alive on First Fridays. If you're hungry, head for Bar + Bistro, which dishes up Latin American fusion food in arty environs.

ARTS FACTORY ➡ BURLESQUE HALL OF FAME

🚌 From Casino Center Blvd, catch the Deuce bus north to Fremont St. Walk one block east of Las Vegas Blvd.

❺ Burlesque Hall of Fame (p187)

Inside the Emergency Arts complex, attached to the Beat coffeehouse and record shop, this two-room gallery has eye-popping photo exhibits on the sultry art and history of burlesque dancing.

BURLESQUE HALL OF FAME ➡ CONTAINER PARK

🚶 Walk one block east along Fremont St.

❻ Container Park (p193)

At this urban park, indie fashion and jewelry shops, art galleries and pop-up eateries and bars are piled on top of one another inside industrial containers connected by catwalks. After 9pm, it's adults-only.

CONTAINER PARK ➡ FREMONT EAST ENTERTAINMENT DISTRICT

🚶 Backtrack one block west on Fremont St.

❼ Fremont East Entertainment District (p189)

Finish the evening with a libation at the speakeasy-style Downtown Cocktail Room), inside the hipster-haven Beauty Bar, at Insert Coin(s) video arcade or on the rooftop patio at Prohibition-era-inspired Commonwealth.

Style in Sin City

Vegas isn't all smoky casinos and themed hotels. Hipsters and high-design fans have a place here too, from the public art collection at CityCenter – the Strip's latest architectural landmark – to the fashionable shopping, bars, shows and nightlife found elsewhere on the Strip, downtown and beyond.

① CityCenter (p93)

Aria casino resort is an architectural show-piece with strikingly designed restaurants and a fabulous public art collection – check out the massive silver sculpture behind the front desk. Next door, Crystals shopping center is another futuristic space with a three-story indoor treehouse.

CITYCENTER ➲ COSMOPOLITAN

🏃 Walk north along the Strip to Cosmopolitan.

② Cosmopolitan (p96)

If you're a cool hunter or a young jetsetter, the Cosmo is where it's at. Amble around the hip casino hotel, with its larger-than-life stiletto heel sculptures and art-supplying vending machines. Have a cocktail at the triple-story Chandelier Bar.

COSMOPOLITAN ➲ PALAZZO

🚌 Cross Las Vegas Blvd on a skybridge, then catch the Deuce bus north to Palazzo.

③ Palazzo (p155)

The Venetian's sister hotel is even more trendsetting than the original. After window shopping at the Grand Canal Shoppes, take a break and sip a glass of Italian wine on the Strip-side terrace at Lavo.

PALAZZO ➲ WYNN

🏃 Walk north across a skybridge to Wynn.

④ Wynn (p168)

This classy casino resort is magnate Steve Wynn's signature showpiece. Stroll through the gorgeous flower-bedecked atrium and gaze out at the Lake of Dreams from the patio of whimsical Parasol Down cocktail bar.

WYNN ➲ ENCORE

🏃 Walk through the Wynn resort to Encore.

⑤ Encore (p168)

The Wynn's younger sister houses more fashion-forward attractions, starting with its shopping promenade. Dine at modish Andrea's or arty Botero steakhouse, then check for last-minute tickets to the aquatic extravaganza *Le Rêve – The Dream*.

ENCORE ➲ GOLDEN NUGGET

🚌 Catch the Deuce or SDX express bus north to downtown.

⑥ Golden Nugget (p190)

Downtown Vegas may be old-school, but the Golden Nugget caters to a younger, more stylish clientele than its Fremont St neighbors. A small swimming pool packs a big punch: spy the waterslide spiraling inside a glass-enclosed shark tank.

GOLDEN NUGGET ➲ HARD ROCK

🚕 Take a taxi (about $20) to the Hard Rock casino hotel.

⑦ Hard Rock (p190)

Finish the night with the SoCal rock 'n' roll crowd at the Hard Rock casino hotel, east of the Strip. Admire the museum-worthy collection of music memorabilia before chowing down at Culinary Dropout and catching a live music show at the Joint concert hall or Vinyl (p203) acoustic lounge.

Crystals (p103), designed by architect Daniel Libeskind
RICHARD CUMMINS/GETTY IMAGES ©

Get Out of Town

When the Vegas hype wears you down, escape into the rugged desert to see one of the world's tallest dams, historic Hoover Dam. It's a quick drive away from Lake Mead, a haven for water-sports enthusiasts, birders and hikers.

① Hoover Dam (p221)

Get an early start from Las Vegas to visit this landmark New Deal project on the Colorado River, completed by thousands of workers in 1936. A memorial nearby pays tribute to the many lives lost while construction was underway.

LAS VEGAS ⊙ HOOVER DAM

🚗 From the Strip, it's about a 45-minute drive. Take I-15 south to I-215 east. Continue to I-515/US 93 & 95, then follow US 93 east of Boulder City. Walk to the dam visitor center from the parking garage ($10).

② Visitor Center (p221)

Beginning inside the visitor center, guided tours give you a chance to ride an elevator more than 50 stories down to see the dam's gigantic power generators. It'll cost you to take the one-hour tour, but engineers and history buffs won't want to miss it.

VISITOR CENTER ⊙ MIKE O'CALLAGHAN–PAT TILLMAN MEMORIAL BRIDGE

🚗 Drive to the free parking lot designated for bridge access, then make the short but steep climb up to the bridge's pedestrian walkway.

③ Mike O'Callaghan–Pat Tillman Memorial Bridge (p222)

Drink in stunning views of the Hoover Dam from this soaring bridge dedicated to Mike

O'Callaghan, a former Nevada mayor, and Pat Tillman, a US football star killed by friendly fire in Afghanistan in 2004. Hold on to the railing when it's windy – this isn't for anyone with a fear of heights.

MIKE O'CALLAGHAN–PAT TILLMAN MEMORIAL BRIDGE ⊙ LAKE MEAD

🚗 Backtrack around 4 miles west on US 93, turning right onto Lakeshore Rd, which enters Lake Mead National Recreation Area.

④ Lake Mead National Recreation Area (p223)

Hiking, birding and water sports such as swimming, fishing, boating, kayaking and stand-up paddle boarding abound at this outdoor playground. It's most popular with locals who need to get away from it all, especially on weekends.

LAKE MEAD ⊙ BOULDER CITY

🚗 Get back on US 93 and head west into Boulder City. Turn left on Nevada Way and left again onto Arizona St.

⑤ Hoover Dam Museum & Boulder City (p222)

This small but interesting museum is located at the Boulder Dam Hotel, where Franklin D Roosevelt and Howard Hughes once slept. After viewing the interactive historical exhibits, stroll around downtown Boulder City, a refreshingly casino-free town that sprang up in the early 1930s to house workers building the dam.

Hoover Dam (p221)
JENNIFER SHARP/GETTY IMAGES ©

Month by Month

February

Chinese New Year
Celebrate the Chinese lunar new year, which falls between late January and mid-February, with festivities at Chinatown Plaza (www.lvchinatown.com) showcasing Chinese acrobats, lion dancers and martial-arts demonstrations; Japanese *taiko* drumming; and pan-Asian folk dancing and food.

Super Bowl Weekend
The busiest time of the year for casinos' sports books happens on the first Sunday in February, when the National Football League (NFL) championship game is broadcast.

March

Nascar Weekend
Rabid stock-car racing fans descend upon the 1.5-mile 'superspeedway' and the dirt track at the Las Vegas Motor Speedway (www.lvms.com), aka the 'Diamond in the Desert,' in early to mid-March.

Las Vegas Restaurant Week
Usually in mid-March, top-shelf restaurants and superstar chefs set showy three-course meals at steeply discounted prices to benefit a nonprofit stop-hunger organization (www.helpoutdineoutlv.org).

St Patrick's Day
On March 17, look for an Irish-green tint to the beer flowing from downtown Vegas casinos, which host a rowdy party on Fremont St. Back on the Strip, New York–New York's Nine Fine Irishmen (p81) pub stages a Celtic Feis festival.

April

Viva Las Vegas
The ultimate rockabilly weekend (www.vivalasvegas.net) happens at the Rio (p16) casino, just west of the Strip, in mid-April. Grease back your hair, fellas, and put on your best pinup dresses, gals, for pool parties, rockin' bands, jive dancing, burlesque competitions and souped-up classic car shows.

May

Cinco de Mayo
Celebrations around town advertise Latin American entertainers, including mariachi bands, *ballet folklorico* (folk dances) and, if you're lucky, *lucha libre* (Mexican stunt wrestling).

Vegas Uncork'd
Rub shoulders with top chefs such as Joël Robuchon, Michael Mina and

Nobu Matsuhisa at this gourmands' culinary gathering in mid-May, with sommelier-led wine tastings, grand dinners and cooking demos.

✈ Helldorado Days

Dating back to the 1930s, this historical five-day hoedown features rodeo events, barbecues, country fiddlers and a cowboy parade downtown (www.elkshelldorado.com).

June

⭐ Electric Daisy Carnival

Three blow-out nights of DJs and live acts bring huge crowds of EDM (electronic dance music) fans to party from dusk till dawn at the Las Vegas Motor Speedway (http://electricdaisycarnival.com).

July

✈ World Series of Poker

High-stakes gamblers, casino employees and celebrities face off in more than 40 tournaments running from late May through mid-July (www.worldseriesofpoker.com). The 10-day Texas hold'em main event earns the winner a cool $8.5 million.

☣ Fourth of July

On this national holiday expect spectacular fireworks after dark on the Strip, a hot lineup of live music and DJs at nightclubs and casinos, sizzling hot sidewalks and melting yard-long margaritas.

August

☣ Def Con

The nation's largest conclave of computer hackers takes place during a long, heavily caffeinated weekend in late July or early to mid-August, with cutting-edge techie tools, guest speakers and book signings (www.defcon.org).

October

✈ Las Vegas BikeFest

The city's largest bike rally brings hogs and heifers, motorcycle-riding poker players and Harley-Davidson fans roaring into town in early October. Barbecues, bikinis, arm wrestling and 'Artistry in Iron' bike-building competitions are all part of the debauchery (www.lasvegasbikefest.com).

☣ Halloween

Haunted houses, masquerade and fetish-fantasy balls, ghoulish outdoor bashes and fantastic freak fests make spending October 31 in Las Vegas a cool idea, especially given the costume-rental options – Elvis in a sequined white jumpsuit, anyone?

November

◉ Aviation Nation

Witness one of the USA's biggest air shows for free in early November, when the USAF Thunderbirds streak through the skies over Nellis Air Force Base. Peruse more than 100 civilian and high-tech military aircraft parked on display.

December

✈ National Finals Rodeo

This hugely popular 10-day event (www.nfrexperience.com) in early to mid-December features top rodeo performers competing in high-stakes steer wrestling, bull riding and more. See Las Vegas get taken over by real cowboys, especially downtown on Fremont St.

☣ New Year's Eve

The Strip becomes a huge party scene as thousands turn out to hear headliner bands and watch fireworks – naturally, fights break out, people faint and everyone drinks too much. Festivities stretch along Las Vegas Blvd and downtown's Fremont Street Experience.

What's New

For this new edition of Discover Las Vegas, our authors hunted down the fresh, the transformed, the hot and the happening. Here are a few of our favorites. For up-to-the-minute recommendations, see lonelyplanet.com/las-vegas.

1 LINQ
On the Strip, just north of Flamingo Rd, this $550-million shopping, dining and entertainment complex has turned heads, and not just for its High Roller – the world's tallest observation wheel, which revolves in the desert sky above Las Vegas Blvd. Hang out and hear indie bands at Brooklyn Bowl, ride the mechanical bull at Chayo's restaurant and tequila bar, then print the perfect Vegas selfie at Polaroid Fotobar. (p44)

2 THE STRIP'S NEW CASINO HOTELS
Adios to the Imperial Palace, Bill's Gamblin' Hall & Saloon and the Sahara. Say hello to the Quad, the boutique Cromwell and the luxury SLS casino hotels, the latter two are opening in 2014. (p51)

3 NOBU
Chef Matsuhisa has brought his brand to Caesars Palace, not only with a signature restaurant but also a boutique hotel where you can have sushi for breakfast in bed. (p135)

4 MGM GRAND RENOVATION
Out with the old, in with the new: plushly redone hotel rooms, sociable bars and dining spaces, and flashy Hakkasan, a combination Chinese restaurant and hot nightclub. (p85)

5 MONTE CARLO & NEW YORK–NEW YORK
The Strip-facing fronts of these two casino hotels are evolving with new, fun-loving bars and eateries (p47; p77).

6 VOODOO ZIPLINE
Suspended sky-high between two hotel towers, the Rio's daring rooftop zipline whisks tandem riders across at more than 30mph. (p216)

7 FREMONT EAST ENTERTAINMENT DISTRICT
Bars, clubs, theaters, art galleries and cafes are blooming in this local nightlife hotspot that's been drawing in-the-know crowds for years. (p189)

8 CONTAINER PARK
Downtown's revitalization project just keeps rolling along, most recently with the addition of this open-air incubator for indie boutique shops, bars and eateries. (p193)

9 SLOTZILLA
Thrill-seekers zoom over pedestrians' heads and neon lights on this zipline suspended from a 12-story slot-machine-themed platform downtown at the Fremont Street Experience. (p185)

10 DOWNTOWN GRAND
The reborn Lady Luck has made a splash on downtown's casino scene, with spiffy rooms, a rooftop pool and arty bars. (186)

11 VEGAS STREATS
On the second Saturday night of each month, local food trucks, graffiti artists, live bands and DJs converge on Fremont St. (p188)

Get Inspired

Books

● **Fear and Loathing in Las Vegas** (Hunter S Thompson) The gonzo journalist's classic was later turned into film gold.

● **The Money and the Power: The Making of Las Vegas and Its Hold on America** (Sally Denton & Roger Morris) A lyrical, haunting investigation of the city's underbelly.

● **Baringing Down the House** (Ben Mezrich) In the early 1990s, six university students counted cards and stole millions playing blackjack.

● **The Green Felt Jungle** (Ed Reid & Ovid Demaris) 1960s exposé uncovering corruption in Sin City's gangster era.

Films

● **Casino** (1995) Master filmmaker Martin Scorsese delves into Vegas' mobster wars.

● **The Hangover** (2009) In this zany comedy, bachelor partygoers try to make what happened in Vegas *stay* in Vegas.

● **Bugsy** (1991) Warren Beatty and Annette Bening bring to life the first Flamingo.

● **Leaving Las Vegas** (1995) A merciless story of a desperate alcoholic and a damaged prostitute.

Music

● **Luck Be a Lady** (Frank Sinatra) Bellagio's fountains dance to this Sinatra classic.

● **The Rat Pack: Live at the Sands** (Frank Sinatra, Dean Martin & Sammy Davis Jr) Relive Vegas' mid-20th-century heyday.

● **I've Got You under My Skin** (Keely Smith & Louis Prima) Sung at the Sahara in the 'Fabulous Fifties.'

● **When I Go to Vegas** (Calvin Harris) EDM anthem for road trippers.

Websites

● **Vegas.com** (www.vegas.com) Overview with reviews and information.

● **Las Vegas Weekly** (www.lasvegasweekly.com) Events and shows.

● **Classic Las Vegas** (www.classicvegas.com) Insider's guide to old-school haunts.

● **Las Vegas: An Unconventional History** (www.pbs.org/wgbh/amex/lasvegas) Companion to an intriguing PBS documentary.

Short on time?

This list will give you an instant insight into Vegas.

Read In 2002's *Neon Metropolis: How Las Vegas Started the Twenty-First Century*, Hal Rothman deconstructs Sin City's spectacular successes and failures.

Watch Steven Soderbergh's 2001 remake of the Rat Pack classic *Ocean's Eleven* sees a star-studded Hollywood cast plot to cheat a string of casinos.

Listen Elvis Presley's playful *Viva Las Vegas* is right on the vintage money.

Log on VegasChatter (www.vegaschatter.com) has the latest rumors and news.

Fountains of Bellagio (p124)
MITCHELL FUNK/GETTY IMAGES ©

Need to Know

Currency

US dollar ($)

Language

English

Visas

Not usually required for citizens of Canada or of the 37 Visa Waiver Program countries with ESTA pre-authorization.

Money

ATM transaction fees inside casino gaming areas are high. Credit cards are widely accepted.

Cell Phones

Must be a multiband GSM model. Buy a prepaid rechargeable SIM card. Cell phones are prohibited in casino race and sports books.

Time

Pacific Standard Time (GMT/UTC minus eight hours)

Wi-Fi

Most casino hotels charge a fee of up to $15 per 24 hours (sometimes only wired access available). Free wi-fi hot spots are more common off-Strip.

Tipping

Tipping is expected, not optional.

For more information, see Survival Guide (p259).

When to Go

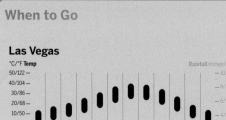

Las Vegas

The question really is when not to go? Most production shows are 'dark' the week before Christmas. Otherwise, the city slows down only slightly during the rainy winter doldrums (November to February) and the dog days of summer (June to August).

Advance Planning

One month before Book flights, a hotel and a rental car if you'll be taking any trips out of town.

Three weeks before Score tickets for production shows, mega-concerts or headliner events.

One week before Book a table at a happening chef's restaurant or sign up for an outdoor adventure tour.

One day before Reconfirm all reservations then get some extra sleep – you'll need it!

Daily Costs

Budget Less than $100

- Downtown casino hotel room on a weekday: $35–90
- Food-court and fast-food meals: $6–12
- 24-hour Deuce & SDX bus pass: $8

Midrange $100–250

- Standard Strip casino hotel room on a weekday: $65–150
- Discounted tickets to a production show: $30–90
- Meal at a casual sit-down restaurant: $20–45
- Three-day monorail pass: $28

Top End More than $250

- Suite at a luxury Strip megaresort: from $200
- VIP tickets to production shows: from $125
- Spa treatments: $75–300
- Taxi between Strip and downtown: $20–25 one-way, plus tip

Arriving in Las Vegas

○ **McCarran International Airport** Shuttle buses run to Strip hotels from $7 one-way, and from $9 to downtown and off-Strip hotels. You'll pay at least $20 plus tip for a taxi to the Strip – tell your driver to use surface streets, not the I-15 Fwy airport connector tunnel ('long-hauling').

○ **Greyhound Terminal** If you're arriving in Vegas via long-distance bus, you'll disembark at a downtown station just off the Fremont Street Experience. To reach the Strip, catch a southbound SDX bus (two-hour pass $6).

○ **Driving into Vegas** Most travelers approach the Strip (Las Vegas Blvd) off the I-15 Fwy. Try to avoid exiting onto busy Flamingo Rd; opt for quieter Tropicana Ave or Spring Mountain Rd.

Getting Around

○ **Bus** Two routes run 24/7 between the Strip and downtown: the double-decker Deuce, which stops more frequently, and the speedier SDX. A 24-hour pass for both is $8.

○ **Car** Though navigating the Strip can be stressful, especially on weekends and at night, self-parking is free almost everywhere. If you're driving between the Strip and downtown, avoid the freeways during rush hours.

○ **Monorail** The monorail links casinos on the east side of the Strip, which is handy if you happen to be staying in one of them, and the city's convention center. Trains run daily until midnight or later. A single-ride ticket is $5.

○ **Taxi** It's illegal to hail a taxi in the street. Cabs queue outside casinos, hotels and malls. Most rides around town cost $15 to $25 plus tip.

Sleeping

With more than 150,000 hotel rooms in Vegas, prices fluctuate according to the season and special events, how many conventions are happening and whether it's a weekday or weekend. For the best deals, book several weeks ahead, then recheck a few days before your trip to see if rates have dropped.

Budget travelers base themselves off-Strip or downtown, though you can sometimes score deals at less fancy Strip casino hotels. Couples and families find good-value rooms at the Strip's classic casino hotels. If money's no object or you're staying with a few friends, splurge on an over-the-top suite at a luxe casino resort.

Useful Websites

○ **Lonely Planet** (www.lonelyplanet.com/hotels) Book hotels and other accommodations.

○ **Travelzoo** (www.travelzoo.com) For discount hotel deals.

○ **Priceline** (www.priceline.com) Lets you bid or 'express' buy your hotel room for less.

○ **Travelworm** (www.travelworm.com) Comprehensive hotel listings and promo offers.

What to Bring

○ **Classy clothes** A dress code (collared shirts for men, and no athletic wear or hats) is enforced at some top nightclubs and restaurants.

○ **Comfortable shoes** If you want to explore the Strip, wear something supportive.

○ **Aspirin or ibuprofen** For hangovers.

Be Forewarned

○ **Smoking** If cigarette smoke bothers you, steer clear of older casinos and gamble at the airier Wynn/Encore, Venetian/Palazzo or Bellagio.

○ **Sex workers** Prostitution is illegal in Clark County, but escorts, call girls and working girls are part of Sin City's high-rolling culture.

○ **Downtown** Away from the Fremont Street Experience, keep your wits about you.

○ **Resort fees** Think you scored a deal on your hotel room? Most hotels add mandatory daily 'resort fees' of $10 to $30, which may cover internet access and fitness-center entry, or nothing much at all. Some also charge $10 for phone reservations.

Walking the Strip

The Strip runs for miles: don't assume you can easily walk from point A to B. Consult a map first and note that pedestrian crossings are punctuated with skybridges and escalators. Take advantage of free trams between casinos whenever possible.

The Strip

Baby, this is where it's at... The Strip, a 4.5-mile stretch of Las Vegas Blvd lined with hulking casino hotels and megaresorts, is so hypnotizing that few visitors venture beyond it. But the famous boulevard is always changing.

The themed casinos built on Las Vegas Blvd in the last half of the 20th century drove home the idea that bigger is better. In 1989 Steve Wynn opened the Mirage, with its erupting volcano and 20,000-gallon tropical aquarium. Other spectacular resorts soon followed, and many classic casinos were abandoned and imploded. In 2005 Wynn reset the Strip's standard with his namesake casino hotel, embodying a new, sophisticated resort style, free of campy themes.

Today, all three varieties of casinos – vintage, themed and high-fashion – are worth your time on a stroll down the Strip.

Dusk on the Strip
145/STUART DEE/CORBIS ©

The Strip Highlights

Welcome to Fabulous Las Vegas Sign (p46)

It's official: you've arrived in Sin City. In the middle of Las Vegas Blvd, the city's most iconic sign announces in vintage style, 'Welcome to Fabulous Las Vegas Nevada.' Of course, when Betty Willis designed it in 1958, the sign wasn't retro – it was modern, with an atomic star-burst on top and, on the back, a friendly reminder to 'Drive Carefully' and 'Come Back Soon.'

MICHAEL PHILLIPS/GETTY IMAGES ©

Stratosphere (p58)

You can spot this futuristic-looking tower from miles around: it's one of the tallest buildings in the country. As you drive by, you might spot tiny human figures swinging out into the air over 100 stories high or bungee jumping off the side of the tower – those are just two of the Stratosphere's action-packed attractions. For a more sedate thrill, try the cocktail lounge on the 107th floor.

RICHARD CUMMINS/GETTY IMAGES ©

Circus Circus (p54)

With the closing of the classic Arabian Nights–themed Sahara casino hotel, Circus Circus become one of the only surviving old-school casinos on the northern Strip. Camp and family friendly, it has a staunchly traditional steakhouse, free circus acts beneath a giant, candy-striped big top and a gazillion old-fashioned carnival and video games. Kids gravitate to the indoor Adventuredome theme park.

3

4

Fashion Show (p59)

All of the Strip could be called a shopaholic's dream, but only one mall can claim to be the biggest in the entire state. Anchoring the north end of the Strip, the Fashion Show is an eye-catching landmark: looking like a flamenco hat, the silver-topped *Cloud* sculpture shades the mall's entrance on sunny desert days. On weekends, step inside for free live runway shows.

5

Flamingo (p56)

Enlivening the Strip even before Sin City's 'Fabulous Fifties' decade, the Flamingo is the stuff of legend: mobsters put up the money to build the place, and Judy Garland later sang onstage here with her daughter Liza Minnelli. Smack in the center of the Strip, this vintage casino hotel is still decked out in outrageous pink neon, with a walk-through wildlife habitat where real flamingos roam.

The Strip Walk

Vegas is famous for its shameless re-creations of famous sights: Egyptian pyramids, the Eiffel Tower, Venetian canals. Jet from Europe to Polynesia and back without changing time zones – or even leaving the Strip.

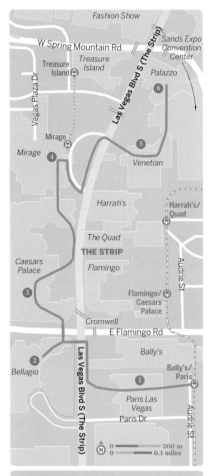

1 Paris Las Vegas

Welcome to the City of Lights. From the monorail station at the back of Bally's, sashay your way into Paris Las Vegas (p114) via the cobblestone shopping arcade Le Boulevard (p119), soaking up *l'atmosphère* and stopping for croissants or crepes. Take a romantic ride up the Eiffel Tower Experience (p116) where you can view the Fountains of Bellagio (p124) from on high.

2 Bellagio

Stay in a European mood by sauntering north to Flamingo Rd, then crossing Las Vegas Blvd on a skybridge to Bellagio (p124). Inside, Dale Chihuly's triumphant glass flower sculptures and seasonal floral displays in the conservatory complement the grand architecture. Strut like an Italian supermodel down the Via Bellagio (p129) shopping promenade, eyeing designer fashions in the glamorous store windows.

3 Caesars Palace

Waltz back in time by taking the skybridge across Flamingo Rd, then riding the escalator down to the plaza outside Caesars Palace (p132), where boozy lemonade is dispensed from the Spanish Steps (p136). Inside this fantasia of classical antiquity, watch cocktail waiters dressed in togas parade underneath faux-frescoed ceilings. Head past the crowds lining up to hear the headliners at the Colosseum (p136) and meander through the vast Forum Shops (p137).

WALK FACTS

- **Start** Paris Las Vegas
- **Finish** Palazzo
- **Distance** 1.1 miles
- **Duration** One or two hours

4 Mirage

Exiting the mall by a grand spiral staircase, amble north along the Strip towards the tropical paradise of the Mirage (p140). Watch the faux volcano explode outside, then step inside the tropically scented hotel lobby to view the 20,000-gallon aquarium and the casino's domed rainforest atrium. If the tropics aren't your thing, channel 1960s London at Cirque du Soleil's show *Beatles LOVE* (p145) and the adjacent Revolution Lounge (p144). In summer, nothing beats mojitos on the Strip-view patio at Rhumbar (p144).

5 Venetian

Wind down your walk on a graceful note by crossing the Strip toward the elegant Venetian (p155), with its flowing canals and mock-marble bridges. Treat yourself to a gondola ride (p164) with a singing gondolier or glide on your own feet through the Grand Canal Shoppes (p163), then indulge in a well-deserved scoop of gelato at busy St Mark's Sq.

6 Palazzo

Keep winding your way through the Grand Canal Shoppes (p164) into the Palazzo (p158), where a photo op in front of the indoor waterfall proves irresistible for many. To get back to where you started, walk outside and head south down the Strip to Harrah's, where you can catch a ride on the monorail once again.

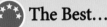 **The Best...**

PLACES TO EAT

Joël Robuchon France's high-flying 'Chef of the Century.' (p89)

Jaleo Modern Spanish tapas, endless sangria and a secret dining room. (p100)

Mon Ami Gabi Sit underneath the Strip's Eiffel Tower at this Parisian bistro. (p117)

Bacchanal All-you-can-eat feast fit for a Roman emperor at Caesars Palace. (p135)

PLACES TO DRINK

Level 107 Lounge You simply can't get any higher on the Strip – sip a martini here at sunset. (p67)

Hyde Bellagio Peer out at the fountain show from this moneyed lounge. (p127)

XS Glam nightclub with world-famous DJs and poolside cabanas. (p174)

FREE ENTERTAINMENT

Fountains of Bellagio Aquatic spectacular evoking *Ocean's Eleven*. (p124)

Mirage Volcano Exploding artificial volcano stopping traffic on the Strip. (p142)

Circus Circus High-wire circus acts overhead in a zany casino. (p54)

Venetian (p155)
SYLVAIN SONNET/GETTY IMAGES ©

★
Don't Miss
LINQ

A mammoth open-air dining, entertainment and retail complex, the $550-million LINQ project has transformed the once-lackluster stretch of the center Strip between the vintage Flamingo and Quad casino hotels. Eclectic shops, buzzing bars, trendy restaurants, live-music venues and even a bowling alley line this pedestrian promenade. Above it all rises the landmark High Roller observation wheel.

Map p48

☏ 800-223-7277

www.thelinq.com

3545 Las Vegas Blvd S

High Roller ride before/after 5:50pm $25/35

⏰ High Roller noon-2pm daily, LINQ restaurant, bar & shop hours vary

monorail Flamingo or Harrah's/Quad

High Roller

The world's largest observation wheel towers 550ft above the LINQ's street-level walkways. Each of the 28 air-conditioned passenger cabins is enclosed by handcrafted Italian glass. Outside, 2000 LED lights glow from dusk until dawn. One revolution takes about 30 minutes, and you'll be sharing the ride with a few dozen strangers. Since this is Vegas, the wheelhouse bar sells boozy drinks to take on board.

Polaroid Museum & Fotobar

Print the perfect Vegas selfie on paper, canvas, bamboo or metal at the Polaroid Fotobar. Then head upstairs to the **Polaroid Museum (adult/child under 12yr $5/ free)**, which showcases historical artifacts such as large-format Polaroid cameras, as well as hosting temporary exhibits like the photographic pop art of Andy Warhol.

Restaurants

Hungry? Good. Brooklyn Bowl dishes up haute American comfort food, while the Yard House pairs upscale pub grub with a variety of microbrews. Chayo's puts a flavorful contemporary spin on Mexican and Southwestern favorites. For quick bites, try brick-oven-fired pizzas from Flour & Barley or grab a posh hot dog at Haute Doggery. For dessert, hit up the 24-hour cupcake ATM outside Sprinkles.

Nightlife

Catch an indie music show at Brooklyn Bowl, down pints while watching the game at the Tilted Kilt or challenge your bros to beer pong at the low roller's casino O'Sheas. Sip a neon-colored daiquiri from Purple Zebra, sing along with piano players at BLVD Cocktail Company and then do shots and ride the mechanical bull at Chayo's.

Shopping

Hand-picked unique boutiques beckon. Browse cutting-edge LA fashions at Kitson, don the perfect hat at Goorin Bros, try on funky eyewear at Chilli Beans, lace up limited-edition kicks from 12am. Run, or get a beauty makeover at the Style Lounge.

Don't Miss List

CHARLEY RYAN, CO-FOUNDER/ CO-OWNER OF BROOKLYN BOWL (P57)

1 **LIVE MUSIC & FOOD AT BROOKLYN BOWL**

We pride ourselves on bringing progressive music to the Strip. Don't miss our upstairs lounge, which has hidden illusions and tricks that you've got to discover for yourself. The brothers from Blue Ribbon Restaurants make the kind of food that they remember from their childhood.

2 **CENTRAL PLAZA**

Brooklyn Bowl's upper-floor patio and terrace both overlook the LINQ's busy Central Plaza. On these outdoor decks, we have telescopes set up just like at the Empire State Building or Grand Canyon, except there's no need for quarters here. You can just walk up and spy on people riding the High Roller in the distance.

3 **HIGH ROLLER**

I got a chance to ride the High Roller observation wheel when it first opened, and it was fantastic fun. The most unexpected feeling happens when your cabin gets to the very top of the wheel's rotation – it feels almost like you're levitating. Tip: the best way to get here if you're not walking the Strip is to get dropped off in back by the taxi stand and valet parking.

4 **YARD HOUSE**

One of Brooklyn Bowl's neighbors at the LINQ is the Yard House, which has 160 craft beers on tap and great food too.

Discover the Strip

⬌ Getting There & Away

○ **Monorail** The monorail connects some casinos along the east side of the Strip, and goes to the city's convention center. Trains run every four to 12 minutes until at least midnight daily.

○ **Bus** The 24-hour Deuce bus line makes all stops along the Strip every 15 to 20 minutes, continuing north to downtown. SDX express buses make limited stops along the Strip before heading north to downtown, running every 15 minutes from 9:30am until midnight daily.

○ **Tram** Free casino trams connect Excalibur, Luxor and Mandalay Bay; the Mirage and Treasure Island; and the Bellagio and Monte Carlo, stopping at CityCenter's Crystals mall and Aria.

○ **Taxi** Taxis queue outside almost all casinos, hotels and shopping malls.

◉ Sights

The boutique **Cromwell** casino hotel, featuring Drai's nightclub and daytime pool club as well as a restaurant by celebrity chef Giada de Laurentis, will open in 2014. So will the luxury SLS casino hotel, rising from the ashes of the vintage Sahara, with high-powered dining concepts from José Andrés and Katsuya Uechi, star-powered shopping at Fred Segal and a branch of LA's Umami Burger with a beer garden. The following sights are listed in geographical order from south to north along the Strip. For more casinos and attractions, peruse the 'Sights' sections of the individual casino resort chapters later in this book.

Circus Circus See p54.	Casino
Flamingo See p56.	Casino
Stratosphere See p58.	Casino
LINQ See p44.	Mall
Fashion Show See p46.	Mall

Welcome to Fabulous Las Vegas Sign   Landmark

Map p48 (5200 Las Vegas Blvd S; ◷24hr; 🚹) In a city famous for neon signs, one reigns supreme: the 'Welcome to Fabulous Las Vegas Nevada' sign, straddling Las Vegas Blvd just south of the Strip. Designed by Betty Willis at the end of the 'Fabulous Fifties,' this Googie-style sign is a classic photo op and a reminder of Vegas' past. Only southbound traffic can pull into the small parking lot.

Welcome to Fabulous Las Vegas Sign
CHRIS HEPBURN/GETTY IMAGES ©

Excalibur
Casino

Map p48 (702-597-7777; www.excalibur.com; 3850 Las Vegas Blvd S; 24hr;) This medieval caricature, complete with crayon-colored towers and a faux drawbridge, epitomizes gaudy Vegas. Inside the mock castle, casino walls are hung with coats of arms and cheap stained-glass imitations depicting valiant knights and lovely damsels. Buried in the Fun Dungeon arcade are Ye Olde carnival games such as skee-ball and joystick joys. The Tournament of Kings dinner show is a demolition derby with hooves and sticky fingers. Parents beware: this place looks more child-friendly than it actually is.

Tropicana
Casino

Map p48 (800-462-8767; www.troplv.com; 3801 Las Vegas Blvd S; 24hr) Open since 1957, the Trop has had half a century to sully its shine, lose its crowds and go the way of the Dunes and the Sands – ashes to ashes, dust to dust. But thanks to a massive facelift and a chic new Miami-meets-Havana theme, it just keeps hanging in there. Out back, the tropically inspired pool complex has multilevel lagoons, streaming waterfalls and classic swim-up blackjack tables. After dark, get your yuks at the Laugh Factory comedy club.

Monte Carlo
Casino

Map p48 (702-730-7777; www.montecarlo.com; 3770 Las Vegas Blvd S; 24hr) Fronted by Corinthian colonnades, triumphal arches, petite dancing fountains and allegorical statuary, this casino is bustling and spacious. The magnificent

Going to the Chapel

A blushing bride says 'I do' every five minutes in Sin City. Scores of celebrity couples have exchanged vows in Vegas, from Elvis Presley and Priscilla Beaulieu to Andre Agassi and Steffi Graf. Why not you, too? After all, the 50:50 odds of a marriage surviving 'till death do us part' start to look pretty good compared with the chances of hitting a royal flush on a video-poker machine.

If you're thinking of officially tying the knot in Las Vegas and want to know what's required, contact Clark County's **Marriage License Bureau** (702-671-0600; www.clarkcountynv.gov/Depts/clerk/Services/Pages/MarriageLicenses.aspx; 201 E Clark Ave; marriage license from $60; 8am-midnight), which gets jammed during crunch times such as weekends, holidays and 'lucky'-number days. For an inexpensive, no-fuss civil ceremony, make an appointment with the county's **Office of Civil Marriages** (702-671-0577; www.clarkcountynv.gov/depts/clerk/pages/ civilmarriages.aspx; 330 S 3rd St, 6th fl; wedding ceremonies from $75; 2-6pm Sun-Thu, 10am-9pm Fri, 12:30pm-9pm Sat).

Expect to pay at least $200 for a basic ceremony at an old-school Vegas wedding chapel. Operating for more than 50 years, **Graceland Wedding Chapel** (Map p186; 800-824-5732, 702-382-0091; www.gracelandchapel.com; 619 Las Vegas Blvd S) created the original Elvis wedding. **Little Church of the West** (800-821-2452, 702-739-7971; www.littlechurchlv.com; 4617 Las Vegas Blvd S; 8am-11pm) features a quaint, quiet little wooden chapel built in 1942 and pictured in *Viva Las Vegas*. At zany **Viva Las Vegas Wedding Chapel** (800-574-4450, 702-384-0771; www. vivalasvegasweddings.com; 1205 Las Vegas Blvd S), you can invite your family and friends to watch your wacky-themed ceremony broadcast live online. Looking like a miniature cathedral, **Vegas Weddings** (Map p186; 800-823-4095, 702-933-3464; www.702wedding.com; 555 S 3rd St; 9am-midnight) offers a walk-up (and drive-thru) wedding window, plus outdoor ceremonies in scenic spots like the Valley of Fire.

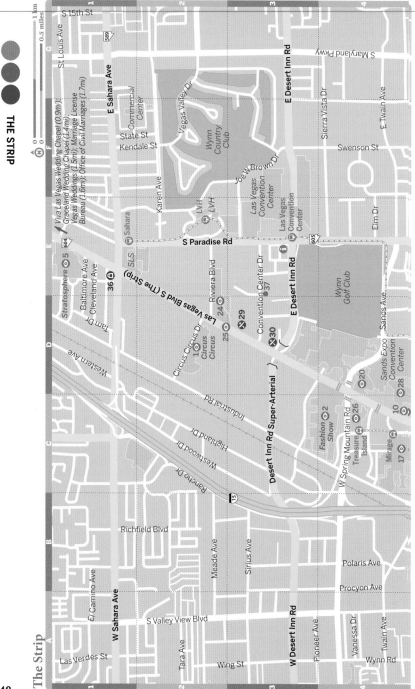

Viva Las Vegas Wedding Chapel (0.9mi);
Graceland Wedding Chapel (1.4mi);
Vegas Weddings (1.5mi); Marriage License
Bureau (1.6mi); Office of Civil Marriages (1.7mi)

S 15th St
S Louis Ave
St Louis Ave
E Sahara Ave
Commercial
Center
State St
Kendale St
Vegas Valley Dr
Wynn
Country
Club
Karen Ave
Joe W Brown Dr
LVH
LVH
Las Vegas
Convention
Center
Sahara
SLS
S Paradise Rd
Baltimore Ave
Cleveland Ave
Riviera Blvd
Convention Center Dr
Stratosphere 5
36
Las Vegas Blvd S (The Strip)
24
29
25
30
37
E Desert Inn Rd
Desert Inn Rd Super-Arterial
Circus Circus Dr
Circus
Circus
Circus
Circus
Industrial Rd
Western Ave
Tam Dr
Fashion
Show 2
Treasure
Island
Mirage
17
W Spring Mountain Rd
26
20
28
10
Sands Expo
Convention
Center
Wynn
Golf Club
Sands Ave
Sands Ave
Highland Dr
Westwood Dr
Rancho Dr
Richfield Blvd
Meade Ave
Sirius Ave
Polaris Ave
Procyon Ave
El Camino Ave
Las Verdes St
W Sahara Ave
S Valley View Blvd
Tara Ave
Wing St
W Desert Inn Rd
S Valley View Blvd
W Desert Inn Rd
Pioneer Ave
Vanessa Dr
Wynn Rd
Twain Ave
E Desert Inn Rd
S Maryland Pkwy
Sierra Vista Dr
Swenson St
E Twain Ave
Elm Dr
E Desert Inn Rd
Las Vegas Convention Center
589
604
605
605
15
THE STRIP
1 km
0.5 miles
N

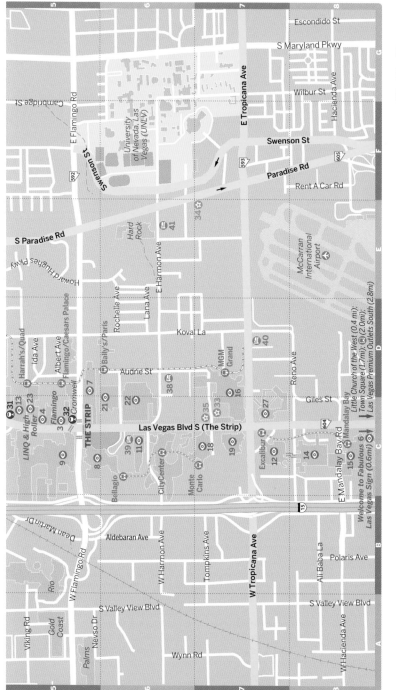

THE STRIP

Las Vegas Blvd S (The Strip)

University of Nevada, Las Vegas (UNLV)

McCarran International Airport

Harrah's/Quad
Flamingo/Caesars Palace
LINQ & High Roller
Flamingo
Cromwell
Bally's/Paris
MGM Grand
Excalibur
Mandalay Bay
Bellagio
CityCenter
Monte Carlo
Hard Rock

E Escondido St
S Maryland Pkwy
E Tropicana Ave
Wilbur St
Hacienda Ave
Swenson St
Paradise Rd
Rent A Car Rd
S Paradise Rd
Howard Hughes Pkwy
Ida Ave
Albert Ave
Rochelle Ave
Lana Ave
E Harmon Ave
Koval La
Reno Ave
Giles St
Audrie St
E Flamingo Rd
Cambridge St
Swenson St

Little Church of the West (0.4 mi);
Town Square (1.7mi); (2.0mi);
Las Vegas Premium Outlets South (2.8mi)

Welcome to Fabulous
Las Vegas Sign (0.6mi)

E Mandalay Bay Rd
E Mandalay Bay Rd

Dean Martin Dr
W Flamingo Rd
Aldebaran Ave
W Harmon Ave
Tompkins Ave
S Valley View Blvd
Ali Baba La
Polaris Ave
S Valley View Blvd
W Tropicana Ave
W Tropicana Ave
W Hacienda Ave
Viking Rd
Nevso Dr
S Valley View Blvd
Wynn Rd
W Hacienda Ave
Gold Coast
Rio
Palms

592
593
605
604
15
15

49

The Strip

marble-floored lobby with Palladian windows and crystal chandelier is vaguely reminiscent of a European grand hotel – but, hey, it's still Vegas, so expect more tastelessness than artistic taste. The family-friendly pool complex out back sports a lazy river ride and a wave pool.

Bally's   Casino
Map p48 (☏702-739-4111; www.ballyslasvegas.com; 3645 Las Vegas Blvd S; ⊙24hr) Unless it's 'bigger is better,' there is no real theme at this time-warped place with a football-field-sized casino overhung by twinkling chandeliers and overstuffed blue velvet chairs. Bally's biggest attraction isn't gaming, it's **Jubilee!** (p57), one of Vegas' long-running showgirl extravaganzas. More than 1000 costumes are worn during the cheesy show; almost 70 stagehands are required to operate the stage, sets, lights and sound equipment; and 4200lbs of dry ice are used each week to create the fog effects.

Discover more technical trivia on a backstage tour, escorted by a real performer from the show.

Quad
Casino

Map p48 (☎702-731-3311; www.thequadlv.com; 3535 Las Vegas Blvd S; ⏰24hr) What was once the Imperial Palace, with a blue-neon-roofed pagoda facade and a faux–Far East theme, has become a theme-free boxy casino hotel called the Quad. On the casino floor, celebrity impersonators still do double duty as 'dealertainers,' jumping up from the blackjack tables to show off their song-and-dance skills. Also inside you'll find the resurrected, lucky leprechaun-themed O'Sheas casino, packed with low rollers and college students.

Harrah's
Casino

Map p48 (☎702-369-5000; www.harrahslas vegas.com; 3475 Las Vegas Blvd S; ⏰24hr) Harrah's may be the friendliest and most playful casino on the Strip – and it's swimming with middle-aged tourists from the Midwest. Entertainment is the name of the game, with genial magician **Mac King** (p57) and the **Improv** (p57) comedy club showcasing headliner comics. Go see lounge lizard Cook E Jarr or 'Big Elvis' impersonator Pete Vallee perform in the piano bar. After dark, get soused in the outdoor **Carnaval Court** (p55), where bartenders juggle fire and cover bands rock the crowds.

Casino Royale
Casino

Map p48 (☎800-854-7666; www.casinoroyale hotel.com; 3411 Las Vegas Blvd S; ⏰24hr) Tired of megaresort casinos stealing your dough courtesy of bad-odds video-poker machines and table games with ridiculous rules that inflate the house advantage (ie 'edge') beyond limits that even mobsters would find respectable? Well, the odds aren't great here either, but at least low minimum bets make it easier to stomach. Cheap drinks and fast food keep you sated.

Riviera
Casino

Map p48 (☎855-468-6748; www.rivierahotel. com; 2901 Las Vegas Blvd S; ⏰24hr) When the Riv opened in 1955, Liberace did the ribbon-cutting honors, and Orson Welles appeared on stage the next year performing – of all things – magic acts.

A host of big-name entertainers once starred here, including Louis Armstrong, Duke Ellington and Tony Bennett. That Hollywood glamour is entirely gone now. Inside the dimly lit, confusingly laid-out casino, cheap slots are pulled by old-as-the-hills clientele. Plug your quarters into the vintage pinball machines over by the food court instead.

Slots-A-Fun
Casino

Map p48 (☎702-734-0410; 2890 Las Vegas Blvd S; ⏰24hr) For cheap booze and cheap thrills, it's tough to beat this lowbrow dive next door to Circus Circus. Grab a coupon book, give the giant slot machine a free spin, play beer pong and scarf down a few hot dogs.

✕ Eating

It's impossible to cover even a fraction of the dining options along the Strip.

For dozens more options, peruse the 'Eating' sections of the individual casino-resort chapters later in this book.

Tacos El Gordo
Mexican $

Map p48 (☎702-641-8228; http://tacoselgordo bc.com; 3049 Las Vegas Blvd S; items $2-10; ⏰9pm-3am Sun-Thu, to 5am Fri & Sat; 🚌Deuce, SDX) This Tijuana-style taco shop from SoCal is just the ticket when it's way late, you've got almost no money left and you're desperately craving carne asada (beef) or *adobada* (chile-marinated pork) tacos in hot, hand-made tortillas. Adventurous eaters order the authentic *sesos* (beef brains), *cabeza* (roasted cow's head) or tripe (intestines) variations.

Stripburger
Burgers $

Map p48 (☎702-737-8747; www.stripburger.com; 3200 Las Vegas Blvd S, Fashion Show; items $4-14; ⏰11am-11pm Sun-Thu, to midnight Fri & Sat; ♿) This shiny silver, open-air diner in the round serves up all-natural (hormone free etc) beef, chicken, tuna and veggie burgers, atomic cheese fries, thick milkshakes, buckets of beer and fruity cocktails, with elevated patio tables overlooking the Strip.

Below: Excalibur (p47); **Right:** High Roller observation wheel (p45)

NM

Café
American, Mediterranean **$$**

Map p48 (📞702-697-7340; www.neimanmarcus.
com; 3200 Las Vegas Blvd S, 2nd level, Neiman
Marcus, Fashion Show; mains $14-22; ⏰11am-6pm
Mon-Sat, noon-5pm Sun; 🚻; 🚌Deuce) At this
contemporary cafe with outdoor terrace
tables hanging above the Strip, the menu
of lighter fare is designed for department-
store shoppers, with composed salads,
club sandwiches, popovers with strawberry
butter, cocktails and Illy espresso.

Peppermill
Diner **$$**

Map p48 (📞702-735-4177; www.peppermilllas
vegas.com; 2985 Las Vegas Blvd S; mains $8-30;
⏰24hr) Slide into a crescent-shaped
booth at this retro casino coffee shop and
revel in the old-school Vegas atmosphere.
You can eavesdrop on Nevada cowboys
and downtown politicos digging into a
gigantic late-night bite or early breakfast.
For tropical tiki drinks, step into the Peppermill's **Fireside Lounge** (p55).

KGB
Burgers **$$**

Map p48 (📞702-369-5065; www.harrahslas
vegas.com; 3475 Las Vegas Blvd S, Harrah's;
mains $12-17; ⏰11am-11pm Sun-Thu, to midnight
Fri & Sat) One of the original competitors
in the Strip's burger wars is chef Kerry
Simon's gourmet burger shop at Har-
rah's, with a tongue-in-cheek Cold War–
era Russian theme and specialty vodkas
behind the bar. Rowdy groups of friends
bite into stuffed jalapeño burgers, slurp
down Cap'n Crunch milkshakes and split
s'mores and cotton candy for dessert.

Roxy's Diner
Diner **$$**

Map p48 (📞702-380-7777; www.stratosphere
hotel.com; 2000 Las Vegas Blvd S, Stratosphere;
mains $8-14; ⏰24hr; 🚻) At this '50s-style
rock 'n' roll diner, waitstaff drop everything
to perform song-and-dance numbers
straight out of *Grease*. It's fun, and the
menu tastes about right for the prices.
Superthick milkshakes come with silver
sidecars, just like when you were a kid.

Top of the World
American $$$

Map p48 (702-380-7711; www.topoftheworldlv.
com; 2000 Las Vegas Blvd S, 106th fl, Strato-
sphere Tower; mains lunch $25-34, dinner $40-79;
11am-11pm) While taking in the cloud-
level views at this revolving romantic roost
perched atop the Stratosphere Tower,
smartly dressed diners enjoy impecca-
ble service and satisfying, if overpriced,
dishes such as Colorado rack of lamb
dusted with Moroccan spices or California
black cod swirled in Thai green curry
sauce. Excellent wine list. Reservations
essential.

Hash House
a Go Go
American $$$

Map p48 (702-254-4646; www.hashhouse
agogo.com; 3535 Las Vegas Blvd S, Quad; mains
breakfast & lunch $8-16, dinner $17-39; 24hr,
except closed 11pm-7am on last Wed night of
month;) Fill up on this SoCal import's
'twisted farm food,' which has to be seen
to be believed. The pancakes are as big
as tractor tires, while farm-egg scrambles
and house-made hashes could knock
over a cow. Meatloaf, pot pies, chicken
'n' biscuits and wild-boar sloppy joes are
what's for dinner, but it's more popular for
breakfast and brunch.

Additional locations downtown at the
Plaza and west of the Strip at the Rio are
open shorter hours.

Andre's
French $$$

Map p48 (702-798-7151; http://andrelv.com;
3770 Las Vegas Blvd S, Monte Carlo; mains $28-
74, tasting menu without/with wine pairings from
$110/190; 5:30-10pm Tue-Sun) Chef André
Rochat's loyal patrons appreciate the
Michelin-starred traditions at this elegant
restaurant with a cigar and cognac lounge
upstairs. Seasonal highlights on the
French provincial menu might include
pan-seared duck foie gras with baked
pumpkin bread pudding and five-spice
crème anglaise. Sommelier-led wine
flights from the world-class cellar are
pricey. Reservations essential; dress well.

Chayo's
Mexican $$$

Map p48 (702-691-3773; http://chayolv.
com; 3545 Las Vegas Blvd S, the LINQ; mains

⭐ Don't Miss
Circus Circus

If you're cruising the bedraggled North Strip, don't overlook Circus Circus. Granted, it's hard to miss, what with the enormous clown-shaped marquee and tent-shaped casino under a striped big top. From the outside, this sprawling resort looks pretty cheesy – and it *is*. It's also overrun by kids, baby strollers and hilariously immature adults.

The decor inside is a riotous carnival of colors, but these days it aims more for commedia dell'arte than Ringling Bros. Three full-sized casinos contain more than 2200 slot machines (keep an eye out for those with spinning carousels), plus wacky table games such as Casino War, with free blackjack, roulette and craps lessons given daily.

Trapeze artists, high-wire workers, jugglers and unicyclists perform excellent free **circus acts** (Map p48; 🕐 shows every 30min, 11am-midnight) above the casino floor. Just show up and take a seat at the **Horse-A-Round Snack Bar** (Map p48; snacks $3-8; 🕐 2:30pm-9pm Mon-Thu, 11:30am-11:30pm Fri & Sun, 11:30am-midnight Sat), made infamous by Hunter S Thompson's *Fear and Loathing in Las Vegas*. Nowadys gonzo fans will have to settle for salty popcorn and a lemonade, as it doesn't serve alcohol anymore. Wrapped around the stage is the **Midway** (Map p48; 🕐 11am-midnight; 🚻), where high-tech video games compete for youngsters' attention with old-fashioned carnival diversions.

Behind the hotel's west tower is **Adventuredome** (www.adventuredome.com; day pass over/under 48in tall $30/17, per ride $5-8; 🕐 10am-6pm daily, later on weekends & May-Sep), packed with thrills and dozens of rides and attractions. Highlights include the double-loop, double-corkscrew Canyon Blaster, gravity-defying El Loco (which packs a whopping -1.5Gs of vertical acceleration), a rock-climbing wall and mini golf. Clowns perform free shows throughout the day.

NEED TO KNOW

Map p48; 📞702-734-0410; www.circuscircus.com; 2880 Las Vegas Blvd S; 🕐24hr; 🚻

$16-32; ⏱11am-11pm Sun-Wed, to 2am Thu-Sat) This stylish Mexican kitchen and tequila bar near the High Roller observation wheel even has a mechanical bull that you can ride. Sink back against a leather banquette and eye the Día de Los Muertos–inspired decor as you feast on inspired modern Mexican dishes like pork tenderloin with cactsus leaves and mole negro sauce. Reservations are helpful.

Happy hour runs 4pm to 7pm daily and from 10pm to midnight on Friday and Saturday. Drop by anytime on Tuesday for two-for-one margaritas and half-price tacos.

Steak House   Steakhouse $$$
Map p48 (☎702-794-3767; www.circuscircus. com; 2880 Las Vegas Blvd S, Circus Circus; mains $28-77; ⏱4-10pm Sun-Fri, to 11pm Sat) All clowning aside, this revered old-school establishment inside Circus Circus takes itself very seriously. Sink into a striped leather chair underneath oil paintings of cows and neo-Victorian stained-glass ceilings. Aged mesquite-grilled steaks, prime rib and lobster tails are cooked to perfection. Reservations recommended.

Capital Grille   Steakhouse $$$
Map p48 (☎702-932-6631; www.thecapitalgrille. com; 3200 Las Vegas Blvd S, 3rd level, Fashion Show; mains lunch $16-35, dinner $28-49; ⏱11:30am-10pm Mon-Fri, noon-10pm Sat, 4-10pm Sun) What sets this upscale chain steakhouse apart is hand-cut, dry-aged beef, carved chops and cracking seafood. For a power lunch, fork into a Maine lobster salad or grilled rib-eye steak sandwich slathered with caramelized onions and Havarti cheese. Reservations recommended, especially for dinner.

🍷 Drinking & Nightlife

Level 107 Lounge   Lounge
Map p48 (☎702-380-7685; www.topoftheworld lv.com; 2000 Las Vegas Blvd S, 107th fl, Stratosphere Tower; ⏱4pm-4am) There's just no place to get any higher in Las Vegas –

without the approval of an air traffic controller – than the lounge overlooking the revolving Top of the World restaurant. Come during happy hour (4pm to 7pm daily) for two-for-one cocktails, half-price appetizers and striking sunset views.

Drai's   Club
Map p48 (☎702-737-0555; www.drais.net; 3595 Las Vegas Blvd S, Cromwell; cover $20-50; ⏱nightclub 10am-5pm Thu-Sun year-round, pool club 10am-7pm Fri-Sun usually May-Sep) Feel ready for an after-hours party scene straight outta Hollywood? Or maybe you just wanna hang out all day poolside, then shake your booty on the petite dance floor while DJs spin hip hop, mash-ups and electronica? This multi-venue club has you covered pretty much all day and night. Dress to kill: no sneakers, tank tops or baggy jeans.

Drai's after-hours DJ parties are legendary, and keep going until 10am on club nights.

Fireside Lounge   Lounge
Map p48 (www.peppermilllasvegas.com; 2985 Las Vegas Blvd S, Peppermill; ⏱24hr) Don't be blinded by the outlandishly bright neon outside. The Strip's most spellbinding retro hideaway awaits at the pint-sized Peppermill casino. Courting couples adore the sunken fire pit, fake tropical foliage and 64oz goblet-sized 'Scorpion' cocktails served by waiters in black evening gowns.

Carnaval Court   Bar
Map p48 (☎702-369-5000; www.harrahslas vegas.com; 3475 Las Vegas Blvd S, outside Harrah's; cover charge varies; ⏱11am-3am) Flair bartenders juggle fire as they keep Harrah's outdoor bar packed with the kind of party people for whom spring break never ends. Live cover acts like the Spazmatics and Mr & Mrs Smith tear up the stage with people dancing below. There's often no cover charge.

Double Barrel Roadhouse   Bar
Map p48 (www.sbe.com/doublebarrel; 3770 Las Vegas Blvd S, Monte Carlo; ⏱11am-2am) With a

RICHARD CUMMINS/GETTY IMAGES ©

⭐ Don't Miss
Flamingo

In 1946 the Flamingo was the talk of the town. Its original owners – all members of the East Coast mafia – shelled out millions to build this unprecedented tropical gaming oasis in the desert. It was prime gangster Americana, initially managed by the infamous mobster Benjamin 'Bugsy' Siegel, who named it after his girlfriend, dancer Virginia Hill (nicknamed 'the Flamingo' for her red hair and long legs).

Siegel died in a hail of bullets at Virginia's Beverly Hills home soon after the Flamingo opened, the victim of a contract killing. The Flamingo had gotten off to a slow start and the casino's investors believed it would ultimately fail, so they 'took care of business' 'They had made a big mistake: the Flamingo not only survived, but it jump-started the modern Strip.

Today the Flamingo isn't quite what it was back when its janitorial staff wore tuxedos, although fantastic clusters of pink and orange neon lights outside the hotel vaguely resemble flamingo feathers – think more *Miami Vice*, less *Bugsy*. It's always manically crowded in the casino, which has more than 1600 gaming tables and slots.

At **Jimmy Buffett's Margaritaville** (p57), Parrot Heads wait for the margarita volcano to overflow into their glasses. Outside in the Flamingo's **wildlife habitat** (Map p48; 📞702-733-3349; ☺8am-dusk, pelican feedings 8am & 2:30pm; 👫) FREE, Chilean flamingos and African penguins wander around, and palm trees and jungle plants flourish in the middle of the desert. On hot summer days, knock back local microbrews at **Sin City Brewing Co** (Map p48; www.sincitybeer.com; Flamingo; ☺11am-2am) or cool off at the Flamingo's adults-only party **Go Pool** (Map p48; www.flamingolasvegas.com; admission $15-25, hotel guests free; ☺hours vary by season).

NEED TO KNOW

Map p48; 📞702-733-3111; www.flamingolasvegas.com; 3555 Las Vegas Blvd S; ☺24hr

Strip-view patio, this double-decker bar and grill anchors the new pedestrian district between the Monte Carlo and New York–New York casino hotels. Staff pour stiff house-made wine coolers into mason jars, cook up Southern comfort food and cheer the live rock bands on stage.

Jimmy Buffett's Margaritaville   Bar

Map p48 (☎702-733-3302; www.margarita ville lasvegas.com; 3555 Las Vegas Blvd S, Flamingo; ⏰11am-1am Sun-Thu, to 2am Fri & Sat) Parrot Heads, you've found your very own paradise on the Strip, with three floors, five bars and a faux volcano exploding hourly, letting frozen margaritas with names such as 'Last Mango in Paris' overflow into big blenders. The tropically themed gaming area extends into the Flamingo's main casino.

⭐ Entertainment

Brooklyn Bowl   Bowling, Live Music

Map p48 (☎702-862-2695; http://vegas. brooklynbowl.com; 3545 Las Vegas Blvd S, the LINQ; 30min lane rental from $25, show tickets $15-70; ⏰11am-2am Sun-Thu, to 4am Fri & Sat) Hipsters gather at NYC import Brooklyn Bowl, which is one part high-tech bowling alley, one part gourmet comfort-food restaurant and one part cool concert venue for the same indie acts you'd hear at Coachella or SXSW music festivals.

Improv   Comedy

Map p48 (☎855-234-7569, 702-777-2782; www. improv.com; 3475 Las Vegas Blvd S, Harrah's; from $30; ⏰8:30pm & 10pm Tue-Sun) The Vegas franchise of this NYC-based chain has the Big Apple's signature red-brick backdrop. The spotlight is firmly cast on touring stand-up headliners of the moment, often polished by recent late-night TV appearances.

Jubilee!   Theater

Map p48 (☎855-234-7469, 702-777-2782; www. ballyslasvegas.com; 3645 Las Vegas Blvd S, Bally's; tickets $63-123; ⏰7pm Sun-Thu, 10pm Sat-Wed) Girls, girls, girls! It's a showgirl production and Vegas wouldn't be Vegas without it. The topless revue features twinkling

rhinestone-bedecked dancers in flashy costumes and enormous headdresses – along with less-than-exciting filler acts. If you can forgive the cheesy undertones, you'll have a riot, especially if you take time for the **backstage tour** (Map p48; ☎702-967-4938; Bally's; tour $15-20; ⏰11am Mon, Wed & Sat) first.

Legends in Concert   Music

Map p48 (☎702-777-7776; www.legendsin concert.com; 3555 Las Vegas Blvd S, Flamingo; adult/child from $50/27; ⏰usually 4pm Sat-Thu & 7:30pm Sat-Mon) Vegas' top pop-star impersonator show features real singing and dancing talent mimicking famous performers such as the Beatles, Elvis, Madonna, James Brown, Britney Spears, Shania Twain and many more.

Mac King   Magic, Comedy

Map p48 (☎855-234-7469, 702-777-2782; www.mackingshow.com; 3475 Las Vegas Blvd S, Harrah's; from $30; ⏰1pm & 3pm Tue-Sat; 🚇Harrah's/Imperial Palace) Redheaded Mac has the most popular afternoon magic and comedy show in town, with lots of PG-13 laughs and sleight-of-hand thrown in. He really rides the crazy train with his bag of tricks, which includes baiting a live goldfish with a Fig Newton cookie.

Thunder from Down Under   Dance

Map p48 (☎702-597-7600; www.thunderfrom downunder.com; 3850 Las Vegas Blvd S, Excalibur; tickets $55-65; ⏰9pm nightly, also 11pm Fri & Sat) At Excalibur, shirtless, stripped-down Australian lads provide nonstop flirting and fun, and bachelorettes often get pulled up on stage. Stick around after the show for photo ops with the boys.

United Artists Showcase Theatre 8   Cinema

Map p48 (☎702-740-4511; www.regmovies.com; 3769 Las Vegas Blvd S, Showcase Mall; adult/child 3-11yr $11.50/8; 👪) It's the only place to see first-run movies on the Strip, which means it's always packed. Although it's hardly the city's most modern cinema, stadium seating and digital sound bring it up to date. Afternoon matinee shows are discounted for adults.

⭐ Don't Miss
Stratosphere

Las Vegas has many buildings over 20 stories tall, but only the Stratosphere exceeds 100. Atop the 1149ft-high tapered tripod tower, vertiginous indoor and outdoor viewing decks afford Vegas' best 360-degree panoramas. There you'll also find **Top of the World** (p53), a revolving restaurant, and the jazzy **Level 107** (p55) cocktail lounge. To get to the top of Vegas' lucky landmark, ride one of America's fastest elevators, lifting you 108 floors in a mere 37 ear-popping seconds.

Once you've snapped some panoramic photos, jump on the tower's high-altitude thrill rides. Insanity swings riders out from the edge of the tower into thin air, then spins its huge claw arms, elevated at an angle of 70 degrees. Rising above it all is the Big Shot, which rockets riders in outward-facing seats up and down a steel spire that forms the pinnacle of the tower itself. X-Scream, which dangles riders teeter-totter style over the side of the tower, can be a letdown, so grab a seat on the right-hand side to increase the fear factor. For maximum effect, do the SkyJump, a bungeelike controlled freefall that drops you 855ft over the side of the tower.

At the base of the tapered tower is a casino favored by a loud-talkin', hard-drinkin' crowd, with low-limit table games and 1200 slots and video-poker machines. Stuff your face with comfort food while being serenaded by the singing waitstaff of **Roxy's Diner** (p52), then spend the rest of your chump change next door at the kingdom of kitsch, **Bonanza Gift Shop** (p59).

NEED TO KNOW

Map p48; ☎702-380-7777; www.stratospherehotel.com; 2000 Las Vegas Blvd S; tower entry adult/child $18/10, all-day pass incl unlimited thrill rides $34, SkyJump from $110; ☺casino 24hr, tower & thrill rides 10am-1am Sun-Thu, to 2am Fri & Sat, weather permitting; ♿

🔒 Shopping

Fashion Show
Mall

Map p48 (www.thefashionshow.com; 3200 Las Vegas Blvd S; ⊙10am-9pm Mon-Sat, 11am-7pm Sun; 👫) Nevada's largest shopping mall is an eye-catcher: topped off by 'the Cloud,' a silver multimedia canopy resembling a flamenco hat, Fashion Show harbors more than 250 chain shops and department stores. Hot European additions to the mainstream lineup include British clothier Topshop (and Topman for men). Live runway shows happen hourly from noon to 5pm on Friday, Saturday and Sunday.

Bonanza Gift Shop
Souvenirs

Map p48 (www.worldslargestgiftshop.com; 2440 Las Vegas Blvd S; ⊙8am-midnight) The self-proclaimed 'purveyors of Las Vegas pop culture' brag about running the world's largest gift shop. Whether or not it's true, it's a blast wading through the truly terrible, 100% tacky selection of souvenirs. Beware that prices for kitsch are higher here than at downtown's Fremont Street Experience.

Las Vegas Premium Outlets South
Mall

Off map p40 (📞702-896-5599; www.premium outlets.com/vegassouth; 7400 Las Vegas Blvd S; ⊙9am-9pm Mon-Sat, to 8pm Sun; 🚌SDX) Bargain hunting is practically a sport at the southern branch of Las Vegas Premium Outlets, where 140 stores cater to families and casual shoppers. Popular brands include DKNY, True Religion, Lucky Brand and several shoe stores. The mall is south of the Strip, past the airport.

Town Square
Mall

Off map p40 (📞702-269-5000; www.my townsquarelasvegas.com; 6605 Las Vegas Blvd S; ⊙10am-9pm Mon-Thu, to 10pm Fri & Sat, 11am-8pm Sun; 👫; 🚌SDX) South of the Strip, this village-style shopping center is geared more to locals than to tourists, with a range of mainstream and upscale chain shops, restaurants, happy-hour bars like Blue Martini and a Whole Foods supermarket. It may be worth the trip if you're traveling with kids just for the playground park, toy train and outdoor films in summer.

🎫 Tours

Vegas Mob Tour
Bus Tour

Map p48 (📞702-807-8036; www.vegasmobtour. com; 99 Convention Center Dr, Royal Resort; 3hr tour $75; ⊙by reservation only) Created with input from real-life mobsters and historians, this bus tour delves into the mafia underworld of Sin City's past, including celebrity scandals, mobster assassinations and other dirty laundry. Tickets include pizza and admission to downtown's **Mob Museum** (p182).

Haunted Vegas Tours
Bus Tour

Map p48 (📞866-218-4935, 702-677-6499; www. hauntedvegastours.com; 99 Convention Center Dr, Royal Resort; 2½hr tour $100; ⊙usually 9:30pm) A pizza party and (borrowed) 'ghost finder' dowsing rods are included on this paranormal hunt at three hot spots around town, including a reputedly haunted house and a creepy park. Tickets include admission to **Madame Tussauds** (p158) wax museum.

Mandalay Bay

Angular and glittering gold, massive Mandalay Bay flanks the far south end of the Strip.

It's the first resort most visitors lay eyes on as their taxicabs roll into Las Vegas – and what better introduction to Sin City than this gleaming high-rise shrine to casino gaming and the luxe life? Though not as over-the-top as some of its rival resorts further down the boulevard, M-Bay has a solid roster of advantages: three high-end hotels, a wave pool and a sandy beach, haute dining rooms presided over by celebrity chefs from Alain Ducasse to Rick Moonen, a futuristic walk-through aquarium, sultry cocktail lounges high above the neon lights of the Strip, and even a poolside casino.

It's the place where well-heeled 30-somethings sunbathe, catch live concerts by pop stars and let themselves be mesmerized by Cirque du Soleil acrobats spinning above a DJ-driven dance floor.

After all, this is Vegas.

ETHAN MILLER/GETTY IMAGES ©

Don't Miss
Mandalay Bay's Best

The 1950s-era Hacienda resort was imploded on New Year's Eve 1996 to clear the way for Mandalay Bay. This casino resort's upscale tropical theme may be subtle, but its grand opening – during which Jim Belushi, Dan Aykroyd and John Goodman cruised through the front doors on motorcycles – certainly wasn't. Today, a Harley-Davidson crew might look out of place in the regal ivory-hued lobby or on the swish casino floor.

Not trying to be any one fantasy, posh Mandalay Bay's standout attractions are many, and include the multilevel **Shark Reef Aquarium** (p64), a walk-through aquarium where overarching windows reveal thousands of tropical fish and a shallow pool that lets you pet pint-sized sharks. Down the resort's romantically lit passageways lie a pair of top-tier spas. World-class chefs have also staked out claims at M-Bay, including atop one of the gold-tinted hotel towers.

With 2700 tons of imported California sand and 6ft waves in a 1.6 million gallon wave pool, at 11-acre **Mandalay Bay Beach** kids float along the lazy river on inner tubes and surf competitions are held on artificial waves. When the stress of gambling in the air-conditioned beachside casino becomes too much, you can retire to a rooftop cabana villa or unwind at Moorea Beach Club, where sultry topless sunbathing happens in summer.

NEED TO KNOW
☎ 702-632-7777; www.mandalaybay.com; 3950 Las Vegas Blvd S; 🕐 24hr

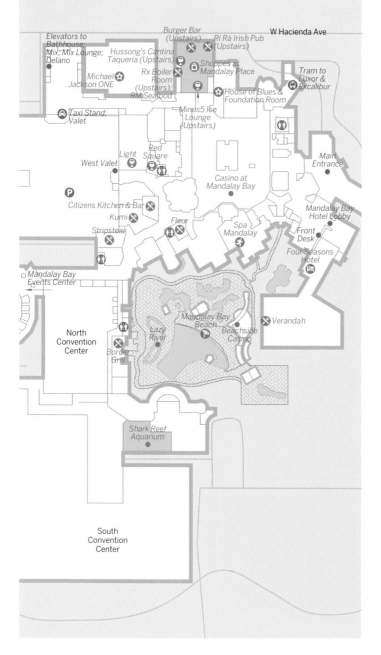

Burger Bar (Upstairs)

Rí Rá Irish Pub (Upstairs)

W Hacienda Ave

Elevators to Bathhouse; Mix; Mix Lounge; Delano

Hussong's Cantina Taqueria (Upstairs)

Shoppes at Mandalay Place

Tram to Luxor & Excalibur

Michael Jackson ONE

Rx Boiler Room (Upstairs); RM Seafood

House of Blues & Foundation Room

Taxi Stand; Valet

Minus5 Ice Lounge (Upstairs)

Light

Red Square

Main Entrance

West Valet

Casino at Mandalay Bay

Citizens Kitchen & Bar

Mandalay Bay Hotel Lobby

Kumi

Fleur

Spa Mandalay

Front Desk

Stripsteak

Four Seasons Hotel

Mandalay Bay Events Center

Mandalay Bay Beach

Verandah

North Convention Center

Lazy River

Beachside Casino

Border Grill

Shark Reef Aquarium

South Convention Center

Discover
Mandalay Bay

Getting There & Away

Tram A free tram connects Mandalay Bay and Excalibur, stopping at Luxor on the way.

Monorail The closest stop to Mandalay Bay is at the MGM Grand, which is a 20-minute walk (save time by taking the tram to Excalibur, then walking across two pedestrian skybridges). Trains run daily until at least midnight.

Bus The Deuce (24-hour) and SDX (9:30am to midnight daily) bus lines, with service along the entire Strip and to downtown, stop outside Mandalay Bay (southbound) and on the opposite side of Las Vegas Blvd (northbound) every 15 to 20 minutes.

Taxi A taxi is your best bet if you're heading downtown. Expect to pay at least $24 (plus tip) one way.

Sights

Mandalay Bay Casino Casino
Map p63 (⊙24hr) Tropical flowers and the sound of running water add a jungle vibe to M-Bay's classy 135,000-sq-ft casino. Well-dressed sports fans find their way to the upscale race and sports book near the high-stakes poker room. Adjacent to Mandalay Bay Beach is the three-story Beachside Casino with a sunlit bar and blackjack, craps and roulette tables overlooking the swimming pool complex.

Shark Reef Aquarium Aquarium
Map p63 (☎702-632-4555; www.sharkreef.com; adult/child 5-12yr $18/12; ⊙10am-10pm Fri & Sat, to 10pm Sun-Thu late May-early Sep, to 8pm Sun-Thu early Sep-late May, last admission 1hr before closing; 👶) M-Bay's unusual walk-through aquarium is home to 2000 submarine beasties, including jellyfish, moray eels, stingrays and, yes, some sharks. Other rare and endangered toothy reptiles on display include some of the world's last remaining golden crocodiles. A staff of scuba-diver caretakers and naturalists are available to chat as you wander around. Better yet, go scuba diving yourself (from $650).

Eating

Dining options range from M-Bay's chef-driven restaurants to more casual eateries in the adjacent Shoppes at Mandalay Place. Reservations are highly recommended at the former; click on www.mandalaybay.com/dining or call 702-632-7200.

Mix (p66)
KELLY-MOONEY/CORBIS ©

Spend the Night

For overnight accommodations, take your pick of three separate hotels. The traditional choice is **Mandalay Bay** (Map p63; ☎702-632-7777, 877-632-7800; www.mandalaybay.com; 3950 Las Vegas Blvd S; r weekday/weekend from $105/130; P ❄ @ 🛜 ♨ 👪), where simple but stylish rooms feature large plasma TVs, high-end linens and warm earth tones. On the highest floors of the Mandalay Bay Tower, and accessible only by private express elevators, the **Four Seasons Hotel** (Map p63; ☎702-632-5000; www.fourseasons.com/lasvegas; Mandalay Bay; r weekday/weekend from $229/289; P ❄ @ 🛜 ♨ 👪) is the picture of elegance. Standard rooms feature deep tubs for soaking and mountain views through floor-to-ceiling windows. In the adjacent tower, with an entrance at the opposite end of the casino, the hip boutique hotel **Delano** (www.delanolasvegas.com; Mandalay Bay; P ❄ @ 🛜 ♨) makes the standard room a suite complete with a wet bar.

The mandatory nightly resort fee ($25 plus tax) includes in-room wi-fi access and entry to a cardio workout room (but not the fitness center at either spa).

Verandah
Mediterranean $$

Map p63 (☎702-632-5121; www.fourseasons. com/lasvegas; Four Seasons Hotel; breakfast & lunch mains $11-22; ⏲6:30am-10pm Mon-Fri, from 7am Sat & Sun) With poolside seating, this upper-crust oasis at the Four Seasons feels far away from the ding-ding-ding of slot machines. During the week, expect delightfully light and fruity breakfasts, an Italian-inspired menu for lunch, a fabulous afternoon tea service (from $34), and happy hour (4pm to 7pm daily) offering specialty cocktails and small plates for $5 each.

Burger Bar
American $$

Map p63 (☎702-632-9364; www.burger-bar. com; Shoppes at Mandalay Place; mains $14-22; ⏲11am-11pm Sun-Thu, to 1am Fri & Sat; 👪) Since when can a hamburger be worth $60? When it's built with Kobe beef, sautéed foie gras and truffle sauce: it's the Rossini burger, the signature sandwich of chef Hubert Keller. Most menu options are more down-to-earth – diners select their own gourmet burger toppings and pair them with skinny fries and a liquor-spiked milkshake or beer float.

Hussong's Cantina
Mexican $$

Map p63 (☎702-632-6450; www.hussongslas vegas.com; Shoppes at Mandalay Place; mains

$14-22; ⏲11am-11pm) This Baja-style cantina brings rowdy, south-of-the-border attitude to Mandalay Bay's mall. Although the original Hussong's down in Ensenada claims to have invented the margarita, the drinks here aren't anything special. Standard tacos, nachos, burritos and other Mexican American standards make up the wooden signboard's menu. Happy hour runs from 3pm to 6pm daily.

Citizens Kitchen & Bar
American $$

Map p63 (☎702-632-7405; http://citizenslas vegas.com; mains $14-24; ⏲24hr) Decent comfort food is what this around-the-clock diner with an attitude is all about. Cure your hangover with a fresh-pressed elixir from the juice bar, or drown your sorrows over losing that big blackjack bet with a huge plate of crispy fried chicken with jalapeno-cheddar waffles. The late-night menu (served after 4:30am) is much less tantalizing.

Kumi
Japanese, Fusion $$$

Map p63 (☎702-632-9100; http://kumilasvegas. com; mains $28-48, small plates & sushi $6-29; ⏲5-10pm Sun-Thu, to 11pm Fri & Sat) Korean-born chef Akira Back's hugely ambitious take on traditional Japanese cuisine results in addictive neo-Asian tastes such as spicy tuna sushi rolls studded with pop rocks, and edamame dipped in kim-chi butter. Backed by photo murals of cherry blossoms, the atmosphere is chic and cool, with sake cocktails and an artful array of dishes for sharing. Reservations are essential.

RM Seafood
Seafood $$$

Map p63 (☏702-632-9300; http://rmseafood. com; Shoppes at Mandalay Place; mains lunch $14-36, dinner $29-89; ☺11:30am-11pm) 🐾 Top chef Rick Moonen is a staunch advocate for sustainable fishing; you won't find farm-raised salmon or bluefin tuna on the menu at this casual cafe. Settle into a mahogany booth or at a table fronting Mandalay Bay's shopping promenade for haute versions of seafood classics such as fish and chips and Maine lobster rolls, or more inventive creations such as catfish sloppy joes.

Happy-hour specials on drinks, sushi and raw-bar dishes are served from 3pm to 7pm daily. Dinner reservations recommended.

Stripsteak
Steak, Seafood $$$

Map p63 (☏702-632-7414; www.michaelmina. net; mains $39-75; ☺5:30-10:30pm, lounge from 4pm) *Esquire* magazine once named chef Michael Mina's butter-poached bone-in-top loin one of the USA's very best steaks. The chef's minimalist steakhouse knifes into an exceptional menu of all-natural Angus and American Kobe beef, taste-awakening appetizers including ahi tuna and hamachi poppers, and classic side dishes with a twist, from truffle mac 'n' cheese to soy-glazed green beans. Reservations essential.

Border Grill
Mexican $$$

Map p63 (☏702-632-7403; www.bordergrill. com; mains $17-36; ☺11am-10pm Mon-Thu, 11am-11pm Fri, 10am-11pm Sat, 10am-10pm Sun; 👪) 🐾 With colorful modern murals and views over Mandalay Beach, this festive eatery dishes up modern Mexican fare designed by chefs from Bravo's *Top Chef Masters* and the Food Network's *Too Hot Tamales*. Come for the weekend brunch of Latin-inspired tapas ($35) with all-you-can-drink mimosas (extra $8). Border Grill uses only hormone-free meat and sustainably caught seafood. Reservations are helpful. A second branch is located at Caesars Palace's Forum Shops.

Fleur
International $$$

Map p63 (☏702-632-9400; www.hubertkeller. com; lunch mains $13-20, small plates $9-27, dinner mains $21-59; ☺lunch 11am-4pm daily, dinner 5-10pm Sun-Thu, to 10:30pm Fri & Sat; 🖋) From French chef Hubert Keller of San Francisco's Fleur de Lys, this soaring space, outfitted with linen curtains and exposed-brick walls, specializes in seasonal small plates inspired by cuisines from around the globe. Get ready for anything, maybe pork-belly fried rice or ancho chili-spiked shrimp and grits, as well as imaginative vegetarian options. Ice cream is dramatically made tableside with liquid nitrogen. Dinner reservations recommended.

Mix
Eurasian $$$

Map p63 (☏702-632-9500; www.alain-ducasse. com; 64th fl; mains $34-54, tasting menu without/with wine pairings $120/175; ☺6-10pm Sun-Thu, to 10:30pm Fri & Sat) A heady glass-elevator ride sets the stage for Mix's sophisticated, space-age decor – check out the two-story chandelier made of 15,000 hand-blown glass globes. The much-hyped kitchen attempts to reproduce dishes from chef Alain Ducasse's Paris and Monaco restaurants. Take your chances, or just go to the sky-high lounge for a cocktail and the same startling Strip views. Reservations essential.

Rx Boiler Room
Gastropub $$$

Map p63 (☏702-632-9900; http://rxboilerroom. com; Shoppes at Mandalay Place; small plates $9-24, mains $18-47; ☺5pm-2am) Upstairs from RM Seafood, chef Rick Moonen's experimental gastropub lures clubby crowds with its steam-punk aesthetic and unusual libations including the Time Traveler's Tea with rum and ginger beer or the Mad Hatter rye cocktail mixed with maple syrup and chocolate bitters. Pastrami sliders, tater tots and other shared plates are more tummy-warming than pricey main courses.

House of Blues
Gospel Brunch
Southern $$$

Map p63 (☎702-632-7600; www.houseofblues.com; adult/child under 11yr $50/27; ⏱seatings 10am & 1pm Sun; ♿) Saturday night sinners can find redemption at HOB's Sunday gospel brunch, where your ticket includes unlimited Bloody Marys and Southern and soul-food favorites such as jambalaya, chicken and waffles, jalapeño cornbread, and warm banana-bread pudding. Buy tickets in advance, as they often sell out.

🍷 Drinking & Nightlife

Mix Lounge
Lounge

Map p63 (64th fl, Mandalay Bay; cover after 10pm $20-25; ⏱5pm-midnight Sun-Tue, to 3am Wed-Sat) High atop one of M-Bay's hotel towers, this is *the* place to go for sunset cocktails. The glassed-in elevator has amazing views on the ride up to the rooftop, and that's before you even glimpse the mod interior design with chocolate-brown leather sofas or the roofless balcony opening up soaring views of the Strip, desert and mountains.

Light
Nightclub

Map p63 (☎702-693-8300; http://thelightvegas.com; cover $20-50; ⏱10:30pm-4am Wed, from 10pm Fri & Sat) Bringing Cirque du Soleil's trademark aerialists, choreographed dancers and special-effects illusions to the Strip's biggest dance floor, Light is not just another Vegas nightclub. Or maybe it is: expect long lines and hard-attitude bouncers who enforce a dress code. Electronica DJs also spin at Daylight, the summertime beach club, and Eclipse concerts on summer nights.

Rí Rá Irish Pub
Pub

Map p63 (☎702-632-7771; www.rira.com/las-vegas; Shoppes at Mandalay Bay; ⏱11am-3am Mon-Thu, 11am-4am Fri, 9am-4am Sat, 9am-3am Sun) Built with salvaged elements from a 19th-century Irish pub that were shipped to America and reassembled on the Strip,

Rí Rá has a wee bit more hospitable spirit than other out-of-the-box Irish pubs in town. Live touring Celtic rock and folk musicians take to the stage around 9pm nightly. Come on weekend mornings for full Irish fry-up breakfasts.

Foundation Room
Nightclub

Map p63 (☎702-632-7631; www.houseofblues.com; 43rd fl; cover usually $30) House of Blues' sophisticated nightclub hosts nightly DJ parties and special events in a stylish space that's half Gothic mansion, half Hindu temple. The expansive views of the Strip are just as impressive as the decor. Look for club promoters around the casino passing out two-for-one drink and free-entry tickets. Dress code enforced.

Minus5 Ice Lounge
Bar

Map p63 (☎702-740-5800; www.minus5experience.com; Shoppes at Mandalay Place; entry with parka, gloves & boot rental $20, incl 2 cocktails $40; ⏱11am-2am Sun-Thu, to 3am Fri & Sat) In a city known for over-the-top gimmicks, this bar has quite a reputation. Don borrowed winter coats and hats before stepping inside the tiny inner sanctum, kept at an arctic chill, where everything is made of ice, from artistic sculptures to the cocktail glasses. No personal cameras allowed. There's another location at the Monte Carlo casino hotel.

Red Square
Bar

Map p63 (☎702-632-7407; ⏱4:30-10pm Sun-Thu, to midnight Fri & Sat) How very

Drink in VIP Views

Level 107 Lounge Stratosphere Tower; p55

Mix Lounge Mandalay Bay; p67

Foundation Room Mandalay Bay; p67

Mandarin Bar & Tea Lounge Mandarin Oriental, CityCenter; p102

ghostbar Palms; p214

post-*perestroika:* a headless Lenin invites you to join your comrades for a tipple behind the blood-red curtains of this Russian restaurant. Behind the solid-ice bar are caviar bowls and more than 200 vodkas mixed with infusions and into cocktails. Sable coats are kept on hand for visiting the private vodka vault. Happy hour runs from 4pm to 7pm daily.

⭐ Entertainment

House of Blues   Live Music
Map p63 (🎵 702-632-7600; www.houseofblues. com; 🕐 box office 9am-9pm) Live blues is definitely not the only game at this imitation Mississippi Delta juke joint. Big-name touring acts entertain the standing-room-only audiences with soul, pop, rock, metal, country, jazz and even burlesque. For some shows, skip the long lines to get in by eating dinner in the restaurant beforehand, then showing your same-day receipt.

Michael Jackson ONE   Theater
Map p63 (🎵 877-632-7400, 800-745-3000; www. cirquedusoleil.com; tickets from $69; 🕐 7pm & 9:30pm Sat-Wed) Cirque du Soleil's musical tribute to the King of Pop blasts onto M-Bay's stage with showstopping dancers and lissome acrobats and aerialists all moving to a soundtrack of Michael Jackson's hits, moon-walking all the way back to his break-out platinum album *Thriller.* No children under five years old allowed.

Mandalay Bay
Events Center   Music, Sports
Map p63 (🎵 702-632-7580; www.mandalaybay. com; 🕐 box office 10am-6pm) Operatic tenor Luciano Pavarotti performed at the opening of this arena-style events center, which hosts championship boxing, ultimate fighting and headliner concerts from Journey to Lady Antebellum.

Left: Shark Reef Aquarium (p64); **Below:** Shoppes at Mandalay Place
(LEFT) YAACOV DAGAN/ALAMY ©; (BELOW) RICHARD CUMMINS/GETTY IMAGES ©

🔒 Shopping

Shoppes at Mandalay Place   Mall
Map p63 (📞702-632-7777; www.mandalaybay.com; 3930 Las Vegas Blvd S, btwn Mandalay Bay & Luxor; 🕙10am-11pm) With a de-stress atmosphere and vaulted ceilings, M-Bay's airy promenade shows off more than two dozen boutiques, including Suite 160 for limited-edition sneakers, Nike Golf, Lush beauty shop, the Art of Shaving and the biggest Guinness-brand store outside of Ireland.

🤸 Spas & Activities

bathhouse   Spa
Map p63 (📞877-632-9636, 702-632-4760; www.mandalaybay.com; 1-/3-/5-day gym pass $15/35/65; 🕙6am-8:30pm) Seducing both sexes, this $25 million minimalist, Asian-inspired spa offers redwood saunas, eucalyptus steam rooms and essential-oil baths. It's a quieter, more intimate alternative to the grander Spa Mandalay. Hotel guests can use the spa facilities by buying a day pass ($25); nonguests must purchase a spa treatment to enter.

Spa Mandalay   Spa
Map p63 (📞702-632-4760, 877-632-7300; day pass for hotel guests $25; 🕙6am-8:30pm) This pampering 30,000-sq-ft spa, outfitted in oak and marble, offers typical massages (get yours with hot stones), body scrubs and facials. Book a treatment and you'll score access to the plunge pools, eucalyptus steam rooms and fitness center. Entry is generally restricted to hotel guests; otherwise, try calling ahead for a weekday appointment.

Luxor

Whether you're arriving in Vegas on an airplane or cruising into town along a desert highway, there's a fixture on the skyline that never escapes the eye: the Luxor's striking 30-story pyramid.

At night a powerful beam of light shoots through the roof 10 miles into the sky like something out of an 1980s sci-fi film – actually, forget cars and planes, the Luxor's beacon is said to be visible from a spaceship.

Despite the high-tech lighting and exterior grandeur – a massive stone Sphinx is poised at the property's entrance – this aging Egyptian-themed casino hotel is no longer one of the Strip's true hot spots. Seemingly constant renovations have brought contemporary eateries and sexed-up nightlife venues, along with spacious swimming pools and a tranquil spa. Today's Luxor has a clamorous and somewhat unrefined vibe that's best suited to party-hearty 20-somethings.

Luxor's pyramid (p72)

TRAVELPIX LTD/GETTY IMAGES ©

⭐ Don't Miss
Luxor's Best

Named after Egypt's splendid ancient city on the east bank of the Nile, the landmark Luxor once had the biggest wow factor on the south Strip. While the theme easily could have produced a pyramid of gaudiness, instead it resulted in a relatively refined shrine to Egyptian art, architecture and antiquities. Some of the more outrageous kitsch has gone the way of the pharaohs, though – in efforts to modernize, the Luxor was 'de-themed' some years ago.

Built in 1993, the 30-story pyramid, housing an enormous atrium and cloaked in black glass, is the main focus. The atrium – the world's largest when it opened – is so voluminous it could accommodate nine Boeing 747s stacked on top of one another. At the apex of the pyramid, a 40-billion-candlepower beacon, the world's most powerful, sends a shaft of bluish-white light 10 miles into the sky, where it's said to be visible to astronauts.

Out in front of the pyramid is a 10-story crouching sphinx and a sandstone obelisk etched with hieroglyphics. The pyramid's interior is adorned with huge Egyptian statues of guards, lions and rams; sandstone walls with hieroglyphic-inscribed tapestries and grand columns; a towering replica of the Great Temple of Ramses II; and a pharaoh's treasure of polished marble.

The King Tut Museum and many of the faux-Egyptian novelties are gone now that MGM Resorts has made over the Luxor with a sleeker, more updated image. Slick-looking restaurants such as **T&T (Tacos & Tequila)** (p74) and **Rice & Company** (p75), rowdy comedian **Carrot Top** (p75) and the happening nightclub **LAX** (p75) bring in a younger crowd.

NEED TO KNOW

☏ 702-262-4000; www.luxor.com; 3900 Las Vegas Blvd S; ⏱ 24hr

LUXOR

Atrium Level

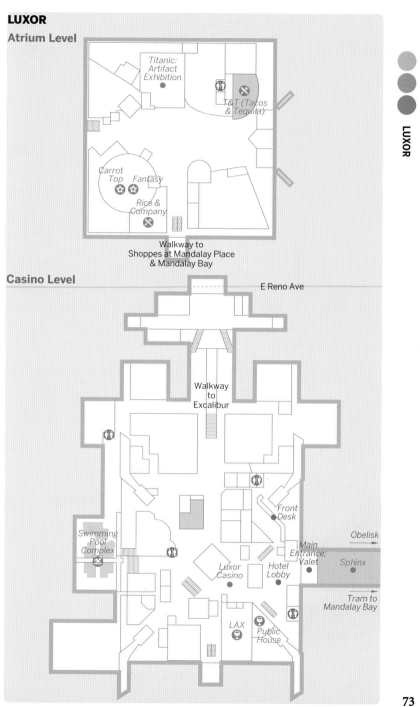

Titanic: Artifact Exhibition

T&T (Tacos & Tequila)

Carrot Top   Fantasy

Rice & Company

Walkway to
Shoppes at Mandalay Place
& Mandalay Bay

Casino Level

E Reno Ave

Walkway
to
Excalibur

Front Desk

Obelisk

Swimming Pool Complex

Main Entrance; Valet

Sphinx

Luxor Casino

Hotel Lobby

Tram to
Mandalay Bay

LAX

Public House

Discover
Luxor

Getting There & Away

○ Tram A free tram connecting Mandalay Bay and Excalibur stops at Luxor. The tram travels north to Excalibur before looping back south to Mandalay Bay. It's quicker to walk to Mandalay Bay through Mandalay Place mall. Luxor is connected to Excalibur by an underground moving walkway.

○ Monorail The closest stop to Luxor is MGM Grand, a 15-minute walk away. Trains run daily until at least midnight.

○ Bus The 24-hour Deuce bus line, servicing the Strip and downtown, stops outside Luxor (southbound) every 15 to 20 minutes. Northbound Deuce) and SDX express buses (9:30am to midnight daily) pick up at Mandalay Bay and MGM Grand.

○ Taxi To get downtown, expect to pay at least $24 (plus tip) one way.

Sphinx and pyramid
ELAN FLEISHER/LOOK/ROBERT HARDING ©

◎ Sights

Luxor Casino
Casino
Map p73 (⊙24hr) With a dark, slightly frenetic feel and confusing layout, the Luxor casino features a few thousand slot and video-poker machines, more than 100 gaming tables, and a race and sports book, plus a few curvaceous female dancers prancing and pirouetting on blackjack and roulette tabletops on weekends.

Titanic: Artifact Exhibition
Exhibit
Map p48 (☑800-557-7428, 702-262-4400; adult/child 4-12yr $32/24; ⊙10am-10pm, last entry 9pm; ⦿) This intriguing exhibition displays more than 250 genuine artifacts salvaged from the RMS *Titanic* – the luxury passenger liner that sank in the chilly Atlantic in 1912. The star attraction is a 15-ton slab of metal once affixed to the ship's starboard hull. Other notable objects include a stunning blue sapphire ring and a champagne bottle plucked from the wreckage.

✖ Eating

The Luxor's dining options aren't scintillating. You're better off walking over to the restaurants in Mandalay Place mall and Mandalay Bay casino resort.

T&T (Tacos & Tequila)
Mexican $$
Map p73 (☑702-262-5225; www.tacosandtequila lv.com; mains $11-24; ⊙11am-11pm) Edgy industrial design pulls a rock 'n' roll crowd upstairs to this popular taqueria inside the Luxor's soaring atrium. Hot-tamale bartenders

Spend the Night

Though the **Luxor** (Map p73; ☏888-386-4658, 702-262-4000; www.luxor.com; r weekday/weekend from $45/85; P✴🗢🏊🛗) isn't one of the Strip's best hotels, you do get to sleep in a pyramid. But with the transition away from a kitschy Egyptian theme and ongoing renovations, staying here is hit-or-miss.

Guest rooms, divided between the pyramid and tower, feature vaguely art-deco furnishings and marble bathrooms. Opt for the newer tower rooms, which have better amenities, including bathtubs. Avoid lower floors in the pyramid, which vibrate all night whenever LAX nightclub is open. If you do stay in the pyramid, you get to ride the Luxor's unusual high-speed elevators, called 'inclinators,' which travel at a 39-degree angle. The mandatory nightly resort fee ($20 plus tax) covers wired in-room internet (currently there's no wi-fi) and fitness-center access.

and tequila temptresses pour shots and pitchers of sangria, while Sunday brunch brings live mariachi bands and two-for-one margaritas and Bloody Marys. Happy hour runs from 2pm to 6pm on weekdays.

Rice & Company
Asian $$

Map p73 (☏702-262-4852; mains $17-28; ◷5-10pm Sun-Thu, to 11pm Fri & Sat) The pan-Asian bistro has a simple motto: 'eat rice, drink tea, slurp noodles, stay healthy.' Prices are inflated for simpler dishes, so go for something more innovative from the Chinese-inspired side of the menu or the sushi list – spice things up with a 'Hot Dang' or 'Crazy Mad Dragon' roll.

🍷 Drinking & Nightlife

LAX
Club

Map p73 (☏702-262-4529; http://angelmg.com/venues/lax; cover $20-40; ◷10:30pm-4am Wed-Sat) Strut your stuff inside this club where the VIP tables border a dance floor that feels like an airport runway between two giant bars – the name is fitting. Nights hosted by Hollywood A-listers and celebutantes are pulse-pounding. Otherwise, there's no reason to pay the cover if you can score a complimentary pass from club promoters in the hotel lobby.

Public House
Sports Bar

Map p73 (www.publichouselasvegas.com; ◷4-11pm) Be wowed by giant-screen TVs while catching NFL games inside this cavernous sports bar, decked out with a patriotic red, white and blue theme.

⭐ Entertainment

Carrot Top
Comedy

Map p73 (☏800-557-7428, 702-262-4400; tickets $50; ◷8:30pm Mon & Wed-Sun) Even if his TV commercials annoyed you to death, this wild and curly orange-haired comedian's shtick could leave your side split and your gut busted. The fast-paced show runs the audience ragged with physical props, dark and twisted stand-up humor and merciless skewering of pop stars, Hollywood celebs and politicians.

Fantasy
Dance

Map p73 (☏702-262-4400, 800-557-7428; www.fantasyluxor.com; tickets from $39; ◷10:30pm) This deliciously trashy topless revue, billed as 'sexy couples' entertainment,' features gorgeous women of many shapes and sizes, and one man for comedic relief. Most of the music is lip-synched, with the exception of the lead siren. Saucy but tame acts mimic Victoria's Secret fashion shows and Playboy Mansion frolics more than anything truly racy.

New York–New York

Give me your tired, your poor, your huddled masses... In this version of New York, the people are tired from walking the Strip, poor from losing at the slot machines, and likely to be huddled over slices of pepperoni pizza in a food court modeled on the real Greenwich Village.

Make no mistake: with its miniature replica skyline and slightly cheesy themed bars, this casino-resort is nothing like the Big Apple – except for the fact that, like its namesake, New York–New York isn't exactly wholesome. This is a place where overgrown frat boys stare up at sexy women dancing on poker tables and Jersey housewives overdo it on martinis in the little 'Times Square.'

Still, the Vegas version, with its eye-catching outdoor monuments such as a pint-sized Statue of Liberty, a scaled-down Brooklyn Bridge and a Coney Island–style roller coaster, is good-spirited fun.

New York–New York

RICHARD I'ANSON/GETTY IMAGES ©

★ Don't Miss
New York–New York's Best

Opened in 1997, the mini-megalopolis of New York–New York features scaled-down replicas of the Big Apple's landmarks, such as the Statue of Liberty and a miniature Brooklyn Bridge. Rising above are perspective-warping replicas of the Chrysler, Empire State and Ziggurat buildings. Wrapped around the hotel's flashy facade is the pièce de résistance: the **Big Apple roller coaster** (p80), with cars resembling NYC taxicabs.

Design elements throughout the property reflect the history, style and diversity of 'Nu Yawk.' Restaurants, bars and retail shops hide behind colorful facades stolen from Park Avenue, Greenwich Village and Times Square storefronts. Claustrophobes, beware: this Disneyfied version of the Big Apple can get even more crowded than the real deal.

Inside, Cirque du Soleil's **Zumanity** (p83) titillates couples with sexy acrobatics. And what would a big bad city be without a few watering holes? The **Bar at Times Square** (p82) is popular with the 40-something crowd for piano sing-alongs; **Nine Fine Irishmen** (p81) proffers well-poured pints and live bands; and **Pour 24** (p82) stocks craft beers. At **Gallagher's Steakhouse** (p81) dig into a New York strip, or pretend you're in Little Italy at **Il Fornaio** (p82). Better yet, act like a real New Yorker and just grab a slice of pizza or a Nathan's Famous Hot Dog to eat on the run.

NEED TO KNOW

☏ 702-740-6969; www.newyorknewyork.com; 3790 Las Vegas Blvd S; ⊘24hr

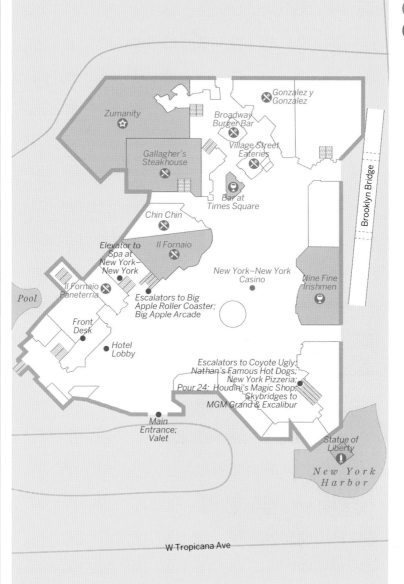

Gonzalez y Gonzalez

Zumanity

Broadway Burger Bar

Gallagher's Steakhouse

Village Street Eateries

Bar at Times Square

Chin Chin

Il Fornaio

Elevator to Spa at New York–New York

New York–New York Casino

Nine Fine Irishmen

Il Fornaio Paneterria

Pool

Escalators to Big Apple Roller Coaster; Big Apple Arcade

Brooklyn Bridge

Front Desk

Hotel Lobby

Escalators to Coyote Ugly; Nathan's Famous Hot Dogs; New York Pizzeria; Pour 24; Houdini's Magic Shop; Skybridges to MGM Grand & Excalibur

Main Entrance; Valet

Statue of Liberty

New York Harbor

W Tropicana Ave

Discover New York–New York

Getting There & Away

Getting There & Away

o **Tram** A skybridge crosses Tropicana Ave to Excalibur, where you can catch a tram south to Luxor and Mandalay Bay.

o **Monorail** The closest stop to New York–New York is at MGM Grand, located across a skybridge on the opposite side of Las Vegas Blvd. Trains run daily until at least midnight.

o **Bus** The 24-hour Deuce bus line, with service along the entire Strip and to downtown, stops outside New York–New York (southbound) and the MGM Grand (northbound) every 15 to 20 minutes. Faster SDX buses (9:30am to midnight daily) stop at MGM Grand (northbound) and Excalibur (southbound).

o **Taxi** A taxi is your best bet if you're heading downtown. Expect to pay at least $23 (plus tip) one way.

New York–New York Casino
ED NORTON/GETTY IMAGES ©

Sights

New York–New York Casino

Casino

Map p48 (⊙24hr) NYNY's casino attracts a mélange of mostly college-aged kids. Gaming tables with so-so odds in the 'Party Pit' are set against a distracting backdrop of go-go dancers and a Michael Jackson impersonator who moon-walks some nights. High-limit wagers are placed in the area wittily named 'Gaming on the Green.'

Big Apple Roller Coaster

Amusement Park

Map p79 (1 ride/day pass $14/25; ⊙11am-11pm Sun-Thu, 10:30am-midnight Fri & Sat; ⛹) This Coney Island–inspired roller coaster makes a heartline twist-and-dive maneuver, producing a sensation similar to that felt by a pilot during a barrel roll in a fighter plane. The rest of the three-minute trip includes stomach-dropping dips, high-banked turns, a 180-degree spiral and blink-and-you'll-miss-it views of the Strip. Hold on tight: your head, back and shoulders will take a beating on this bumpy ride. All riders must be at least 54in tall.

More than a million people ride this roller coaster each year, including blushing brides and grooms who get hitched on board (wedding ceremonies from $600).

Big Apple Arcade

Arcade

Map p79 (⊙8am-11pm Sun-Thu, to 2am Fri & Sat; ⛹) Above the casino floor, a gargantuan carnival-esque arcade offers something for kids (and kids at heart) with 200-plus video games ranging from '80s classics including Ms Pac-Man to the latest Japanese

Spend the Night

Though guest rooms and suites at **New York–New York** (Map p79; ☎866-815-4365, 702-740-6969; www.newyorknewyork.com; r weekday/weekend from $50/110; P✿🛜@☃) aren't exactly standouts on the Strip, they generally get positive reviews. The smallest 'Park Avenue' and marginally bigger 'Madison Avenue Deluxe' rooms all have flat-screen TVs and marble baths. If you're able to spend more, splash out on a Marquis suite with a four-person whirlpool tub and Strip views.

The mandatory nightly resort fee ($20 plus tax) covers fitness-center access and wi-fi both in guest rooms and throughout the property.

imports, plus laser tag. Just be aware that little ones might see the scantily clad babes dancing on tables downstairs in the casino.

 Eating

NYNY has the best-value eats on the southern Strip. By the pedestrian skybridge entrance on the mezzanine level, a cluster of fast-food stands sell Nathan's Famous Hot Dogs, Tropicana juice smoothies and 99¢ cups of coffee.

Il Fornaio Paneterria
Bakery, Cafe $

Map p79 (snacks & drinks $3-8; ⏱6am-6pm) Sip espresso and pick up delectable, freshly baked goods such as lemon-pecan scones, cinnamon coffee cake and hazelnut pastries at this bakery-cafe near the hotel lobby.

New York Pizzeria
Pizza $

Map p79 (mains $5-10; ⏱10am-1am Sun-Thu, to 4am Fri & Sat; 👶) This no-frills pizzeria turns out piping-hot garlic knots and large, dripping slices of pizza, mini calzones and overstuffed stromboli. Open late, it's perfect for a quick stop after you've been drinking at the bars.

Village Street Eateries
International $$

Map p79 (mains $5-20; ⏱7am-3am, restaurant hrs vary; 👶) The cobblestone streets of

NYNY's Greenwich Village are bursting with budget options: authentic **Greenberg & Sons Deli**; **Broadway Burger Bar** for patties made with grass-fed beef sourced from a ranch in Uruguay; bargain slices from **Sirrico's Pizza**; **Chin Chin** for take-out-quality Chinese dishes and Japanese sushi; and **Gonzalez Y Gonzalez**, a tequila-soaked Tex-Mex cantina.

Gallagher's Steakhouse
Steakhouse $$$

Map p79 (☎702-740-6450; www.gallaghers nysteakhouse.com; mains $28-50; ⏱4-11pm Sun-Thu, to midnight Fri & Sat) This reproduction of a classy NYC steakhouse (the original Gallagher's dates from 1927) drums up a serious dinner menu with lobster bisque, wedge salads, dry-aged bone-in sirloin (the house specialty, which you'll see hanging in glass-fronted meat lockers out front) and side dishes including house-made potato chips. The circular bar is an atmospheric spot for a martini.

Nine Fine Irishmen
Pub $$$

Map p79 (☎702-740-6463; www.ninefine irishmen.com; mains $15-30; ⏱11am-11pm; 🛜) Dig into finessed country cooking at this authentic Irish bar, which offers a decent but overpriced menu of lamb stew, bangers and mash, corned-beef sandwiches and other pub grub, washed down with pints of Guinness. Vegetarians aren't totally left out, with herb-crusted goat cheese salad, baked brie with oven-roasted tomatoes and fried pickles on the menu.

Il Fornaio
Italian $$$

Map p79 (☎702-740-6403; www.ilfornaio.com; mains breakfast $9-12, dinner $14-40; ⊙7:30-10:30am & 11:30am-midnight) Take a bite of wood-fired pizza, pasta and salads at this classic NY-style Italian joint. House specialties include lasagna layered with porcini mushrooms; cannelloni stuffed with rotisserie chicken, organic spinach and smoked mozzarella; and spicy linguine tossed with clams, mussels, prawns and scallops. Gourmet omelets bring out the breakfast crowd.

🍷 Drinking & Nightlife

After dark, New York–New York takes on an atmosphere that's more frenetic frat-boy than sophisticated urbanite.

Nine Fine Irishmen
Pub

Map p79 (☎702-740-6463; www.ninefineirish men.com; ⊙11am-2:45am, live music from 9pm; 📶) Built in Ireland and shipped piece by piece to America, this pub has cavernous interior booths and outdoor patio tables beside NYNY's Brooklyn Bridge. Genuine stouts, ales, ciders and Irish whiskeys are always stocked at the bar. Live entertainment is a mix of Celtic rock and traditional Irish country tunes, occasionally with sing-alongs and a champion Irish dancer.

Pour 24
Bar

Map p79 (⊙24hr) Upstairs next to the sky-bridge entrance, Pour 24 looks like just any other standard casino bar. The draw is the long list of American craft beers – including Dogfish Head's 60 Minute IPA and Big Sky's Moose Drool – on draft and in bottles, or create your own tasting flight.

Bar at Times Square
Bar

Map p79 (☎702-740-6466; cover $10-25, free until 7pm; ⊙11am-2:30am, live music 8pm-2am) Baby boomers dig the sing-along vibe at this packed dueling piano bar with polished wooden floors. Show up early for live music or risk waiting outside in Greenwich Village, where latecomers

Il Fornaio

strain to catch a glimpse of the drunken festivities inside. Happy hour runs from 3pm to 7pm on weekdays, when the 'Sax Man' croons.

Coyote Ugly   Bar
Map p79 (www.coyoteuglysaloon.com; cover $10, free before 9pm; ☺6pm-2am Sun-Thu, to 3am Fri & Sat) Just like in the movie – well, sort of – this rowdy bar features voluptuous female bartenders dancing on the bar while pouring shots of liquor into the mouths of the mostly male crowd. There's a steady stream of drunken dudes stumbling out of this dive in the wee hours. Happy hour runs from 6pm to 9pm daily.

⭐ Entertainment

Zumanity   Theater
Map p79 (☏888-693-0763, 866-815-4365; www.zumanity.com; tickets $69-105, love seats per couple $250; ☺7pm & 9:30pm Fri-Tue) Billed as 'the sensual side of Cirque du Soleil,' this human zoo amps up the energy, contorted acrobatics and flirtatious eroticism of the troupe's other risk-taking Strip shows. It won't take your breath away, though. So what's the hook? Maybe it's the curvilinear thrust stage, uninhibited costumes or the aphrodisiacal cocktail menu. No guests under 18 years old admitted.

🔒 Shopping

Houdini's Magic Shop   Children
Map p79 (www.houdini.com; ☺10am-midnight Mon-Thu, to 1am Fri & Sat, 9am-midnight Sun) Let yourself be roped into this real-deal magic shop by the staff who perform illusions and card tricks out front for sometimes inebriated passersby (they're easy marks). Magician memorabilia and DIY magic kits are sold inside. There are other branches at MGM Grand, Planet Hollywood's Miracle Mile Shops and the Grand Canal Shoppes at the Venetian.

🏃 Spas & Activities

Spa at New York–
New York   Spa
Map p79 (☏702-740-6955; www.newyork newyork.com/spa; 3rd fl, near Empire Elevator; guests/nonguests day pass $10/20; ☺6:30am-7pm) In New York–New York's top-rated fitness room, the cardio machines have personal TVs, while weight machines overlook the outdoor swimming pool. Both the men's and women's spas offer steam rooms and saunas (men also get a whirlpool), but they're diminutive. Massage and spa treatments are a la carte.

MGM Grand

For an idea of the scope of billion-dollar MGM Grand, consider that when it opened in 1993 39 armored cars delivered $3.5 million in quarters to the casino's slot machines.

Despite its overwhelming size (it takes 15 minutes just to walk to the monorail station) many places in this gargantuan property manage to feel surprisingly intimate, even clubby. Trend-setting restaurants and nightlife justify the glowing emerald green resort's motto 'Maximum Vegas,' along with a giant pool complex sporting the longest lazy river ride in town. The resort's developers have had to keep up with the Joneses, though – a gigantic hotel in Moscow recently snatched the title of the largest hotel in the world.

In the past few years ever-evolving MGM Grand has embarked on an ambitious 'grand renovation,' adding contemporary style and technology to guest rooms and revamping the resort's endlessly entertaining amenities.

MGM Grand

PAUL CHESLEY/GETTY IMAGES ©

⭐ Don't Miss
MGM Grand's Best

Owned by movie company Metro-Goldwyn-Mayer, the MGM Grand liberally borrows Hollywood themes. Check out the casino resort's Strip-side entrance, where flashing LED screens and computerized fountains add extra theatrics to the 100,000lb, 45ft-tall bronze lion statue – naturally, it's the largest bronze statue in the country. Star-worthy 'Maximum Vegas' attractions include Cirque du Soleil's martial-arts-inspired spectacular **Kà** (p91) and the massive **MGM Grand Garden Arena** (p91), which stages championship boxing and mega concerts by pop stars.

For many, the MGM Grand's biggest draw is the Grand Pool complex out back, with four swimming pools and a few whirlpools. At this fabulous outdoor playground, children splash in shallow aqua pools, bikini beauties sunbathe on chaise longues, college students slurp from yard-long strawberry daiquiris and last night's party crowd recovers under beach umbrellas. The highlight is an 8000ft-long lazy river – the longest in Vegas – that snakes around the pools, passing through spraying waterfalls and underneath bridges draped with tropical foliage. Rent an inner tube or just let the gentle current sweep you along. During summer, **Wet Republic** (p90) is the Strip's most MTV-worthy pool club.

Back inside, stroll past an impressive lineup of celebrity chefs' restaurants, bars and nightlife venues, none more dazzling than **Joël Robuchon** (p89), where you'll dine inside a faux Parisian mansion, and newcomer **Hakkasan** (p89), a glam Chinese restaurant and nightclub. A handful of low-key attractions, namely **CSI: The Experience** (p88) and **CBS Television City** (p88), add a family-oriented atmosphere.

NEED TO KNOW
☎702-891-1111; www.mgmgrand.com; 3799 Las Vegas Blvd S; ⏰24hr

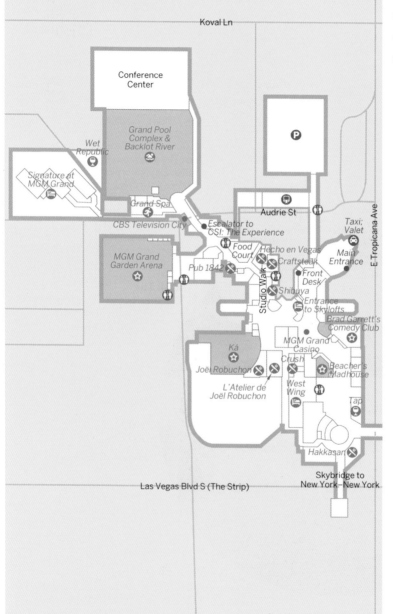

Koval Ln

Conference Center

Grand Pool Complex & Backlot River

Wet Republic

Signature at MGM Grand

Grand Spa

CBS Television City

Escalator to CSI: The Experience

Audrie St

Taxi; Valet

Main Entrance

E Tropicana Ave

Food Court

Hecho en Vegas

Craftsteak

Front Desk

MGM Grand Garden Arena

Pub 1842

Studio Walk

Shibuya

Entrance to Skylofts

Brad Garrett's Comedy Club

Ká

Joël Robuchon

L'Atelier de Joël Robuchon

MGM Grand Casino

Crush

Beacher's Madhouse

West Wing

Tap

Hakkasan

Las Vegas Blvd S (The Strip)

Skybridge to New York–New York

Discover
MGM Grand

Getting There & Away

○ **Monorail** The monorail connects the MGM Grand with select casino hotels along the east side of the Strip, as well as with the city's convention center. Trains arrive every four to 12 minutes, operating daily until at least midnight.

○ **Bus** The Deuce (24 hour) and faster SDX (9:30am to midnight daily) bus lines, with service along the Strip and to downtown, stop outside the MGM Grand (northbound) and Excalibur (southbound) every 15 to 20 minutes.

○ **Taxi** A taxi is your best bet if you're heading downtown. Expect to pay at least $23 (plus tip) one way.

Sights

MGM Grand Casino Casino
Map p48 (📞877-880-0880; www.mgmgrand.com; 3799 Las Vegas Blvd S) Astoundingly, this resort contains no fewer than 18,000 doors, 7778 beds and 93 elevators. The casino can feel labyrinthine, with thousands of slot machines and hundreds of gaming tables. Near the race and sports book, decked out with skyboxes and giant-screen plasma TVs, the MGM's hot poker room is open around the clock, offering tableside massages and free Texas hold'em lessons daily.

CSI: The Experience Exhibit
Map p87 (📞877-660-0660, 702-891-7006; www.csitheexperience.org; Studio Walk; adult/child 4-11yr $28/21; ⊙9am-9pm, last entry 8pm; 👪) Following the conceit of the prime-time TV series, this hands-on science exhibit lets visitors play sleuth, collecting evidence from a fake crime scene and analyzing it in an interactive 'lab' to crack the case. Although it's small, overpriced and not always fully functional, hard-core CSI fans may enjoy it. Not recommended for children under 12 years old.

CBS Television City Exhibit
Map p87 (📞702-891-5752; www.tvcityresearch.com; Studio Walk; ⊙usually 10am-8:30pm; 👪) **FREE** This tech-forward attraction features a video wall, logo souvenir shop and several futuristic theaters where viewers watch TV pilot episodes for market re-

MGM Grand Casino

Spend the Night

At the **MGM Grand** (Map p87; ☎877-880-0880, 702-891-1111; www.mgmgrand.com; r weekday/weekend from $70/140; 🅿❄@🛜🏊🚹), 5040 rooms and suites are spread out among four 30-story towers. But is bigger better? Yes and no. In a hotel this big, guest services tend to be sluggish and you might get lost trying to find your room. But the 'Grand Renovation' has done away with the slightly cheap looking decor of the old Hollywood-themed rooms by adding pop art, jewel-toned furnishings, bronze fixtures and high-tech media hubs.

Stylish hideaways within the MGM Grand complex include the West Wing, where modish design rules and walk-in showers for two spice things up; Stay Well rooms, which offer Vitamin C-charged showers, hypoallergenic bedding and aromatherapy; and the extravagant **Skylofts** (Map p48; ☎877-646-5638, 702-891-3832; www.skyloftsmgmgrand.com; ste from $1000; 🅿❄@🛜🏊), where an overnight stay includes a personal butler. Occupying three towers nearby is the **Signature at MGM Grand** (Map p48; ☎877-727-0007, 702-797-6000; www.signaturemgmgrand.com; 145 E Harmon Ave; weekday/weekend ste from $95/170; 🅿❄@🛜🏊), a non-gaming, non-smoking, all-suites condo hotel.

The mandatory nightly resort fee ($25 plus tax) includes in-room wi-fi and cardio-room access.

search, sometimes donning 3D eyewear. Children must be at least 10 years old to attend most screenings.

🍴 Eating

The MGM Grand is a dining powerhouse. For reservations click on www.mgmgrand.com/restaurants or call ☎877-660-0660.

Joël Robuchon — French $$$

Map p87 (☎702-891-7925; www.joel-robuchon.com/en; tasting menu per person $120-425; ⏰5:30-10pm Sun-Thu, to 10:30pm Fri & Sat) The acclaimed 'Chef of the Century' leads the pack in the French culinary invasion of the Strip. Adjacent to the high-rollers' gaming area, Robuchon's plush dining rooms, done up in leather and velvet, feel like a dinner party at a 1930s Paris mansion. Complex seasonal tasting menus promise the meal of a lifetime – and they often deliver.

Reservations are essential for dinner here, as well as at the slightly less-expensive **L'Atelier de Joël Robuchon**

Map p87 (☎702-891-7358; www.joel-robuchon.com/en; mains $41-97, tasting menu without/with wine pairings $159/265; ⏰5-11pm) next door, where bar seats front an exhibition kitchen.

Hakkasan — Chinese $$$

Map p87 (☎702-891-7888; http://hakkasan.com/lasvegas; mains $16-68; ⏰5-11pm Sun-Thu, to midnight Fri & Sat) For see-and-be-seen dining or a splashy date night, few restaurants on the Strip beat this dramatic Chinese restaurant, with futuristic neo-Asian accents visible everywhere, from patterned upholstery to screened-in dining 'cages.' Michelin-starred chef Ho Chee Boon's mainly Cantonese menu darts off in unexpected ways, like the roasted cod with champagne and honey. Mixologist cocktails are designed to wow.

Reservations essential.

Pub 1842 — Gastropub $$$

Map p87 (☎702-891-3922; http://michaelmina.net; mains brunch $11-16, lunch & dinner $18-49; ⏰11:30am-10pm Sun-Thu, to midnight Fri & Sat) At chef Michael Mina's casual gastropub, don't let the cabin-in-the-woods decor, with plaid-patterned booths and wooden-slat walls, fool you. Extraordinarily tasty, whimsical comfort food – try a lobster corn dog or a gourmet burger topped with peanut butter and bacon jam – goes above and beyond. So do the barrel-aged cocktails and craft beer flights from the bar. Happy hour runs from 3pm to 6pm daily. Dinner reservations recommended.

Craftsteak
Steakhouse $$$

Map p87 (☏702-891-7318; www.craft restaurantsinc.com; mains $36-70, tasting menu $120-160; ⏰5:30-10pm Sun-Thu, to 10:30pm Fri & Sat) This richly wood-laden steakhouse lacks exclusivity, what with all the monorail riders walking by. Celeb chef Tom Colicchio's menu of grass-fed steaks, grilled bison and 24-hour braised short ribs, plus bounty from the sea such as Australian lobster tail, is sometimes a letdown in its execution. Drown any disappointments with a huge array of top-shelf bourbon and scotch. Reservations essential.

Shibuya
Japanese $$$

Map p87 (☏702-891-3001; tasting menus $55-120; ⏰5:30-10pm Sun-Thu, to 10:30pm Fri & Sat; ⏰) Come for the stellar sake cellar, dramatic interior design and taste-bud-awakening hot and cold appetizers, such as crab seaweed salad with crispy lotus chips. Specialty sushi rolls and family-style *teppanyaki* (grill) menus are the best value, but you'll still pay through the nose. Reservations recommended.

Crush
Mediterranean $$$

Map p87 (☏702-892-3222; pizzas & small plates $14-18, mains $16-65; ⏰5:30-10:30pm Sun-Thu, to 11:30pm Fri & Sat; ⏰) Off the casino floor, an airy dining room and a cozy wine-cellar room compose this casual eatery and wine bar. On the seasonal Mediterranean menu, crispy 700°F wood-oven-fired pizzas, rich pasta and both raw and roasted *antipasti* are more satisfying than meatier mains. Vegetar-

ian, vegan, dairy-free and gluten-free options aim to please everyone.

Hecho en Vegas
Mexican $$$

Map p87 (☏702-891-3200; mains $16-42; ⏰5-10pm Sun-Thu, to 11pm Fri & Sat) An offshoot of Tucson's El Charro Cafe, this lofty cantina by the monorail station hosts festive groups with pitchers of margaritas. Handmade tamales, tortillas and torta bread stand out on an average menu that also includes chimichangas, Sonoran hot dogs, and fajita platters with ancho-chili-rubbed skirt steak or shrimp diablo.

🍷 Drinking & Nightlife

Hakkasan
Club

Map p87 (☏702-891-3838; http://hakkasanlv. com; cover $20-75; ⏰10pm-4am Thu-Fri & Sun, 9pm-4am Sat) At this lavish Asian-inspired nightclub, international jet-set DJs including Tiësto and Steve Aoki rule the jam-packed main dance floor bordered by VIP booths and floor-to-ceiling LED screens. More offbeat sounds spin in the intimate Ling Ling Club, revealing leather sofas and backlit amber glass. Bouncers enforce the dress code: upscale nightlife attire (no athletic wear); collared shirts required for men.

Wet Republic
Pool Club

Map p87 (☏702-891-3715; http://wetrepublic. com; cover $20-40; ⏰usually Mar-Sep, hrs vary) Think of Wet Republic, the city's biggest 'ultra pool,' as a nightclub brought out into the sunlight. The mostly 20- and 30-something crowd in stylish swimwear show up for EDM tunes spun by megawatt DJs such as Calvin Harris, fruity cocktails and bobbing oh-so-coolly around saltwater pools while checking out the bikini-clad scenery. Book ahead for VIP bungalows, daybeds and cabanas.

Tap
Sports Bar

Map p87 (☏702-891-1111; 11am-11pm) Within swinging distance of the casino's race and sports book, this clubhouse plasters the walls with sports memorabilia. Order a round of craft beers and a plate of beer-can chicken while you watch the big game on five dozen HDTV screens.

⭐ Entertainment

Kà
Theater

Map p87 (☏800-929-1111, 702-531-3826; www. cirquedusoleil.com; adult $69-150, child 5-12yr $35-75; ☺7pm & 9:30pm Tue-Sat; ♟) Cirque du Soleil makes this sensuous story of imperial twins, mysterious destinies, love and conflict one of the Strip's hottest tickets. Instead of a stage, there's a $200 million grid of moving platforms elevating a frenzy of martial-arts-styled performances. Children under five years old are not allowed.

Beacher's Madhouse
Theater, Comedy

Map p87 (☏702-891-3577; http://beachers madhouse.com; tickets $75-125; ☺10:30pm Wed, Fri & Sat) Spotting celebs in the VIP box may steal your attention from this wild interactive show, where you might get pulled up on stage to boogie with the red-hot Beacher's Babies. Expect frenetic frat-boy antics, sick stand-up and a little magic in this bawdy, short-attention-span sideshow.

MGM Grand Garden Arena
Music, Sports

Map p87 (☏877-880-0880; www.mgmgrand. com/entertainment; ticket prices vary; ☺box office 9am-8:30pm) Madonna, U2, Lady Gaga, Bruce Springsteen and the Rolling Stones have all rocked the stage of this 17,000-seat arena, which also hosts championship boxing tournaments and fight nights.

Brad Garrett's Comedy Club
Comedy

Map p87 (☏866-740-7711; www.bradgarrett comedy.com; tickets $45-90; ☺8pm) TV sit-com star Brad Garrett and a rotating line-up of stand-up comedians do their schtick at this clubby theater with red-velvet curtains. It's pricey, so check out who's appearing before you plunk down your credit card.

🤸 Spas & Activities

MGM Grand Spa
Spa

Map p87 (☏702-891-3077; gym pass $10, gym & spa day pass $25; ☺6am-7pm Mon-Thu, to 8pm Fri-Sun) A two-hour 'Dreaming Ritual,' employing Australian Indigenous healing and massage techniques, is the signature treatment at this sprawling 29,000-sq-ft spa, which soothes with design accents such as bamboo, rock walls and elemental wood. Spa day passes are for hotel guests only; nonguests may make spa appointments for Monday through Thursday.

CityCenter & Cosmopolitan

Goodbye kitsch and cigarettes, hello high modern style.

On the Strip, themed casino hotels compete to outdo each other, but CityCenter beats the competition by not competing at all. This contemporary mini 'city' of cutting-edge hotels, restaurants and designer boutiques is a towering, luxury playground. Its high-minded public artwork has transformed both the skyline and the cultural landscape of the Strip.

Add to the mix a Japanese-style spa, offbeat Cirque du Soleil show, catwalk designers such as Christian Dior, and buzzing restaurants and nightlife at the Cosmopolitan casino resort next door, and it's obvious that CityCenter wants you to have it all. In this megalopolis, where neon lights burn brightly and millions of air conditioners pump around the clock, it's not easy being ecoconscious. But forward-thinking CityCenter, with Gold LEED (Leadership in Energy & Environmental Design) certification and official status as one of the world's largest sustainable developments, attempts the impossible – that's another reason to drop by.

CityCenter & Cosmopolitan Highlights

Fine Art Collection (p98)

Worth more than $40 million, CityCenter's thought-provoking collection of modern and contemporary fine art is freely displayed throughout the complex's public spaces. You can pick up a self-guided brochure from hotel and shopping mall concierge desks or download a free mobile walking-tour app, but the real appeal is stumbling on unexpected works around every corner. Nancy Rubins' sculpture *Big Edge*, Vdara Hotel & Spa

② Cosmopolitan (p96)

The Strip's hippest casino resort for now, Cosmo avoids utter pretension, despite the constant wink-wink, arty-retro flourishes such as the Art-o-Mats (vintage cigarette machines hawking original art rather than nicotine), the help-yourself pool tables surrounded by old-school leather armchairs and the larger-than-life red stiletto heel that you can climb into for a tongue-in-cheek Vegas photo op.

Crystals (p103)

The structure of CityCenter's dazzling shopping mall is an architectural and cultural attraction in its own right. Admire the angular glass canopy jutting onto Las Vegas Blvd, then walk inside to find a three-story 'treehouse' made of smooth, dark wood, as well as a kid-friendly, high-tech art installation composed of neon tube lights and glass-encased funnels of swirling water. Daniel Libeskind's Crystals shopping mall

Mandarin Oriental & Vdara (p102)

Despite all its frenetic energy, CityCenter also enfolds two hushed oases, the Mandarin Oriental and all-suites Vdara hotels, where you can get away from the ding-ding-ding of the slot machines. Even if you're not staying overnight, ride the elevator to the Mandarin Oriental's 23rd-floor 'sky lobby' to take in nighttime views of the Strip's neon lights while you sip champagne cocktails.

Aria (p101)

CityCenter's architectural showpiece, Aria has a sophisticated casino accented with sleek chrome, polished stone and dark wood. It's a fitting backdrop for visually stunning restaurants, many run by top chefs. Energy-efficient design features and ecoconscious amenities don't come at the price of luxuries, whether you find them at the East-meets-West spa or inside your own cocoon-like hotel room or suite.

SHAY VELICH/PHOTOSTOCK-ISRAEL/ALAMY ©

⭐ Don't Miss
Cosmopolitan's Best

Hipsters who thought they were too cool for Vegas finally have a place to go where they don't need irony to endure – or enjoy – the aesthetics of the Strip. Like the new Hollywood 'It Girl', the Cosmopolitan casino looks absolutely fabulous at all times. A steady stream of ingenues and entourages parade through the lobby, along with anyone else who adores contemporary art and design.

Dangling like a glimmering ornament in the center of the Cosmo is the gorgeous **Chandelier Bar** (p102), a three-tiered cocktail bar fringed by glowing glass-bead curtains. Perched on a velvet loveseat, you'll feel like you're sipping champagne inside a rosy jewelry box. **Marquee** nightclub (p102) and the **Shops at Cosmopolitan** (p103) draw fashion plates too. In warmer months, bikini-clad babes lounge under cabanas at the outdoor **Boulevard Pool**, where indie-music stars give concerts under the stars.

Lighthearted eateries include the **Wicked Spoon Buffet** (p100), Chinese-Mexican **China Poblano** (p99), gourmet burgers at **Holsteins** (p99), Spanish tapas at **Jaleo** (p100) and the experimental supper club **Vegas Nocturne at Rose.Rabbit.Lie** (p102). The morning after, melt away your hangover inside the **Sahra Spa & Hammam** (p103).

NEED TO KNOW
📞 702-698-7000; www.cosmopolitanlasvegas.com; 3708 Las Vegas Blvd S; 🕐 24hr

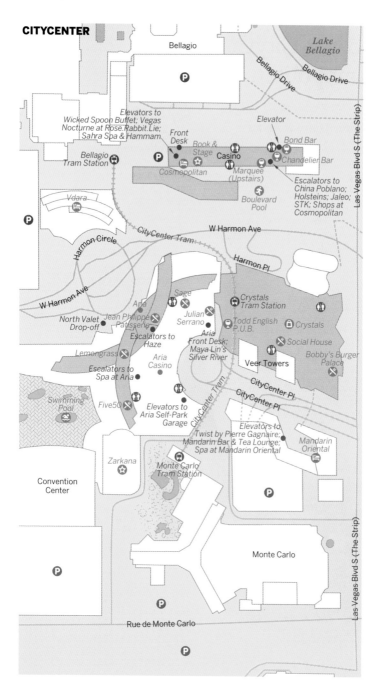

CITYCENTER

Bellagio

Lake Bellagio

Bellagio Drive

Bellagio Drive

Elevators to Wicked Spoon Buffet; Vegas Nocturne at Rose.Rabbit.Lie; Sahra Spa & Hammam

Front Desk

Book & Stage

Casino

Elevator

Bond Bar

Chandelier Bar

Bellagio Tram Station

Cosmopolitan

Marquee (Upstairs)

Escalators to China Poblano; Holsteins; Jaleo; STK; Shops at Cosmopolitan

Boulevard Pool

Vdara

W Harmon Ave

Las Vegas Blvd S (The Strip)

CityCenter Tram

Harmon Circle

W Harmon Ave

Harmon Pl

Harmon Pl

Sage

Aria

Crystals Tram Station

North Valet Drop-off

Jean Philippe Patisserie

Julian Serrano

Todd English P.U.B.

Crystals

Escalators to Haze

Aria Front Desk; Maya Lin's Silver River

Social House

Lemongrass

Aria Casino

Veer Towers

Bobby's Burger Palace

Escalators to Spa at Aria

CityCenter Pl

CityCenter Pl

Swimming Pool

Five50

Elevators to Aria Self-Park Garage

CityCenter Tram

Elevators to Twist by Pierre Gagnaire; Mandarin Bar & Tea Lounge; Spa at Mandarin Oriental

Mandarin Oriental

Zarkana

Monte Carlo Tram Station

Convention Center

Monte Carlo

Las Vegas Blvd S (The Strip)

Rue de Monte Carlo

Discover CityCenter & Cosmopolitan

Getting There & Away

o **Tram** Free trams connect Bellagio with CityCenter from 8am to 4am daily, stopping at Crystals and Monte Carlo en route. Trams arrive every seven to 15 minutes.

o **Monorail** Cross Las Vegas Blvd and walk about 15 minutes to the monorail station at the back of Bally's or MGM Grand. The monorail connects selected casinos along the east side of the Strip with the city's convention center. Trains operate daily until at least midnight.

o **Bus** The 24-hour Deuce bus line, with service along the entire Strip and to downtown, stops outside the Monte Carlo (southbound) and Planet Hollywood (northbound) every 15 to 20 minutes.

o **Taxi** A taxi is your best bet if you're heading downtown. Expect to pay at least $21 (plus tip) one way.

Sights

CityCenter Fine Art Collection
Public Art

Map p97 (CityCenter; 24hr) FREE With a striking range of large-scale art installations, contemporary sculptures and larger-than-life abstract paintings, CityCenter curates one of the biggest collections of corporately owned art anywhere in the world. Notable artists include Claes Oldenburg, Coosje van Bruggen, Nancy Rubins, Frank Stella and Maya Lin, whose 84ft-long reclaimed-silver cast of the Colorado River hangs behind the Aria hotel's front desk.

Aria Casino
Casino

Map p97 (Aria, CityCenter; 24hr) Smartly designed and seductively illuminated, CityCenter's star casino is a sophisticated place to throw your money away. Look for all the usual suspects, plus exclusive spaces such as the Spin high-limit slot-machine room and high-stakes blackjack and baccarat in the invitation-only Salon Privé. Aria's poker room hosts nightly tournaments.

Eating

CityCenter's Aria casino hotel, Mandarin Oriental luxury hotel and Crystals shopping center all draw epicureans, as does the neighboring Cosmopolitan casino resort. To make a reservation at Aria, visit www.aria.com/dining/restaurants or call ☎877-230-2742; for Cosmopolitan, visit www.cosmopolitanlasvegas.com/taste.aspx or call ☎877-893-2003.

Aria (p101)

Spend the Night

Want to hang your hat at CityCenter? As long as you're not looking for a bargain, there's something for everyone. The **Cosmopolitan** (Map p97; ☏ 855-435-0005, 702-698-7000; www.cosmopolitanlasvegas.com; r/ste from $160/220; 🅿️❄️📶@🏊👶), with its hot dining and nightlife and stylish, tech-friendly suites, is where 20- and 30-somethings blow out their budgets. The tailored accommodations at **Aria** (Map p97; ☏ 866-359-7757 , 702-590-7757; www.arialasvegas.com; r weekday/weekend from $129/189; 🅿️❄️📶@🏊👶) attract a sophisticated, if more mature, clientele. Business travelers and high rollers check into the five-star **Mandarin Oriental** (Map p97; ☏ 888-881-9578, 702-590-8888; www.mandarinoriental.com/lasvegas; r/ste from $225/435; 🅿️❄️📶@🏊), while eco-conscious urbanites book the spacious apartment-style suites at non-gaming hotel **Vdara** (Map p97; ☏ 866-745-7767, 702-590-2111; www.vdara.com; ste weekday/weekend from $119/179; 🅿️♿❄️📶@🏊✒️).

Jean Philippe Patisserie
Bakery, Desserts $

Map p97 (Aria, CityCenter; snacks & drinks $4-11; ⏰6am-midnight Mon-Thu, to 2am Fri & Sat, to 1am Sun; 👶) Handily located next to Aria's casino, this master pastry chef's shop churns out chocoholic truffles, sweet crepes, house-made gelati and other snacks until late at night. Pick up coffee and espresso to go.

Bobby's Burger Palace
Burgers $

Map p97 (☏702-598-0191; http://bobbysburgerpalace.com; Crystals, CityCenter; items $4-10; ⏰10am-midnight) Hey, it's no palace, but it's half the price of some star chefs' burger joints on the Strip. Get the Napa Valley Burger topped with goat's cheese and Meyer lemon-honey mustard, plus hand-cut fries and a pistachio milkshake or a frozen cactus-pear margarita.

China Poblano
Mexican, Chinese $$

Map p97 (☏702-698-7900; Cosmopolitan; shared plates $5-20; ⏰11:30am-11:30pm) Noodles and tacos, together? An eye-catching fusion eatery from chef José Andrés mixes two unlikely cuisines – Chinese and Mexican – in a lively, hipster-friendly space where the glow of neon signs brightens darkened booths and bar stools. Inspired street food riffs include duck tongue tacos with lychee and red-chili-braised pork buns.

Holsteins
Burgers $$

Map p97 (☏702-698-7940; http://holsteinslv.com; Cosmopolitan; items $6-18; ⏰11am-midnight, to 2am Fri & Sat; 👶) At graffiti-covered Holsteins, handcrafted burgers are championship worthy, as are all-American classics with a gourmet twist – fried pickles, truffle lobster mac 'n' cheese, and milkshakes spiked with chocolate vodka. Pick from the 'big buns' or 'tiny buns' (sliders) lists of beef, chicken, lamb, pork and veggie patties. Reservations recommended.

Five50
Pizza $$

Map p97 (Aria, CityCenter; shared plates $9-18, pizzas $22-29; ⏰11am-midnight) Near Aria casino's race and sports book, this chef-owned pizza bar is far better than expected. Be bewildered by the choices on the extra-large menu of craft beers and cocktails, artisanal meat and cheese platters, garden-fresh salads, hot antipasti such as pepperoni *arancini*, and crispy, thin-crust pizzas with smoky char marks. Take-out pizza slices are available after closing time.

Lemongrass
Asian $$

Map p97 (Aria, CityCenter; most mains $14-29, tastings menus $39-59; ⊘11am-2am; 🍽️👶) Visually high impact, this Thai and pan-Asian kitchen offers a satay bar and quasi-authentic soups, curries and noodle dishes, from *tom kha* chicken to drunken noodles with seafood. Use caution when ordering spice level 10 – it's mouth-searing.

Jaleo
Spanish, Tapas $$$

Map p97 (📞702-698-7950; www.jaleo.com; Cosmopolitan; shared plates $5-35; ⊘noon-midnight; 🍽️) The Vegas version of pioneering Spanish chef José Andrés' flagship restaurant in DC brings modern tapas to a lighthearted setting with a rustic-chic look: recycled wooden tables with mismatched chairs, whimsical glassware and colorful details left and right. Try the potent sangria and a few traditional small plates or more innovative tastes such as gin-and-tonic Pacific oysters. Reservations essential.

To dine in the chef's private dining room on a sky's-the-limit tasting menu, make reservations via email one month in advance for **é** (www.ebyjoseandres.com).

Julian Serrano
Spanish, Tapas $$$

Map p97 (📞702-590-8520; Aria, CityCenter; shared plates $4-39, mains $24-50, tasting menus $39-59; ⊘11:30am-11pm Sun-Thu, to 11:30pm Fri & Sat; 🍽️) A splash of sunset colors stolen straight from Ibiza enlivens this sociable tapas bar, positioned for prime people-watching just off Aria's hotel lobby. Start off with white sangria, then choose several small plates: marinated olives, stuffed *piquillo* peppers, freshly grilled calamari or Iberian black pig ribs. Paellas are more than enough to feed two. Dinner reservations recommended. Happy hour runs from 4pm to 5:30pm Sunday through Thursday.

Twist by Pierre Gagnaire
French $$$

Map p97 (📞888-881-9367; Mandarin Oriental, CityCenter; mains $45-95, tasting menus $95-295; ⊘6-10pm Tue-Thu, to 10:30pm Fri & Sat) If romantic Twist's sparkling nighttime Strip views don't make you gasp, the modern French cuisine by this three-star Michelin chef just might. Seasonal tasting menus may include squid-ink *gnocchetti* topped with carrot gelée or langoustine with grapefruit fondue, finished off with bubble-gum ice cream with marshmallow and green-tea crumbles. Reservations essential; dress code is business casual.

Sage
American $$$

Map p97 (📞702-590-8690; Aria, CityCenter; mains $35-54, tastings menus $59-150; ⊘5-11pm Mon-Sat) Chef Shawn McClain brings seasonal Midwestern farm-to-table cuisine to the Strip. The backlit mural over the bar almost steals the scene, but creative twists on meat-and-potatoes classics – imagine pork terrine with blue corn succotash and salsa verde – and seafood and pasta also shine. After dinner, sip absinthe poured from a rolling cart. Reservations essential; business-casual dress.

Wicked Spoon Buffet
Buffet $$$

Map p97 (Cosmopolitan; per person $26-40; ⊘brunch 8am-2pm Mon-Fri, to 3pm Sat & Sun, dinner 5-9pm Mon-Thu, 5-10pm Fri, 3-10pm Sat, 3-9pm Sun; 👶) Wicked Spoon makes casino buffets seem cool again, with freshly prepared temptations served on individual plates for you to grab and take back to your table. The spread has all the expected meat, sushi, seafood and desserts, but with global upgrades – think roasted bone marrow and a gelati bar. Weekend brunch adds unlimited champagne mimosas or Bloody Marys (surcharge $10).

Social House
Asian, Sushi $$$

Map p97 (📞702-736-1122; www.socialhouselv.com; Crystals, CityCenter; prix-fixe lunch $20-25, shared plates $5-50, dinner mains $25-50; ⊘lunch noon-5pm daily, dinner 6-10pm Sun-Thu, to 11pm Fri & Sat) You won't find a sexier sushi bar and pan-Asian grill anywhere on the Strip. Low-slung tatami cushions, faded Japanese woodblock prints and a sky terrace inside Crystals mall add up to a seductively date-worthy atmosphere. Be

YAACOV DAGAN/ALAMY ©

★ Don't Miss
Aria's Best

CityCenter revolves around Aria, a thoroughly contemporary casino resort with a deluxe, design-savvy casino surrounded by tempting restaurants. Key pieces of CityCenter's priceless **art collection** (p98) are also found here. Look for poet-sculptor Tony Cragg's stainless-steel column sculptures near the tram boarding area and Jenny Holzer's *Truisms* scrolling across large LED panels near the north valet stand.

Delve even deeper inside Aria to find its Japanese-inspired **spa** (p103), Cirque du Soleil's imaginative show **Zarkana** (p102) and CityCenter's only nightclub, **Haze** (p102), where reality-TV stars such as Pauly D might pop in.

At the chic but casual **Julian Serrano** (p100) tapas restaurant, located just off the hotel lobby, you can quaff sangria and share small plates of stuffed olives while watching the comings and goings of big-shot gamblers. Chicago chef Shawn McClain's **Sage** (p100) specializes in sustainable farm-to-table cuisine, while his **Five50** pizzeria (p99) is equally applauded.

NEED TO KNOW
Map p97; ☎702-590-7111; www.aria.com; 3730 Las Vegas Blvd S, CityCenter; ⏰24hr

thrilled by the imported sake list. Dinner reservations recommended.

STK   Steakhouse **$$$**
Map p97 (☎702-698-7990; http://togrp. com/togrp-stk; Cosmopolitan; mains $29-59; ⏰5:30-11pm Sun-Thu, to midnight Fri & Sat)

With the motto 'Not your daddy's steak-house' and flush with fashionistas, high rollers and hipsters, Cosmo's STK rocks a nightclub vibe with DJs that you'll either love or hate. Faux animal-skin fabrics, white leather banquettes and cinematic lighting appeal to swinging bachelor/ette parties. ~~The mostly solid~~ steakhouse menu is spiced up with creative tastes such as jalapeno onions and bacon butter.

Drinking & Nightlife

Marquee
Club

Map p97 (📞702-333-9000; http://marquee lasvegas.com; Cosmopolitan; 🕙10pm-5am Thu-Sat & Mon) The Cosmopolitan's glam nightclub cashes in on its multimillion-dollar sound system and a happening dance floor surrounded by towering LED screens displaying light projections that complement EDM tracks hand picked by famous-name DJs. From late spring through early fall, Marquee's mega-popular daytime pool club heads outside to a lively party deck overlooking the Strip, with VIP cabanas and bungalows.

Chandelier Bar
Cocktail Bar

Map p97 (Cosmopolitan; 🕙24hr) Towering high in the center of Cosmopolitan, this ethereally designed cocktail bar is inventive yet beautifully simple, with three levels connected by romantic curved staircases, all draped with glowing strands of glass beads. The second level is headquarters for molecular mixology (order a martini made with liquid nitrogen), while the third specializes in floral and fruit infusions.

Mandarin Bar & Tea Lounge
Lounge, Bar

Map p97 (Mandarin Oriental, CityCenter; 🕙lounge 10am-10pm daily, bar 5pm-1am Mon-Thu, 4:30pm-2am Fri & Sat, 5-11pm Sun) With glittering Strip views from the panoramic windows of the hotel's 23rd-floor 'sky lobby,' this sophisticated lounge serves exotic teas by day and champagne cocktails by night. Make reservations for afternoon tea (from $36, available 1pm to 5pm daily).

Haze
Club

Map p97 (📞702-693-8300; www.hazelas vegas.com; Aria, CityCenter; cover $20-40; 🕙10:30pm-4am Thu-Sat) At CityCenter's almost passé nightclub, occasional headliners include hip-hop artists and celebutante wannabe DJs. Go-go dancers in boudoir-inspired get-ups writhe to a mash-up of tunes above a claustrophobic dance floor.

Todd English P.U.B.
Pub

Map p97 (www.toddenglishpub.com; Crystals, CityCenter; 🕙11am-2am Mon-Fri, from 9:30am Sat & Sun) Twice-daily happy hours (3pm to 6pm, and 10pm until midnight) with half-price pints and cheap wings, oysters and sliders keep barstools filled at this cozy brick-walled pub with an outdoor patio. The kitchen closes at 11:30pm daily.

Bond Bar
Bar

Map p97 (Cosmopolitan; 🕙10am-3am) At futuristic Bond, sip a blood-orange-infused house cocktail or pop open a craft beer as DJs spin electronic beats and 21st-century video-art installations catch the eye.

Entertainment

Vegas Nocturne at Rose.Rabbit.Lie
Theater

Map p97 (📞877-677-0585; http://roserabbit lie.com; Cosmopolitan; cover for midnight show $30; 🕙show 8pm, 10pm & 12am) Newfangled supper club, Rose.Rabbit.Lie tosses vintage cocktails together with throwback dishes such as lobster Newburg and oysters Rockefeller. But the real star is Vegas Nocturne, a cabaret variety show that goes on stage three times nightly. Lucky patrons are escorted into secret rooms for private sideshows. Dress code is 'casual elegant' (collared shirt preferred for men).

Go before midnight to avoid paying the cover (one-drink minimum still applies).

Zarkana
Theater

Map p97 (📞855-927-5262; www.cirquedu soleil.com; Aria, CityCenter; tickets $69-180; 🕙7pm & 9:30pm Fri-Tue; 👪) Set in a bizarre fantasy world, *Zarkana*'s story engages with the themes of lost love, abandonment and redemption – but of course you're really here to see 70 of Cirque du Soleil's world-class acrobats, aerialists, jugglers and trapeze artists do their thing. Don't jump out of your seat when you see the slithering snake lady and spider woman emerge. Children aged 5 years and up may attend the show, although loud noises and periods of darkness may frighten them.

Book & Stage
Live Music

Map p97 (Cosmopolitan; ⊙10am-3am, live music usually from 10pm Wed-Sat) At Cosmo's race and sports book, sink into an easy chair and bet on the big game while you catch up-and-coming indie bands, often live rock or acoustic acts. No cover charge.

🔒 Shopping

Crystals
Mall

Map p97 (www.crystalsatcitycenter.com; 3720 Las Vegas Blvd S, CityCenter; ⊙10am-11pm Sun-Thu, to midnight Fri & Sat) Design-conscious Crystals, by architect Daniel Libeskind, is the most striking shopping center on the Strip. Win big at blackjack? Waltz inside Christian Dior, Dolce & Gabbana, Prada, Hermès, Harry Winston, Paul Smith or Stella McCartney showrooms at CityCenter's shrine to haute couture. For sexy couples with unlimited cash to burn, Kiki de Montparnasse is a one-stop shop for lingerie and bedroom toys.

Shops at Cosmopolitan
Fashion

Map p97 (Cosmopolitan; ⊙10am-11pm Sun-Thu, to midnight Fri & Sat) Hipster-loving boutiques gather inside the Cosmopolitan resort: CRSVR sneaker boutique, DNA2050 denim bar, AllSaints Spitalfields from the UK, Molly Brown's swimwear, Retrospecs & Co eyewear, Skins 6|2 Cosmetics and Kidrobot for DIY toys and pop-culture collectibles. Rent the Runway can be a lifesaver for women who forgot to pack the right dress for a big night out (bachelorette parties welcome).

🏃 Spas & Activities

Sahra Spa & Hammam
Spa

Map p97 (☎855-724-7258, 702-698-7171; Cosmopolitan; day pass fitness center $20, spa $30-40; ⊙8am-7pm) The Cosmopolitan's spa specializes in extravagant rituals and 'transformations' inspired by Middle Eastern traditions of bathing and detoxification – just the ticket after a wild night of clubbing. Rent the heated-stone hammam for just yourself or with a few friends, followed up by a clay wrap scented with cardamom, a full-body scrub or a rub-down massage. Book appointments in advance.

Spa at Aria
Spa

Map p97 (☎702-590-9600; Promenade Level, Aria, CityCenter; spa & fitness center day pass $30-40; ⊙spa 5:30am-8pm, salon 9am-7pm) Promoting its Japanese-style water gardens, heated-stone beds and a co-ed salt-therapy room, Aria's spa is both Zen-like and hyper-modern. Specialized spa services include Ashiatsu pressure-point and Thai poultice massage (the latter relaxes the muscles with a soothing application of lemongrass and ginger), green-tea eye compresses, coconut-oil scalp treatments and seaweed body wraps.

Spa at Mandarin Oriental
Spa

Map p97 (☎888-881-9530, 702-590-8886; Mandarin Oriental, CityCenter; ⊙spa 10am-8pm Mon-Thu, 9am-9pm Fri-Sun, fitness center from 5am) The Mandarin Oriental's serene spa is designed to capture the opulence of 1930s Shanghai, offering a luxurious grab bag of a laconium, a women's rhassoul mud bath, steam rooms and an ice fountain. Situated beside a fully equipped gym, the Strip-view fitness studio will pump you up with Pilates or mellow you out with yoga.

Planet Hollywood

Rock 'n' roll history was made at this address.

Planet Hollywood stands on the hallowed ground of the original Aladdin casino hotel, the swinging 1960s-era resort where Elvis Presley and Priscilla Beaulieu tied the knot. The Aladdin was dramatically imploded in 1998 and replaced with the new Aladdin megaresort, retooled to target the Asian and European jet set.

But only 13 months after its grand opening, the owners made what was then the largest bankruptcy filing in Nevada history, with an outstanding debt of more than $600 million. Planet Hollywood snatched up the resort in 2003, then took their sweet time stripping the hotel of all its Arabian Nights trappings and rebranding the Miracle Mile Shops.

For fans of vintage Vegas, that felt like a crime. But for trend-conscious shoppers, Paris Hilton imitators and 20-somethings who like a contemporary casino, the new PH pretty much fits the bill.

Planet Hollywood

★ Don't Miss
Planet Hollywood's Best

The Aladdin resort was swimming in a sea of debt when Planet Hollywood bought it in 2003. Wayne Newton owned the Aladdin for a while, Johnny Carson tried to buy it and, before the economic bubble burst in the Land of the Rising Sun in the 1980s, a Japanese businessperson controlled it. But no one has ever made a mint with this hexed property – not yet, anyway.

The genie's newest masters have shifted the casino hotel's theme from Istanbul to Hollywood. PH pays homage to the casino resort's past, however, with the Moroccan-styled **Spa By Mandara** (p111). They've also kept a few of the Aladdin's gold-star attractions: the **Spice Market Buffet** (p110) and **Miracle Mile Shops** (p111), formerly Aladdin's Passage. (Fun fact: Barbara Eden of *I Dream of Jeannie* TV fame hosted the grand opening of the shopping center when the new Aladdin opened in 2000.)

The Hollywood theme is relatively subtle: you'll see film memorabilia displayed around the resort, including inside the guest rooms. The developers' efforts to achieve a more glamorous modern look is clearly evident in the massive lobby, where black granite, spotless glass and massive columns create drama, and eight chandeliers glitter with 66,000 hand-strung crystals each.

Meanwhile dining, nightlife and entertainment options are still evolving. A show-stopping **burger bar** (p109) from *Hell's Kitchen* chef Gordon Ramsay and a va-va-va-voom headliner show from pop diva Britney Spears have recently upped the ante.

If the slick new property has you feeling nostalgic for days gone by, head downtown to Fremont St. The huge neon genie lamp that once stood outside the Aladdin, rescued and restored by the **Neon Museum** (p184), still glows outside the Neonopolis.

NEED TO KNOW
☎702-785-5555; www.planethollywoodresort.com; ⏱24hr

PLANET HOLLYWOOD

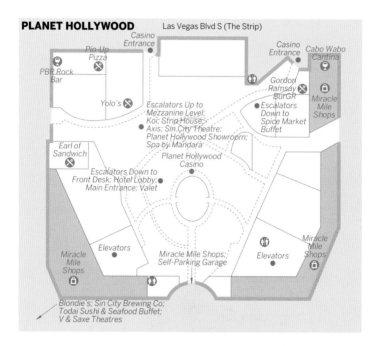

Las Vegas Blvd S (The Strip)

Casino Entrance

Pin-Up Pizza

PBR Rock Bar

Yolo's

Escalators Up to Mezzanine Level; Koi; Strip House; Axis; Sin City Theatre; Planet Hollywood Showroom; Spa by Mandara

Earl of Sandwich

Escalators Down to Front Desk; Hotel Lobby; Main Entrance; Valet

Casino Entrance

Cabo Wabo Cantina

Gordon Ramsay BurGR

Miracle Mile Shops

Escalators Down to Spice Market Buffet

Planet Hollywood Casino

Miracle Mile Shops

Elevators

Miracle Mile Shops; Self-Parking Garage

Elevators

Miracle Mile Shops

Blondie's; Sin City Brewing Co; Todai Sushi & Seafood Buffet; V & Saxe Theatres

Discover
Planet Hollywood

 Getting There & Away

Monorail The walk from Planet Hollywood to the nearest monorail station, at the back of Bally's casino hotel, takes at least 15 minutes. The monorail stops at selected casinos along the east side of the Strip, as well as at the city's convention center. Trains arrive every four to 12 minutes, operating daily until at least midnight.

Bus The 24-hour Deuce and faster SDX (9:30am to midnight daily) bus lines, with service along the entire Strip and to downtown, stop outside Planet Hollywood (northbound) and across and up the street at Bellagio (southbound) every 15 to 20 minutes.

Taxi A taxi is your best bet if you're heading downtown. Expect to pay at least $19 plus tip one way.

Sights

Planet Hollywood Casino
Casino

Map p48 (⊙24hr) Inside the flashy casino, nearly 90 table games and almost 3000 slot and video poker machines await. Players in the 'Pleasure Pit' are tended to by dealers and go-go dancers in lingerie-inspired getups. Ensconced by walls of disco-like LED lights are a race and sports book and a high-impact poker room with unbelievably plush chairs and daily Texas hold'em tournaments.

Eating

Neither Planet Hollywood nor the adjacent Miracle Mile Shops are among Sin City's memorable dining spots: there are no truly exceptional eateries here. Foodies should walk across the pedestrian skybridge to Cosmopolitan or CityCenter.

Earl of Sandwich
Deli $

Map p107 (www.earlof sandwichusa.com; items $2-7; ⊙24hr; 🚻) Pennypinchers sing the praises of this super-popular deli next to the casino, which pops out sandwiches on toasted artisan bread, tossed salads, wraps and a kids' menu, all with quick service, unbeatable opening hours and some of the lowest prices on the Strip.

Pin-Up Pizza
Pizza $

Map p107 (items $3-6; ⊙11am-2am Sun-Thu, to 4am Fri & Sat; 🚻) Have a hankering for crispy, thin-crust NYC-style pizza hand made from authentic Neapolitan-flour

Planet Hollywood's Casino
ED NORTON/GETTY IMAGES ©

Spend the Night

With 2600 recently renovated rooms, **Planet Hollywood** (Map p107; ☎866-919-7472, 702-785-5555; www.planethollywoodresort.com; r weekday/weekend from $59/160; ⓟ❄️📶@♿️🎱) is not one of the Strip's most family-friendly hotels, but it's nearly perfect for young couples and bachelor/ette parties. Amenities in standard 'Hollywood Hip' rooms include quirky film memorabilia, flat-screen TVs, luxury bedding with leather headboards and huge bathrooms featuring deep soaking tubs. Though many guest rooms are on the dark side, they're also quiet and spacious. You'll pay more for for views of the Strip or Bellagio's dancing fountains.

The mandatory nightly resort fee ($20 plus tax) covers daily fitness-center access and in-room wi-fi for one laptop or mobile device.

dough right before your eyes? This Strip-front pizza shop will more than satisfy your drunk, ravenous self, especially if you buy a buttery garlic knot or sugar-dusted cannoli too.

Yolo's
Mexican $$

Map p107 (☎702-785-0122; www.arkvegas.com/restaurant/yolos-mexican-grill; mains $12-22; ⏱11:30am-10pm Sun-Thu, to midnight Fri & Sat, bar till 1am Sun-Thu, to 4am Fri & Sat) Duck underneath a searingly yellow sign into this casino cantina, where the Mexican and Southwestern menu holds surprises that include comparatively fair prices and unusual dishes such as roasted vegetable enchiladas with adobo sauce and slow-roasted pork in citrus-chili marinade. Lunch and late-night specials are just $10 each. Happy hour (3pm to 6pm on weekdays) brings $5 bites and drinks.

Karaoke takes over the bar on Thursday, Friday and Saturday nights – anyone brave enough to sing gets a free shot!

Gordon Ramsay BurGR
Burgers $$

Map p107 (☎702-785-5555; www.gordonramsay.com; mains $13-18; ⏱11am-midnight Sun-Thu, to 2am Fri & Sat) Even the special-effects window installation at the entrance looks like it's on fire at this hot, hot burger joint by the *Hell's Kitchen* chef. Open wide and bite into Gordon's 'farm burger' topped with duck-breast bacon, a fried egg and English cheddar cheese, accompanied by truffled parmesan fries and a caramel-toffee milkshake on the side. It's casual, but reservations help.

Koi
Sushi $$$

Map p107 (☎702-454-4555; www.koi restaurant.com; mains $12-60; ⏱5:30-10:30pm Sun-Thu, 5:30-11:30pm Fri & Sat, lounge open later; ✈) While the paparazzi won't lunge at you outside the front door like they do at the ubercool LA hot spot of the same name, Koi still makes waves with its stylish looks, fusion sushi rolls and long list of hot and cold appetizers. Bite into a tiny dragon roll while you down a blood orange sunset cosmo in the chic environs. Reservations are helpful.

Order half-off food and drink specials during happy hour (5pm to 7pm daily). The lounge often stays open late for drinks, DJs and dancing.

Strip House
Steakhouse $$$

Map p107 (☎702-737-5200; www.striphouse.com; mains $29-54; ⏱5-11pm Sun-Thu, to 11:30pm Fri & Sat) With a sexy 1920s cabaret vibe and glowing red boudoir lamps, this dramatic steakhouse is the opposite of stuffy. Sit down with your bachelor/bachelorette party, or maybe just you and your sweetie, to fork into a classic NY strip or kosher rib-eye steak with housemade sauce and goose-fat potatoes. The star of the dessert menu is a tall 24-layer chocolate cake. Reservations essential.

Spice Market Buffet
Buffet $$$

Map p107 (buffet per adult $22-36, per child 4-12yr $13-20; ◷7am-11pm; 🅿️🚹) Middle Eastern, Asian, Italian and Mexican fare are thrown into the global mix at this jewel of a buffet, a throwback from the original Aladdin resort. Attentive service, above-average desserts and live-action cooking stations justify the often very long waits to be seated.

Todai Sushi & Seafood Buffet
Buffet $$$

Map p107 (📞702-892-0021; www.todai.com; Miracle Mile Shops; buffet per adult/child lunch $24/12, dinner $36/18; ◷11:30am-2:30pm daily, 5:30-9:30pm Sun-Thu, 5:30-10pm Fri & Sat; 🚹) Patronize this all-you-can-eat 160ft-long spread of Japanese, Chinese and Korean fare for dozens of sushi selections, sizzling seafood, cool salads and bowls of Hawaiian *poke*. Lobster, shellfish and crab legs get added to the mix at dinnertime.

🍷 Drinking & Nightlife

Sin City Brewing Co
Bar

Map p107 (📞702-732-1142; www.sincitybeer.com; Miracle Mile Shops; ◷10am-11pm Sun-Thu, to midnight Fri & Sat) Drop off anyone who thinks shopping is hell at this made-in-Vegas microbrew bar, then come back for them once they're angelically soused on pints of *weisse* wheat, blonde, amber or stout.

Cabo Wabo Cantina
Bar

Map p107 (www.cabowabocantina.com; ◷8am-midnight) Started by rock musician Sammy Hagar of Van Halen fame, Cabo Wabo Cantina is a mini-chain Mexican bar and grill with a killer Strip-view patio. Dip into a bowlful of fresh guacamole with tortilla chips and sip a signature blue 'Waborita' as you watch the world walk by.

Blondies
Sports Bar

Map p107 (www.blondieslasvegas.com; Miracle Mile Shops; ◷usually 24hr) This straight-up sports bar pulls in the punters with

Miracle Mile Shops

beer pong, waitstaff in short-skirted cheerleader outfits and all-you-can-drink happy hours ($20) from 3pm to 6pm on weekdays. Expect big crowds during NFL football and international soccer games.

PBR Rock Bar
Bar

Map p107 (www.pbrrockbar.com; ◎8am-3am) It's not the flavorless BBQ plates that you come to this country-and-western theme bar for. It's the spacious Strip-view patio and chance to ride the mechanical bull, rodeo-style. Live bands, DJs and karaoke liven things up late at night.

⭐ Entertainment

Axis, Sin City Theatre & Planet Hollywood Showroom
Performing Arts

Map p107 (☏855-234-7469, 702-777-2782; www.planethollywoodresort.com/shows.html; prices vary) Three different on-site venues at the Planet Hollywood casino resort – the Axis, Sin City Theatre and Planet Hollywood Showroom – host headliners such as Britney Spears, as well as stand-up comics, R-rated variety acts, celebrity tribute artists like Purple Reign and touring musicians from Tool to CeeLo Green. Check the website for upcoming shows and to buy tickets in advance.

V & Saxe Theaters
Performing Arts

Map p107 (☏866-932-1818, 702-260-7200; www.vtheaterboxoffice.com; Miracle Mile Shops; tickets $79-99; ◎7pm & 9pm) The energetic extravaganza *Vegas! The Show,* featuring a live orchestra and a cast of more than 40 showgirls, dancers, singers and celebrity impersonators, tells the story of how Vegas became an entertainment capital. Cheaper comedy and magic

shows, musical acts such as Recycled Percussion and hokey zombie burlesque revues also go on stage at the mall's twin theaters. Browse current shows online, but don't pay full price – get discount coupons from freebie tourist magazines.

🔒 Shopping

Miracle Mile Shops
Mall

Map p107 (☏888-800-8284, 702-866-0703; www.miraclemileshopslv.com; 3663 Las Vegas Blvd S, ◎10am-11pm Sun-Thu, to midnight Fri & Sat) This sleekly redesigned shopping mall is still a staggering 1.2 miles long. With 170 retailers, the focus is on contemporary chains, especially urban apparel, jewelry and gifts. Standout shops include Bettie Page for 1940s and '50s pinup and vintage-style dresses; Brit import H&M; LA denim king True Religion; and Vegas' own rock-star boutique, Stash, for both women and men.

🏃 Spas & Activities

Spa By Mandara
Spa

Map p107 (☏702-785-5772; www.mandara spa.com; ◎7am-7pm, fitness center from 6am, salon from 8am) The Moroccan-inspired Spa by Mandara, furnished with palm trees and painted with rich red and gold hues, has the usual spa offerings and more – are you ready for a coconut-milk body wrap? For the spa-goer who has done it all, the indulgent 'Mandara Four Hands Massage,' features, you guessed it, the simultaneous attention of two massage therapists.

Fitness center access comes complimentary with a spa treatment more than $50.

Paris
Las Vegas

Napoleon once said, 'Secrets travel fast in Paris.' In Las Vegas this casino hotel, which opened in 1999, is no secret anymore.

Paris Las Vegas aims to capture the essence of the real grande dame by recreating her most famous landmarks, including the Eiffel Tower, Arc de Triomphe and Maritime Fountain from the Place de La Concorde. The Gallic caricature evokes the gaiety of the City of Light – right down to the accordion players.

Tongue-in-cheek fake Francophonic signs such as 'Le Buffet' point the way to a dozen French restaurants and cabaret and piano bars that are mostly frequented, like the resort itself, by a mature crowd. Many visitors to Vegas pass through at least once, though, to visit the top of Paris' signature attraction – the Eiffel Tower Experience. It's a perfect vantage point for watching the Bellagio's fountain show, day or night.

Paris Las Vegas
CHRIS HEPBURN/GETTY IMAGES ©

⭐ Don't Miss
Paris Las Vegas' Best

Welcome to the City of Light, Vegas-style. This mini-version of the French capital may not exude the true charm of Paris – it feels like a themed section of Disney World's Epcot – but efforts to emulate the city's great landmarks, including a 34-story Hotel de Ville replica and famous facades from the Paris Opera House and the Louvre, make it a fun stop for families and Francophiles who've yet to see the real thing.

Naturally, the signature attraction is the **Eiffel Tower Experience** (p116). How authentic is this half-scale tower? Gustave Eiffel's original drawings were consulted, but the 50-story steel replica is welded rather than riveted. It's also fireproof and engineered to withstand a major earthquake. Visitors ascend in a glass elevator to the tower's observation deck for panoramic views of the valley, desert mountains and the Strip, with the dancing fountains of Bellagio across the street. To savor the gorgeous views, reserve a table at the **Eiffel Tower Restaurant** (p118).

If you'd rather dine on solid ground, gorge at **Le Village Buffet** (p117) or snag an alfresco Strip-side table at **Mon Ami Gabi** (p117). Indulge in a frangipani body wrap at the **Spa by Mandara** (p119), then sip the crème de la crème bubbly waiting on ice at **Napoleon's** champagne bar (p118). At night, watch beautiful people ascending the grand staircase to **Chateau Nightclub & Gardens** (p118), or enjoy free lounge entertainment at **Le Cabaret** (p118).

NEED TO KNOW
📞702-946-7000; www.parislasvegas.com; 3655 Las Vegas Blvd S; 🕓24hr

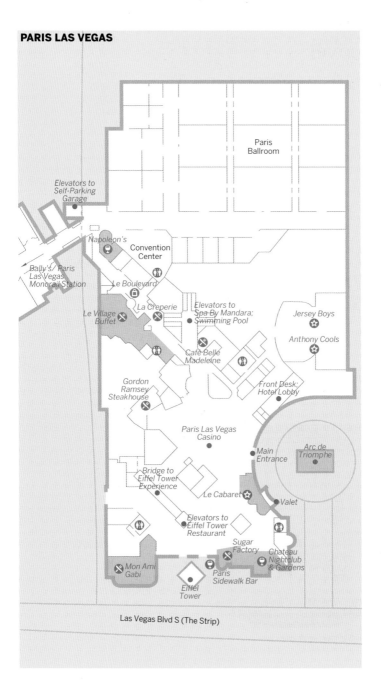

Paris Ballroom

Elevators to Self-Parking Garage

Napoleon's

Convention Center

Bally's / Paris Las Vegas Monorail Station

Le Boulevard

La Creperie

Le Village Buffet

Elevators to Spa By Mandara; Swimming Pool

Jersey Boys

Anthony Cools

Café Belle Madeleine

Gordon Ramsey Steakhouse

Front Desk; Hotel Lobby

Paris Las Vegas Casino

Main Entrance

Arc de Triomphe

Bridge to Eiffel Tower Experience

Le Cabaret

Valet

Elevators to Eiffel Tower Restaurant

Sugar Factory

Chateau Nightclub & Gardens

Mon Ami Gabi

Paris Sidewalk Bar

Eiffel Tower

Las Vegas Blvd S (The Strip)

Discover
Paris Las Vegas

Getting There & Away

o **Monorail** Paris Las Vegas is connected to Bally's casino hotel and its monorail station by the quaint cobblestone Le Boulevard, an indoor passageway. The monorail links various casinos along the east side of the Strip with the city's convention center. Trains arrive every four to 12 minutes, operating daily until at least midnight.

o **Bus** The 24-hour Deuce and SDX (9:30am to midnight daily) bus lines, with service along the entire Strip and to downtown, stop outside Paris Las Vegas (northbound) and across the street at the Bellagio (southbound) every 15 to 20 minutes.

o **Taxi** A taxi is your best bet if you're heading downtown. Expect to pay at least $18 plus tip one way.

Sights

Paris Las Vegas Casino   Casino
Map p115 (⊙24hr) Surrounded by Parisian street scenes, this bustling vaulted casino with ceilings that simulate sunny skies is home to 100 gaming tables, more than 2000 slot machines and a race and sports book next to Le Bar du Sport. In the high-limit gaming area, authentic French roulette wheels, which have no 0 or 00, slightly improve your odds of winning.

Eiffel Tower Experience   Tower
Map p115 (✆888-727-4758; adult/child 12yr & under/family $10.50/7.50/32, after 7:15pm $15.50/10.50/47; ⊙9:30am-12:30am Mon-Fri, to 1am Sat & Sun, weather permitting) Families and lovers flock to Vegas' ersatz Eiffel Tower, lining up for grated views from a wind-blown observation deck. It's cheaper to take a ride on the tower's elevators during the day, but nighttime panoramas of the Strip, with casinos' neon signs glowing and the Bellagio's dancing fountains lit up, are worth paying extra for. Get free admission on your birthday with photo ID.

Eating

Café Belle Madeleine   Cafe, Bakery $
Map p115 (items $3-8; ⊙6am-1am; 🛜)
Quick food options abound in Le Boulevard shopping arcade. Some of the most authentically Parisian options include fresh-baked croissants, flaky pastries and slices of quiche from this winsome store-front cafe, which also brews hot tea and espresso. For gluten-free desserts, just ask.

Paris Las Vegas hotel
SYLVAIN SONNET/GETTY IMAGES ©

Spend the Night

Don't let the grand reception area fool you at **Paris Las Vegas** (Map p115; 877-796-2096, 702-946-7000; r weekday/weekend from $60/135; 🅿️❄️📶@☁️🐾). Although they're clean and serviceable (and some are pet-friendly), standard 'luxury' rooms, with their odd royal-blue carpeting and slightly faded bedskirts, are only a step up from any run-of-the-mill chain hotel. To feel the Parisian flair, upgrade to an atmospheric Red Room, outfitted with plasma TVs and rich Moulin Rouge–inspired decor, including whimsical puckered-lips-shaped sofas in rooms with king beds.

The mandatory nightly resort fee ($20 plus tax) covers in-room wi-fi, as well as entry to the fitness center and Paris' unique octagonal swimming pool near the base of the Eiffel Tower.

La Creperie
French $$

Map p115 (crepes $10-12; ⏱️7am-11pm) Cheap? No. Crazily delicious? Yup. This crepe stand justifies a detour down Le Boulevard (it's near the entrance to Le Village Buffet). Dessert crepes with fillings such as Nutella, caramelized apple, and strawberries with chocolate are more addictive than savory options such as roast chicken with pesto.

Sugar Factory
American $$

Map p115 (📞702-331-5100; http://sugarfactory.com/las-vegas-paris-hotel; most mains $12-20; ⏱️brasserie 24hr, candy shop 10am-midnight Sun-Thu, 9am-1am Sat & Sun) Fruit Loops panna cotta, giant goblet cocktails adorned with gummy bears and 'Fat Elvis' waffles topped with peanut-butter mousse, caramelized bananas and bacon are just a sugary sampling of what's in store at this all-night brasserie. Pop into the Wonka-esque candy shop next door for custom-mixed milkshakes and sparkly 'couture pops' that celebutantes lick.

Gordon Ramsay Steak
Steakhouse $$$

Map p115 (📞702-946-4663, 877-346-4642; www.gordonramsay.com; mains $32-105, tasting menu without/with wine pairings $145/220; ⏱️4:30-10:30pm daily, bar to midnight Fri & Sat) Carnivores, leave Paris behind and stroll through a miniaturized Chunnel into British chef Gordon Ramsay's steakhouse. Ribboned in red and and domed by a jaunty Union Jack, this is one of the top tables in town. Fish, chops and signature beef Wellingtons round out a menu of Himalayan salt-room-aged steaks. No reservation? Sit at the bar instead.

Mon Ami Gabi
French $$$

Map p115 (📞702-944-4224; www.monamigabi.com; mains $12-40; ⏱️7am-11pm Sun-Thu, to midnight Fri & Sat) Think très charming Champs Élysées bistro. Breezy patio tables in the shadow of the Eiffel Tower are parfait for alfresco dining and people-watching. Though spotty service is far from magnifique, it's got classic steak frites, mussels, crepes, quiches and salads, plus a respectable wine list and a special gluten-free menu. Reservations recommended for indoor seating; the patio is first-come, first-served.

Le Village Buffet
Buffet $$$

Map p115 (📞702-946-7000; buffet per adult $22-34, child 4-8yr $13-20; ⏱️7am-10pm; 🍷👶) An incredible array of fruits and cheeses, a toasty range of breads and pastries, and macaroons for dessert

117

make this one of the best-value buffets on the Strip. Distinct cooking stations are themed by France's various regions, with an emphasis on seafood. Breakfasts are excellent, as are weekend brunches.

Eiffel Tower Restaurant

French $$$

Map p115 (702-948-6937; www.eiffeltowerrestaurant.com; mains lunch $14-32, dinner $32-89, tasting menu without/with wine pairings $125/205; 11:30am-4pm & 5-10:30pm Mon-Thu, 11:30am-4pm & 5-11pm Fri, 11am-4pm & 5-11pm Sat, 11am-4pm & 5-10:30pm Sun) At this *haute cuisine* eatery midway up its namesake tower, the Francophile wine list is vast, the chocolate soufflé is unforgettable, and views of the Strip and Bellagio's fountains are breathtaking. Chef Joho's contemporary renditions of French classics, however, falter from time to time.

Lunch is your best bet, but it's more popular to come for sunset. Reservations essential.

🍷 Drinking & Nightlife

Chateau Nightclub & Gardens

Nightclub, Bar

Map p115 (702-776-7770; www.chateaunightclublv.com; 4pm-2am) Hip-hop prevails at this rooftop venue landscaped to look like Parisian gardens. Views over the Strip are divine from tiered outdoor terraces while, back inside, go-go dancers do their thing above a small dance floor, which can be half empty even on weekends. Sometimes on summer days the lounge space on the open-air deck doubles as a beer garden.

Napoleon's

Bar

Map p115 (4pm-1am) Whisk yourself off to the never-never land of 19th-century France, with decor including a mosaic floor and overstuffed sofas as luxurious as the menu of 100 types of bubbly (with vintage Dom Pérignon for big spenders). Dueling pianos draw a crowd; there's no cover charge, but expect a two-drink minimum.

Paris Sidewalk Bar

Bar

Map p115 (hrs vary by season) Have you spotted Strip-walkers drinking strawberry daiquiris out of plastic 'Eiffel Tower' cups and colorful ceramic hot air balloons? They're sold at this open-air bar near the casino's front entrance.

⭐ Entertainment

Jersey Boys

Theater

Map p115 (855-234-7469, 702-777-2782; www.jerseyboysinfo.com; tickets $60-200) This Tony Award–winning Broadway musical follows the rise of Frankie Valli and the Four Seasons to chart-topping stardom in the 1960s. Join the audience and sing along with oldies such as 'Can't Take My Eyes off You' and 'Sherry.' Note this show isn't recommended for children under 13, and those under five are not allowed.

Anthony Cools

Comedy

Map p115 (855-234-7469, 702-777-2782; www.anthonycools.com; tickets $56-89; 9pm Tue & Thu-Sun) It's a wicked adults-only scene at this R-rated comedic hypnotist's stage show, where audience members are gamely tested for suggestibility, then hauled up on stage to become the laughingstocks of that night's raunchy, raw and uncensored 90-minute session. Of all Vegas' hypnotists, Cools has the biggest cult following.

Le Cabaret

Live Music

Map p115 (9pm-1am Sun-Thu, to 2am Fri & Sat) Just off the casino floor, the intimate Le Cabaret hosts a nightly schedule of

Mon Ami Gabi (p117)

RICHARD CUMMINS/GETTY IMAGES ©

live jazz and sultry lounge singers or DJs. Grab a cafe table underneath leafy artificial trees strung with festive lights. There's typically no cover charge.

🔒 Shopping

Le Boulevard   Mall
Map p115 (⊙most shops 10am-11pm Sun-Thu, to midnight Fri & Sat) Along a winding cobblestone replica of the Rue de la Paix, leading onto a promenade that connects to Bally's casino hotel, popular stops include L'Apothecaire beauty shop; Les Eléments home decor; Les Enfants, for French children's fashions and toys; La Cave wine seller; Davidoff Boutique cigar shop; and Presse newsstand.

🏃 Spas & Activities

Spa By Mandara   Spa
Map p115 (☎702-946-4366; www.mandara spa.com; fitness center day pass for nonguests $25; ⊙7am-7pm, fitness center from 6am, salon from 8am) At this full-service salon and spa, which mixes Balinese and European influences, the most luxurious treatment rooms have handcrafted tropical hardwood, Matisse-style artworks and silk carpets. Couples can opt for the romantic 'Paris for Lovers' treatment package, delivered with a whirlpool tub made for two. Complimentary fitness-center access comes with spa treatments over $50.

You'll find newer Mandara spas inside the Tropicana and Planet Hollywood casino hotels.

Bellagio

Fans of eye-popping luxury, along with movie buffs who liked *Ocean's Eleven*, won't want to miss Steve Wynn's original opulent Vegas pleasure palazzo.

Inspired by the beauty of a lakeside Italian village, and built on the site of the legendary Dunes, the Bellagio is now a classic fixture on the Strip. Famous for its ornate Tuscan architecture and 8-acre artificial lake, it's the graceful antithesis of what most people expect of Las Vegas. A thousand dancing fountains spring from the lake's waters every 15 to 30 minutes throughout the afternoon and evening. In a nearby courtyard, the hotel's distinctive pool area is surrounded by private cabanas and accented by carved Italian columns and artfully formed citrus and parterre gardens.

Although the nouveau riche stink can be heady, the secret delight of Bellagio is that romance is always in the air.

Fountains of Bellagio (p124)
HOWARD T FANG/GETTY IMAGES ©

SYLVAIN SONNET/GETTY IMAGES ©

⭐ Don't Miss
Bellagio's Best

Fringed by the Bellagio's famous dancing fountains, the resort's butter-yellow buildings seem to have been plucked from Italy's Lake District. Beyond the glass-and-metal porte cochere awaits a stable of world-class restaurants, a swish shopping concourse, a European-style casino, a **fine-arts gallery** (p125) and much more.

The hotel's gasp-worthy lobby is adorned with a backlit glass sculpture, *Fiori Di Como*, by Dale Chihuly, composed of 2000 hand-blown flowers in vibrant colors that hang from the ceiling. Adjacent to the lobby is the **Bellagio Conservatory & Botanical Gardens** (p124), where artistic and whimsical arrangements of towering greenery and showy blooms change with the seasons. Real flowers, cultivated in a gigantic onsite greenhouse, brighten countless vases throughout the property.

Springing out of the faux Italian lake fronting the resort are the dancing **Fountains of Bellagio** (p124). For front-row seats, head to **Hyde Bellagio** lounge (p127) for happy hour and lean over the balcony to almost feel the spray, or reserve an outdoor patio table at one of the Bellagio's lakefront restaurants. Afterward, stroll over to **Jean Philippe Patisserie** (p125), just so you can say you've seen the world's largest chocolate fountain up close.

Sprawling behind the hotel, Bellagio's lushly landscaped five-pool complex evokes the Mediterranean. As only hotel guests are able to experience it, and no unaccompanied children under 14 years old are allowed, it's also a relatively tranquil pool scene for Vegas. To unwind even more, hotel guests can book rejuvenating treatments at **Spa Bellagio** (p129).

NEED TO KNOW

☎ 888-987-6667; www.bellagio.com; 3600 Las Vegas Blvd S; 🕐 24hr

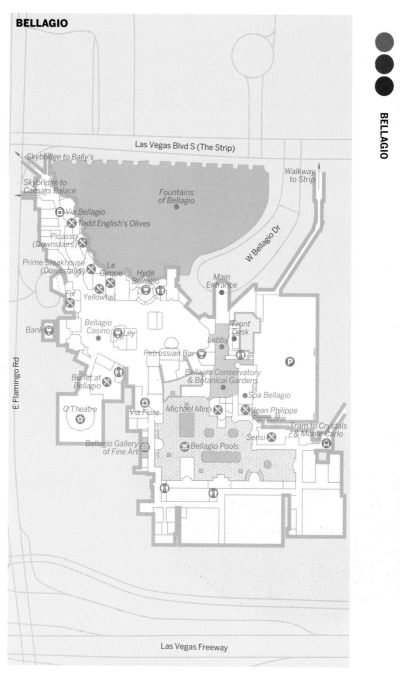

BELLAGIO

Las Vegas Blvd S (The Strip)

Skybridge to Bally's

Skybridge to Caesars Palace

Walkway to Strip

Fountains of Bellagio

W Bellagio Dr

Via Bellagio

Todd English's Olives

Picasso (Downstairs)

Prime Steakhouse (Downstairs)

Le Cirque

Hyde Bellagio

Main Entrance

Fix

Yellowtail

Bank

Bellagio Casino

Lily

Front Desk

Lobby

Petrossian Bar

Bellagio Conservatory & Botanical Gardens

E Flamingo Rd

Buffet at Bellagio

Spa Bellagio

O'Theatre

Via Fiore

Michael Mina

Jean Philippe Patisserie

Tram to Crystals & Monte Carlo

Bellagio Gallery of Fine Art

Sensi

Bellagio Pools

Las Vegas Freeway

Discover Bellagio

Getting There & Away

○ **Tram** Free trams connect Bellagio to CityCenter between 8am and 4am daily, stopping at Crystals and Monte Carlo en route. Trams arrive every seven to 15 minutes.

○ **Monorail** Cross Las Vegas Blvd and walk to the monorail station at the back of Bally's casino hotel. The monorail connects various casinos along the east side of the Strip with the city's convention center. Trains operate daily until at least midnight.

○ **Bus** The 24-hour Deuce and faster SDX (9:30am to midnight daily) buses serve the entire Strip and downtown, stopping outside Bellagio (southbound) and Paris Las Vegas (northbound) every 15 to 20 minutes.

○ **Taxi** A taxi is your best bet if you're heading downtown. Expect to pay at least $20 (plus tip) one way.

◉ Sights

Bellagio Casino
Casino

Map p48 (888-987-6667; www.bellagio.com; 3600 Las Vegas Blvd S; 24hr) This posh European-style casino has high-limit gaming tables and 2400 slot machines with very comfortable seats but highly unfavorable odds. A stop on the World Poker Tour, Bellagio's tournament-worthy poker room offers 24-hour tableside food delivery for card sharks.

Fountains of Bellagio
Fountain

Map p123 (www.bellagio.com; shows every 30min 3-7pm Mon-Fri, noon-7pm Sat & Sun, every 15min 7pm-midnight daily;) With a backdrop of Tuscan architecture, the Bellagio's faux Lake Como and dancing fountains are the antithesis of the Mojave Desert – although the resort does use reclaimed water. The fountain show's recorded soundtrack varies, so cross your fingers that it will be Italian opera or Ol' Blue Eyes crooning 'Luck Be a Lady,' instead of country-and-western twang.

Bellagio Conservatory & Botanical Gardens
Gardens

Map p123 (24hr;) **FREE**

Changing with the seasons, Bellagio's conservatory displays ostentatious floral arrangements that are bizarrely installed by crane through a soaring 50ft-high ceiling. The effect is unnatural, but that doesn't stop crowds from gawking, and the aroma of fresh blooms is enchanting. Peek around the periphery of the conservatory for classic paintings re-created with buds and flowers instead of oil paints.

Bellagio Casino
SYLVAIN SONNET/GETTY IMAGES ©

Spend the Night

With classic elegance, recently renovated rooms and suites, and a mid-Strip location, **Bellagio** (Map p123; 📞888-987-6667, 702-693-7111; www.bellagio.com; r weekday/weekend from $169/239; P ❄ 🛜 🏊) is one of the most glamorous places to sleep in Vegas. For such a large hotel, guest services are impressively smooth and personalized: check-in is a breeze and the polished, white-glove room service is a delightful indulgence.

A $70 million overhaul of the hotel's main tower has brought a fresher, more contemporary look to oversized resort rooms, plus high-tech amenities such as media hubs, as well as ecoconscious touches including LED lighting and organic carpeting. Incredibly soft beds come with Bellagio's signature cashmere pillow-top mattresses. Super-sized bathrooms, outfitted in Italian marble and black granite, feature deep soaking tubs and luxe bath products.

The mandatory nightly resort fee ($25 plus tax) covers in-room wi-fi and high-speed wired internet access, as well as fitness-center entry.

Bellagio
Gallery of Fine Art
Gallery

Map p123 (📞877-957-9777, 702-693-7871; adult/child under 12yr $16/free; ⏱10am-7pm, last entry 6:30pm) The Bellagio's petite art gallery hosts blockbuster traveling shows from nationally renowned art museums. Free docent-guided tours are usually given at 2pm daily. Check what's currently showing on the website before you make a special trip. Original masterworks also hang inside the resort's Picasso restaurant, although you'll be lucky to get inside without booking a table.

🍴 Eating

Bellagio's stable of kitchen heavyweights is starting to show its age. Still, foodies make a beeline for some of these Vegas classics – Picasso earned two Michelin stars, while Le Cirque and Michael Mina each earned one, and the resort as a whole has four James Beard award-winning chefs and three master sommeliers. Bellagio's culinary team stays on the cutting edge of the food and wine scene, teaching high-end cooking classes at its 'Epicurean Epicenter' and hosting events such as Vegas Uncork'd with *Bon Appétit* magazine in May. For information and reservations, visit http://bellagio.com/restaurants or call 📞866-259-7111. Note that children aged five to 18 years are allowed at only some of Bellagio's restaurants.

Jean Philippe
Patisserie
Bakery, Desserts $

Map p123 (www.jpchocolates.com; snacks & drinks $4-11; ⏱7am-11pm Mon-Thu, to midnight Fri-Sun; 👶) As certified by the *Guinness Book of World Records,* the world's largest chocolate fountain cascades inside the front windows of this champion pastry-maker's shop, known for its fantastic sorbets, gelati, pastries and chocolate confections. Coffee and espresso are above the Strip's low-bar average.

Todd English's
Olives
Mediterranean $$$

Map p123 (www.toddenglish.com; mains lunch $17-29, dinner $25-49; ⏱restaurant 11am-2:45pm & 5-10:30pm, bar 3-5pm; 🖊) East Coast chef Todd English pays homage to the ancient life-giving fruit at this Italian-inflected eatery. Flatbread pizza, house-made pasta and grilled meats get top billing. The chef's table faces a bustling open kitchen, while the patio overlooks Lake Como. With an exceptional wine list and flamboyant desserts, it's always packed – come for lunch but make reservations first.

Prime Steakhouse
Steakhouse **$$$**

Map p123 (mains $36-70; ⏱5-10pm) Slightly past its prime, this lakeside steakhouse, adorned with gilt chandeliers and plush velvet curtains, reveals a fantastic menu of not just traditional cuts, but also the likes of short ribs with poblano-cheddar croquettes and roasted sea bass with mushroom-*yuzu* (Japanese citrus) sauce. The elegant bar keeps a bold wine inventory dominated by Californian and French reds.

Reservations are recommended, especially for outdoor patio tables. Dress is business casual (no shorts).

Le Cirque
French **$$$**

Map p123 (☎702-693-8100; www.lecirque. com; prix-fixe dinner without/with wine pairings $100/150, tasting menus from $135/205; ⏱5:30-10pm Tue-Sun) A legendary name from NYC, Le Cirque pairs artful *haute cuisine* with bountiful French wines in a joyous, intimate lakeside setting under a silk-tented ceiling. Foie gras parfait, crispy veal sweetbreads and sea urchin with panna cotta are among the delicious dishes. Service is remarkably attentive. Reservations essential; business casual dress (no shorts or athletic wear).

Michael Mina
Seafood **$$$**

Map p123 (☎702-693-7223; www.michaelmina. net; mains $42-78, tasting menu without/with wine pairings $115/180; ⏱5:30-10pm Thu-Tue; 🍴) An adventurous menu of ocean catch such as phyllo-crusted sole and Maine lobster pot pie with truffle cream. Order a root beer float with a plate of warm cookies for a nostalgic dessert. The overall experience often measures up to the sky-high prices, but the dining room is too close to the crushing conservatory crowds.

Fix
Steakhouse **$$$**

Map p123 (www.fixlasvegas.com; mains $36-77; ⏱11am-2pm Fri-Sun, 5-10:30pm daily) The fix is in: Fix is a perfect pre-clubbing launch pad, or just the venue for eyeing celebs and the action on the casino floor. This trendy, high-flying steakhouse hybrid makes gourmet comfort-food goodies such as lobster tacos, Kobe chili cheese fries, and crispy waffles with duck confit and maple-bourbon syrup. Reservations are essential, especially on weekends.

Sensi
International **$$$**

Map p123 (mains $28-50, tasting menu without/with wine pairings $80/125; ⏱restaurant 5:30-10:30pm, bar menu from 4pm) 🌿 At this soothing spot tucked inside the Bellagio's spa tower, minimalist architecture and waterfall wall screens complement a globally harmonious menu of seafood, chops, pasta and salads, equally influenced by Europe and Asia. Unlike at most Vegas restaurants, the ingredients are all natural, organic and sustainably sourced whenever possible, and herbs come from the restaurant's rooftop garden.

Rumor has it that this restaurant will soon be rebranded.

Yellowtail
Japanese **$$$**

Map p123 (http://yellowtaillasvegas.com; shared plates $10-55, tasting menu without/with sake pairings $150/205; ⏱5-10pm Mon-Thu, to 11pm Fri-Sun, lounge closes 1hr later) The entrance to this sleek sushi bar is heralded by a massive bronze sculpture of a yellowtail fish. Local maverick chef Akira Back buys top-drawer seafood and ingredients imported from markets all over the globe. Dip into an extensive sake cellar and savor a long list of cold and hot shared dishes while watching the Bellagio's fountain show. Reservations recommended.

Picasso
Mediterranean **$$$**

Map p123 (prix-fixe dinner menu without/with wine pairings $115/175; ⏱5:30-9:30pm Wed-Mon) Five-star chef Julian Serrano delivers artistic Franco-Iberian fusion in a museum-like setting. Original masterpieces by Picasso regrettably overshadow the indulgent, yet miniature entrées, such as the signature sautéed fallow deer medallions, roasted pigeon and milk-fed veal chops. The vegetarian tasting menu is extortionately priced – just forget about it. Reservations essential; business casual dress (no shorts).

Buffet at Bellagio   Buffet $$$
Map p123 (www.bellagio.com; per person $19-40; ⏲7am-10pm) Bellagio once competed for honors among Vegas' live-action buffets, but lately it has become second-tier. It's most satisfying at breakfast or lunch. The more varied dinnertime spread features seafood and creative dishes from around the world – too bad they don't all taste as good as they look.

🍷 Drinking & Nightlife

Bottoms up: Bellagio sells more wine than any other hotel in the USA, with 20 different cellars stocking bottles valued collectively at over $30 million.

Hyde Bellagio   Lounge, Nightclub
Map p123 (📞702-693-8700; www.hyde bellagio.com; cover $20-40, usually free before 10pm; ⏲lounge 5-11pm daily, nightclub 10pm-4am Tue, Fri & Sat) Cutting-edge design icon Philippe Starck brought his unique vision to Bellagio's most svelte nightspot. His signature flair is everywhere: dramatic chrome chandeliers, soaring arches illuminated with LED lights, carved black wood, oversize mirrors and eclectic sculptures. Kick back on a plush loveseat or just stand on the balcony, awestruck, as the Bellagio's fountains create a wall of water just outside.

On some nights, the lounge converts to a nightclub, with guest celebrity DJs, confetti falling over a pint-size dance floor and glow sticks giving it a rave atmosphere. Show up before 10pm to avoid paying the cover charge.

Petrossian Bar Lounge

Map p123 (☎702-693-7111; ⏲24hr) Even though it's just off the casino floor, this elegant cocktail bar feels sheltered from the cacophony of the slot machines – especially when a talented pianist is playing the Steinway grand. It's the place for a classic martini or a glass of champagne, or come for the afternoon tea service between 1pm and 4pm daily (from $35, reservations required).

Bank Club

Map p123 (☎702-693-8300; www.thebanklasvegas.com; cover $20-30, hotel guests free; ⏲10:30pm-4am Thu-Sun) The reincarnation of Light is cloaked in onyx walls with gold accents, although the mixed-ages crowd doesn't look wealthy. Lavish multi-tiered VIP booths are layered around a stand-and-pose dance floor where hi-NRG pop and hip-hop mixes dominate. Professional hosts push the top-shelf bottle service. Dress code (upscale nightlife attire) not always enforced.

Lily Lounge

Map p123 (www.lilylv.com; ⏲5pm-4am) Three elements make this lounge seductive: serious mixology (the seasonal cocktail list is a knock-out), easy access (it's located right in the middle of the casino floor) and unique decor (imported Spanish stone tabletops). Sink into a plush sofa and kick off the evening with a drink or two.

☆ Entertainment

O Theater

Map p123 (☎888-488-7111, 702-693-8866; www.cirquedusoleil.com; tickets $99-155; ⏲7:30pm & 10pm Wed-Sun) Phonetically speaking, it's the French word for water (*eau*). With a lithe international cast performing in, on and above water, Cirque du Soleil's *O* tells the tale of theater through the ages. It's a spectacular feat of imagination and engineering, and you'll pay dearly to see

it – it's one of the Strip's few shows that rarely sells discounted tickets.

Children less than 18 years old must be accompanied by an adult; those under five are not allowed into the theater.

🔒 Shopping

Via Bellagio   Mall
Map p123 (⏱10am-midnight) Bellagio's swish indoor promenade, Via Bellagio, is home to a who's who of fashion-plate designers: Bottega Veneta, Chanel, Dior, Fendi, Giorgio Armani, Gucci, Hermès, Prada, Louis Vuitton and Tiffany & Co. If you've been bewitched by Dale Chihuly's colorful blown-glass sculptures, drop by his signature gallery shop on the Via Fiore, a much shorter shopping promenade not far from the conservatory.

🏃 Spas & Activities

Spa Bellagio   Spa
Map p123 (📞702-693-7472; spa day pass for hotel guests $29; ⏱6am-8pm) Bellagio's spa cocoons hotel guests in gorgeous surrounds, making anyone feel like a queen (or king) for a day. On the far-reaching menu of spa treatments, expect to see Thai yoga massage and deluxe hydrotherapy, including coconut milk and seaweed baths. Sign up for boot camp, body sculpting, Pilates fusion or kickboxing sessions in the fully equipped fitness center.

Caesars Palace

Ancient Rome and Las Vegas have one theme in common: decadence.

So it's fitting that Sin City's first fully real-ized megaresort took on a Greco-Roman fantasyland look when it debuted on New Year's Eve in 1967, capturing the world's attention and upping the luxury ante for the gaming industry with full-size marble reproductions of classical statuary such as Michelangelo's *David,* scantily costumed cocktail waitstaff and a Strip-side row of towering fountains.

Later, it took a star turn in blockbuster Hollywood movies such as *Rain Man* and *The Hangover*. Thanks to megabucks renovations, Caesars continues redefining its swanky self. With a spiffed-up outdoor Roman Plaza facing the Strip and neon lights replaced by hand-painted murals, Caesars is competing to rule the Strip's frenetic empire of luxury megaresorts once again. Yet, with the cocktail waitstaff continuing to roam the casino in skimpy togas, the Palace remains, for many, quintessentially kitschy Vegas.

Roman-style architecture, Caesars Palace

PICTURENET / CORBIS ©

⭐ Don't Miss
Caesars Palace's Best

Despite recent upgrades that have lent the once-gaudy Palace a more sophisticated air, some of the resort's original features from the swinging '60s have survived. Out front are the same spritzing fountains that daredevil Evil Knievel made famous when he jumped them on a motorcycle on December 31, 1967 (and ended up with a shattered pelvis and a fractured skull. More than two decades later, his son Robby repeated the attempt – more successfully).

The likes of Celine Dion, Shania Twain and Elton John perform at the **Colosseum** (p136), a gigantic showroom modeled after its Roman namesake and custom-built for lavish theatrical spectacles. Nearby, fashionistas saunter around inside the **Forum Shops** (p137). In the hotel's fabulous Garden of the Gods Pool Oasis, goddesses proffer frozen grapes in summer; Roman-eqsue statuary surrounds the circular Temple Pool; and topless sunbathing happens at Venus Pool Club.

The Palace and Forum Shops also feature dining venues fit for an emperor, including the gut-busting buffet **Bacchanal** (p135) and high-flying celebrity chef outposts such as **Nobu** (p135), **Restaurant Guy Savoy** (p135) and Bobby Flay's **Mesa Grill** (p136). Afterward, sip rum on a floating boat inside **Cleopatra's Barge** (p136), get giddy over champagne cocktails at **Fizz** (p136) or do double-takes at the riotous variety show **Absinthe** (p137).

NEED TO KNOW

☎702-731-7110; www.caesarspalace.com; 3570 Las Vegas Blvd S; ⏰24hr

CAESARS PALACE

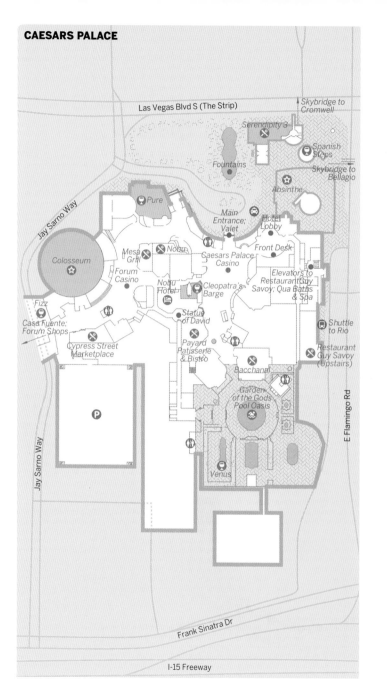

Las Vegas Blvd S (The Strip)

Skybridge to Cromwell

Serendipity 3

Spanish Steps

Skybridge to Bellagio

Fountains

Absinthe

Pure

Main Entrance; Valet

Hotel Lobby

Mesa Grill

Nobu

Front Desk

Colosseum

Caesars Palace Casino

Forum Casino

Elevators to Restaurant Guy Savoy; Qua Baths & Spa

Nobu Hotel

Cleopatra's Barge

Fizz

Casa Fuente; Forum Shops

Statue of David

Shuttle to Rio

Cypress Street Marketplace

Payard Patisserie & Bistro

Restaurant Guy Savoy (Upstairs)

Bacchanal

Jay Sarno Way

Garden of the Gods Pool Oasis

E Flamingo Rd

Venus

Frank Sinatra Dr

I-15 Freeway

133

Discover
Caesars Palace

🔄 Getting There & Away

○ **Monorail** Walk across Las Vegas Blvd to the monorail station at the back of the Flamingo casino hotel. The monorail connects selected casinos along the east side of the Strip with the city's convention center. Trains arrive every four to 12 minutes, operating daily until at least midnight.

○ **Bus** The 24-hour Deuce bus line, with service along the entire Strip and to downtown, stops outside Caesars Palace (southbound) and the Flamingo (northbound) every 15 to 20 minutes. Faster SDX buses (9:30am to midnight daily) stop at Bellagio (southbound) and Paris Las Vegas (northbound) every 15 minutes.

○ **Taxi** A taxi is your best bet if you're heading downtown. Expect to pay at least $18 (plus tip) one way.

◎ Sights

Caesars Palace　　Casino
Map p48 (⊗24hr) Enclosed under soaring ceilings adorned with faux frescoes, this imperial casino and its twin, the Forum Casino, offer more than 100 card tables and thousands of slots. Caesars Palace claims to be the site of more million-dollar slot machine jackpots than any other casino in the world. There's also a state-of-the-art race and sports book and a pro-worthy poker room.

✖ Eating

Claiming a handful of fine-dining institutions, Caesars Palace has a solid restaurant reputation. More standard options await in the adjacent Forum Shops. Make reservations online at www.caesarspalace.com or by calling ☎877-346-4642.

Cypress Street Marketplace　　Fast Food $
Map p133 (mains $6-12; ⊗11am-11pm; 👪) Conveniently charge those made-to-order pizzas and salads, Tex-Mex tacos and Asian stir-fries, along with beer and wine, to a 'smart' card, then pay upon exiting the food court, where tables perch over the casino floor.

Serendipity 3　　Desserts $$
Map p133 (☎702-731-7110; www.serendipity3.com; desserts $10-18; ⊗8am-11pm Sun-Thu, to midnight Fri & Sat; 👪) At this pink candy-striped soda fountain with shady terrace seating overlooking the Strip, sink your sweet tooth into frozen hot chocolate and opulent ice-cream

Cupcakes, Serendipity 3
DAVID BECKER/GETTY IMAGES ©

Spend the Night

Although Caesars Palace has been a status symbol on the Strip for more than a half century, guest rooms at the **hotel** (Map p133; ☎ 866-227-5938, 702-731-7110; www.caesarspalace.com; r weekday/weekend from $90/125; P❋ 🖥 @ 🏊 🐾) aren't as magnificent as the resort itself. Spread out across five towers, the functional rooms aren't overly spacious but some allow pets. Recently renovated rooms in the Augustus and Octavius Towers offer more luxury amenities including spa tubs.

Or feel like a VIP at Nobu Hotel, a boutique hotel inside the Centurion Tower that brings a shot of high style and concierge-level service to what are otherwise quite compact rooms. The stylish rooms and suites come with VIP check-in, exotic sleep oils, welcome tea service and a unique in-room dining menu designed by **Matsuhisa** (p135), the Iron Chef himself.

The mandatory nightly resort fee ($25 plus tax) covers in-room wi-fi and daily fitness center access.

sundaes. Take a pass on the rest of the all-American menu.

Nobu
Japanese, Fusion $$$

Map p133 (☎ 702-785-6628; www.nobu restaurants.com; shared plates $5-60, lunch mains $22-50, dinner tasting menus $90-500; ⏰ lunch 11am-3pm Sat & Sun, dinner 5-11pm Sun-Thu, to midnight Fri & Sat, lounge 5pm-1am Sun-Thu, to 2am Fri & Sat) Iron Chef Matsuhisa's new sequel to his NYC establishment is almost as good as the original. The setting is postmodern Zen, with glowing yellow lanterns, private dining 'pods' and sociable *teppanyaki* grill tables. Stick with Nobu's classics such as black cod with miso, South American-influenced *tiradito* (a lighter version of ceviche), spicy edamame and fusion sushi rolls. Reservations essential.

If you can't afford a full meal, grab one of the 300-odd seats in the lounge and order cocktails and appetizers.

Restaurant Guy Savoy
French $$$

Map p133 (☎ 702-731-7286; www.guysavoy. com; Augustus Tower, mains $80-110, tasting menus $120-350; ⏰ 5:30-10:30pm Wed-Sun) With Strip-view picture windows, this exclusive dining room is the only US restaurant by three-star Michelin chef

Guy Savoy. Both the culinary concepts and the prices reach heavenly heights. If you just want a small taste, perhaps of artichoke black-truffle soup or crispy-skinned sea bass, sit in the Cognac Lounge for drinks and nibbles. Dinner reservations are essential.

Bacchanal
Buffet $$$

Map p133 (buffet per adult $26-54, child 4-10yr $15-27; 🎫 👪) As over-the-top as Caesars Palace's statuary of Roman gods and goddesses, this is the Strip's most expansive and expensive buffet. An all-you-can-eat feast of king crab legs, house-made sushi and dim sum, oak-grilled BBQ, baked-to-order souffles and so much more that goes beyond what you could ever possibly taste in just one sitting. Windows overlook the Garden of the Gods pools.

Payard Patisserie & Bistro
French $$$

Map p133 (☎ 702-731-7292; www.payard.com; drinks & snacks $5-11, mains $16-30, prix-fixe 3-course dinner $48; ⏰ bistro 6:30am-2:30pm daily, 5-10pm Wed-Sun, patisserie 6am-11pm daily; 👪) Operated by third-generation French chef and chocolatier Françoise Payard, this spot offers tastes as rich as the handcrafted woodwork, leather banquettes and crystal chandelier in the dining room. Relish fresh takes on bistro classics at breakfast and lunch, or indulge in outrageous desserts such as éclairs layered with vanilla-kirsch cream and handmade espresso from the gleaming pastry counter out front.

Mesa Grill — Southwestern $$$

Map p133 (702-731-7731; www.mesagrill.com; mains brunch & lunch $13-24, dinner $32-50; 11:30am-2:30pm & 5-11pm Mon-Fri, 10:30am-3pm & 5-11pm Sat & Sun;) While star chef Bobby Flay doesn't cook on the premises, his bold signature menu of spicy Southwestern fare is usually satisfying, whether it's a New Mexican green-chili cheeseburger, blue-corn pancakes with barbecued duck, or ancho-chili and honey-glazed salmon. Lunch and weekend brunch are better value than dinner.

🍷 Drinking & Nightlife

Fizz — Lounge

Map p133 (702-776-3200; 5pm-2am Sun-Thu, noon-4am Fri & Sat) Towering black-and-gold rectangular doors open into this lavish bubbly palace co-created by Elton John's partner, David Furnish. Silk-covered walls are hung with photographs from the couple's personal collection. Slide into a moon-shaped, cream-colored leather booth, then peruse the menu of champagne by the glass and high-end fizzy cocktails, with canapes and caviar on the side. Upscale dress recommended.

Venus — Pool Club

Map p133 (702-650-5944; http://angelmg.com/venues/venus-pool-club; admission free-$20; hrs vary by season) Expect a more sultry, adults-only scene at Caesars Palace's pool club, where topless sunbathing is encouraged and women always get in free. The atmosphere is chill, with DJs spinning electronica and hip-hop, and a flirty co-ed 30-something crowd.

Cleopatra's Barge — Bar, Lounge

Map p133 (bar 5pm-3am, lounge from 8pm Sun-Thu, from 11pm Fri & Sat) The miniature ship inside a candlelit cocktail lounge looks like something straight out of *Pirates of the Caribbean,* setting the mood for mischief. On closer inspection, it's a scaled-down replica of the Egyptian queen's royal transportation down the Nile. There's no cover charge for live bands or late-night DJs and dancing on the boat.

Spanish Steps — Bar

Map p133 (11am-2am Sun-Thu, to 3am Fri & Sat, weather permitting) Outside Caesars Palace fronting Las Vegas Blvd, order a fruity frozen mojito, margarita or boozy lemonade while you sit and watch the world waltz by. It's an almost irresistible stop on sticky, hot summer days.

Casa Fuente — Bar

Map p133 (www.casafuente.com; Forum Shops; 10am-11pm Sun-Thu, to midnight Fri & Sat) Wicker sidewalk chairs and a petite bar serving tropical cocktails makes this 'money' cigar shop feel like a little slice of Miami. A walk-in humidor stocks Arturo Fuente cigars from the Dominican Republic.

⭐ Entertainment

Colosseum — Music, Comedy

Off Map p133 (866-227-5938; www.the colosseum.com; tickets $55-500) A high-tech version of ancient Rome's famous arena, this spectacular 4100-seat venue has state-of-the-art sound and lighting systems fit for the first-class performers who take the stage here, including chanteuse Celine Dion, pianist Elton John and comedian Jerry Seinfeld. Thanks to the circular layout, there's hardly a bad seat in the house, with the audience seated no further than 120ft from the stage.

SYLVAIN SONNET/GETTY IMAGES ©

Absinthe
Theater

Map p133 (📞800-745-3000; www.absinthe vegas.com; Roman Plaza, tickets $99-125; 🕒7:30pm & 9:30pm Wed-Sun) An experimental new breed of raucous variety show, one-of-a-kind Absinthe mixes bawdy and surreal comedy with burlesque, cabaret and Cirque du Soleil–style acrobatics, all roped together by the foul-mouthed emcee Gazillionaire. It has an explicit erotic vibe: no one under 18 years is allowed inside the big-top tent set up outside Caesars Palace.

🔒 Shopping

Forum Shops
Mall

Off Map p133 (www.simon.com; 🕒10am-11pm Sun-Thu, to midnight Fri & Sat) Caesars' fanciful nod to ancient Roman marketplaces houses 160 designer emporia, including catwalk wonders Armani, DKNY, Jimmy Choo, John Varvatos and Versace; trend-setting jewelry and accessory stores; and one-of-a-kind specialty boutiques such as Agent Provocateur lingerie, Bettie Page pin-up fashions, MAC cosmetics and Kiehl's bath-and-body shop. Don't miss the spiral escalator, a grand entrance for divas strutting off the Strip.

🏃 Spas & Activities

Qua Baths & Spa
Spa

Map p133 (📞866-782-0655; fitness -enter day pass $25, incl spa facilities $45; 🕒6am-8pm) Qua evokes the ancient Roman rituals of indulgent bathing. Try a signature 'bath liqueur,' a personalized potion of herbs and oils poured into your own private tub. The women's side includes a tea lounge, a herbal steam room and an arctic ice room where artificial snow falls. On the men's side, there's a barber spa and big-screen sports TVs.

Fitness-center entry is complimentary with spa treatments over $75.

Mirage

No desert hallucinations here: that is indeed a faux volcano erupting.

It's the dramatic yet playful hallmark of the Mirage, a fixture on the Strip since it opened in 1989. Casino mogul and then-owner Steve Wynn boasted that his goal was to create a property 'so overriding in its nature that it would be a reason in and of itself for visitors to come to Las Vegas.'

It cost many times more than any Strip megaresort had up to that point. The Mirage today still captures the imagination although its glories have been largely outshone by Wynn's newer casino megaresorts up the street. Still, the Mirage keeps up with the times with several cutting-edge eateries, a Kanye-endorsed nightclub and one of the best Cirque du Soleil shows on the Strip.

Few visitors leave the Mirage unimpressed, although its subtle appeal is most appreciated by a well-heeled older crowd.

⭐ Don't Miss
Mirage's Best

Inside, the Mirage's paradisiacal setting is replete with a huge rain forest atrium under a conservatory dome filled with jungle foliage, meandering streams and soothing cascades. Woven into the tropical waterscape are scores of bromeliads enveloped in sunlight and fed by a computerized misting system. Tropical scents also waft through the hotel lobby, which features a 20,000-gallon saltwater aquarium filled with 60 species of coral-reef critters from Fiji to the Red Sea, including puffer fish, tangs and pygmy sharks.

Even more tropical greenery, meandering lagoons, poolside bars and the tiny, topless Bare daytime club (p144) make the Mirage's outdoor pool complex a Vegas classic. But the new theme here is 'remixed,' with an emphasis on innovative entertainment. Hits include Cirque du Soleil's **Beatles LOVE** (p145); the psychedelic Fab Four-inspired **Revolution Lounge** (p144); mojitos on the Strip-view patio at **Rhumbar** (p144); and an NYC-import nightclub, **1 OAK** (p144).

Out front in a lagoon splashed down beside Las Vegas Blvd, the Mirage's fiery, revamped trademark **volcano** (p142) erupts with a roar at the top of every hour after dark, often startling pedestrians who just happen to be passing by, lighting their faces with childish delight.

Kids will beg their parents to visit the cramped wildlife exhibits at **Siegfried & Roy's Secret Garden & Dolphin Habitat** (p142). Though the dynamic duo of magicians and animal tamers is no longer performing on stage following an infamous mauling incident in 2003, you can see their royal white tigers and magical 'white lions' here, if you must.

NEED TO KNOW

📞702-791-7111; www.mirage.com; 3400 Las Vegas Blvd S; 🕐24hr

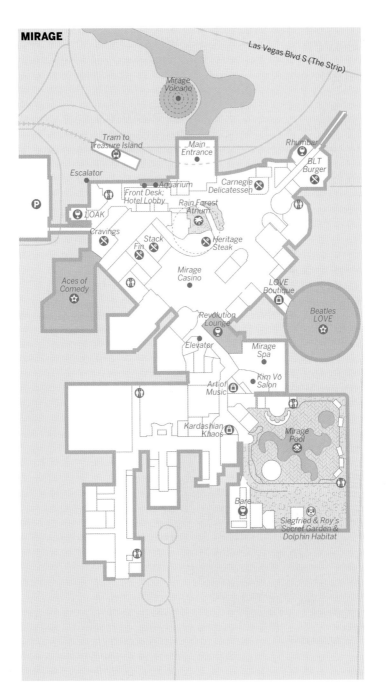

MIRAGE

Las Vegas Blvd S (The Strip)

Mirage Volcano

Tram to Treasure Island

Main Entrance

Rhumbar

BLT Burger

Escalator

Aquarium

Carnegie Delicatessen

Front Desk; Hotel Lobby

Rain Forest Atrium

1OAK

Cravings

Stack

Heritage Steak

Fin

Mirage Casino

LOVE Boutique

Aces of Comedy

Beatles LOVE

Revolution Lounge

Elevator

Mirage Spa

Kim Vô Salon

Art of Music

Kardashian Khaos

Mirage Pool

Bare

Siegfried & Roy's Secret Garden & Dolphin Habitat

Discover Mirage

Getting There & Away

○ **Tram** A free tram glides over to Treasure Island every 15 minutes or so between 7am and 2am daily.

○ **Monorail** Cross Las Vegas Blvd to board the monorail at the back of Harrah's casino hotel. The monorail links selected casinos along the east side of the Strip with the city's convention center. Trains arrive every four to 12 minutes, operating daily until at least midnight.

○ **Bus** The 24-hour Deuce bus line, with service along the entire Strip and to downtown, stops outside the Mirage (southbound) and across Las Vegas Blvd at Harrah's (northbound) every 15 to 20 minutes.

○ **Taxi** A taxi is your best bet if you're heading downtown. Expect to pay at least $17 plus tip one way.

Sights

Mirage Casino
Casino
Map p48 (⊙24hr) Splashed with tropical hues, the Mirage's airy casino manages to feel less hurried, with more than 100 table games and more than 2000 slot machines. Inside the 10,000-sq-ft race and sports book, big-screen TVs are tuned to every major sporting event. The poker room is one of the Strip's classiest, offering daily tournaments and complimentary lessons.

Mirage Volcano
Landmark
Map p141 (⊙shows hourly 6pm, 7pm or 8pm-11pm or midnight; ♿) FREE When the Mirage's trademark artificial volcano erupts with a roar out of a 3-acre lagoon, it inevitably brings traffic on the Strip to a screeching halt. Be on the lookout for wisps of smoke escaping from the top, signaling that the fiery Polynesian-style inferno, with a soundtrack by a Grateful Dead drummer and an Indian tabla musician, is about to begin.

Siegfried & Roy's Secret Garden & Dolphin Habitat
Zoo, Aquarium
Map p141 (📞702-791-7188; adult/child 4-12yr $20/15; ⊙11am-6:30pm Mon-Fri, from 10am Sat & Sun; ♿) All of the feats of conservation claimed by this place can't compensate for enclosures built much too small for majestic predators such as spotted leopards, black panthers and white lions and tigers, who prefer to roam the world's wildest places. The claustrophobic Atlantic bottlenose dolphin pools may also concern animal lovers, so we recommend giving this overpriced but popular attraction a miss.

Mirage Volcano
H & D ZIELSKE/GETTY IMAGES ©

Spend the Night

Renovated recently, guest rooms at the **Mirage** (Map p141; ☎800-374-9000, 702-791-7111; www.mirage.com; r weekday/weekend from $95/130; P ❄ 🛜 @ ≋) have a whimsical yet sophisticated look: the swirling patterns call to mind the psychedelic spin of Cirque du Soleil's *Beatles LOVE,* while flat-screen TVs, iPod docks and fluffy beds make it feel fresh and contemporary. If you upgrade to a 'Tower Suite,' you'll get a whirlpool tub. The mandatory nightly resort fee ($25 plus tax) includes in-room wi-fi and access to the fitness center at the spa.

🍴 Eating

Make reservations via www.mirage.com/restaurants or by calling ☎866-339-4566. Epicures eagerly await the opening of Iron Chef Morimoto's new restaurant in late 2014.

BLT Burger
American $$

Map p141 (☎702-792-7888; www.bltburger.com; items $7-17; ⏱11am-2am Sun-Thu, to 4am Fri & Sat; 🍴) French-trained NYC chef Laurent Tourondel is the man behind this lively burger house featuring Black Angus beef, lamb, chicken, salmon and veggie burgers with all the trimmings. Also on the menu are dozens of craft beers, liqueur-spiked 'adult' milkshakes, crisp sweet-potato fries and deep-fried Oreos with frozen custard and blackberry jam.

Carnegie Delicatessen
American $$

Map p141 (mains $12-25; ⏱24hr; 🍴) Late risers appreciate the anytime breakfasts at this diner with patterned black-and-white floor tiles and maroon high-backed booths. Unbelievably huge pastrami deli sandwiches and slices of NYC cheesecake are big enough for two, maybe three, friends to split and still have leftovers. Sit down only if you're very hungry.

Heritage Steak
Steakhouse $$$

Map p141 (☎702-791-7111; www.craftrestaurantsinc.com; mains $35-80; ⏱5-10:30pm, lounge to 11pm Sun-Thu, to 11:30pm Fri & Sat) Top chef Tom Colicchio's second Strip steakhouse flies higher than his MGM Grand outpost. All-natural, open-flame-grilled American steaks, charred octopus and ash-roasted bone marrow are just a sampling of carnivorous treats on a cutting-edge contemporary menu. The throwback cocktail list is just as unusual as what's for dessert, including sweet-corn ice cream. Reservations essential.

Stack
Eclectic $$$

Map p141 (www.lightgroup.com; mains $28-79, small plates $15-21; ⏱5-10pm Sun & Tue-Thu, 5-11pm Mon, Fri & Sat) The striking interior of this hybrid steakhouse is dominated by curved hardwood walls that seem to undulate above the fashionistas downing cucumber martinis at the long bar. Order shared plates of adult tater tots and king crab and jalapeño tacos, or settle in for a Kobe beef burger, a dry-aged, bone-in steak or Maine lobster curry. Reservations strongly recommended.

Fin
Chinese $$$

Map p141 (mains $16-40, prix-fixe dinner $50; ⏱5-10pm Thu-Mon) With ocean-colored glass baubles strung from the ceiling, this dining room feels like a glorious fishbowl. Sit regally surrounded by hand-painted silk wallpaper and feast on an odd mix of sophisticated modern cuisine and Americanized take-out classics like General Tsao's chicken. Seafood is remarkably fresh, whether you taste the steamed sea bass or spicy shrimp. Reservations advised.

Cravings
Buffet $$$

Map p141 (per adult $16-32, per child 5-10yr $12-22; ⏰7am-9pm Mon-Fri, from 8am Sat & Sun) Not the very best, but far from the worst of the Strip's buffets, Cravings will probably leave you feeling your got your money's worth, with 11 live-action cooking stations, Goose Island IPA on tap and life-changing chocolate croissant bread pudding for dessert. Rather eat in your room? Ask about the take-out special ($16) that lets you fill up a to-go box.

🍷 Drinking & Nightlife

1 OAK
Club

Map p141 (📞702-588-5656; www.1oaklasvegas.com; cover $20-40; ⏰10:30pm-4am Tue & Thu-Sat) The Mirage's reincarnated nightclub is the second location for 1 OAK (an acronym for 'one of a kind') after NYC. The main staircase was made for strutting down onto a throbbing dance floor where paper 'snowflakes' rain on clubbers grooving to hip-hop and pop mash-ups. Too crowded? Get your groove on in the hidden side room.

Revolution Lounge
Lounge

Map p141 (📞702-693-8300; http://lightgroup.com; cover free-$20; ⏰10pm-4am Thu-Tue) At this psychedelic Beatles-themed ultra lounge, DJs spin downtempo house, Brit pop, hip-hop, world music and remixes of classic rock, disco and '80s new wave. Live bands take over some nights. 'Revolution Sundays' put on LGBTQ dance parties.

Rhumbar
Cocktail Bar

Map p141 (📞702-792-7615; www.rhumbarlv.com; ⏰usually 1pm-midnight Sun-Thu, to 2am Fri & Sat, weather permitting) Mojitos, capirinhas and daiquiris are pure mixology magic at this Caribbean-flavored bar and cigar lounge – needless to say, these cocktails are a big step up from the sugary, yard-long frozen drinks sold along the Strip. Cool off with your poison of choice in the minimalist bright-white bar or at breezy lounge tables on the Strip-view patio.

Bare
Pool Club

Map p141 (📞702-588-5656; www.barepoollv.com; cover $10-40; ⏰hrs vary by season) A teensy pool club with 'European-style' (ie topless) sunbathing, chaise lounges and palm trees waving overhead isn't worth the steep price of admission for most guys, but gorgeous women often get in free with no waiting. Fruity cocktails and party platters enhance a flirtatious atmosphere.

Cirque du Soleil's *Beatles LOVE*
GEORGE ROSE/GETTY IMAGES ©

MIRAGE DRINKING & NIGHTLIFE

⭐ Entertainment

Beatles LOVE
Theater

Map p141 (📞702-792-7777, 800-963-9634; www.cirquedusoleil.com; tickets $79-180; 🕐7pm & 9:30pm Thu-Mon; ♿) Another smash hit from Cirque du Soleil, *Beatles LOVE* started as the brainchild of the late George Harrison. Using *Abbey Road* master tapes, the show psychedelically fuses the musical legacy of the Beatles with Cirque's high-energy dancers and signature aerial acrobatics. Come early to photograph the trippy, rainbow-colored entryway and grab drinks at Abbey Road bar, next to Revolution Lounge. No ticket discounts for children; those under age five are not allowed in the theater.

Aces of Comedy
Comedy

Map p141 (📞800-963-9634, 702-792-7777; www.mirage.com; tickets $40-100; 🕐sched-ules vary, box office 10am-10pm Thu-Mon, to 5pm Tue & Wed) You'd be hard pressed to find a better A-list collection of famous stand-up comedians than this year-round series of appearances at the Mirage, which delivers the likes of Jay Leno, Kathy Griffin and Lewis Black to the Strip. Buy tickets in advance online or by phone, or go in person to the Mirage's Cirque du Soleil box office.

🔒 Shopping

LOVE Boutique
Gifts

Map p141 (🕐10am-6pm Tue & Wed, to midnight Thu-Mon) Can't get enough of Cirque du Soleil and the Fab Four? Swing inside this themed boutique for colorful souvenirs such as T-shirts and buttons, musical CDs and rare autographed Beatles memorabilia.

Art of Music
Antiques, Gifts

Map p141 (http://deals.artofmusiclv.com; 🕐9am-11pm) Autographed memora-bilia from TV, movie, music and sports superstars hang on the walls and can be bought for a sum. Check online for upcoming in-store signings, usually championship fighters or retired professional ball players.

Kardashian Khaos
Gifts

Map p141 (http://kardashiankhaos.com) This cheesy, celebrity-craze store peddles home decor, beach towels, glassware and accessories officially endorsed with images of the reality TV family.

🏃 Spas & Activities

Mirage Spa & Kim Vō Salon
Spa

Map p141 (📞702-791-7472; day pass hotel guests/nonguests $28/50; 🕐salon 9am-7pm, spa 6:30am-7pm) Recently made over, the Mirage's elemental spa specializes in deluxe body treatments with essential ocean minerals or fruits. Feel even more like money at Hollywood A-list celebrity stylist Kim Vō's salon where you can get a Moroccan oil scalp massage. Available only to hotel guests, spa and fitness-center day passes include complimentary yoga classes.

Non-guests may book spa appointments for Monday through Thursday (fitness-center entry is combined with some spa treatments).

Treasure Island

Free-flowing rum, piles of golden coins and lots o' booty.

Welcome to the Vegas version of Treasure Island, often referred to simply as 'TI,' where a total overhaul has put the 'sin' back in casino, taking the resort from family-friendly to bawdy.

Although traces of Treasure Island's (TI) original swashbuckling skull-and-crossbones theme linger (if you look hard), don't let the pirate ship out front fool you into thinking you're at Disneyland. The re-imagined TI is a classier, terra-cotta-hued resort aiming for a Caribbean hideaway appeal, and it practically screams 'leave the kids at home.'

But that doesn't make for an atmosphere of stuffed shirts, not by a long shot. Revamped eateries and bars with Strip-view patios are crowded with festive 20- and 30-somethings, while all ages line up to see *Mystère*, the longest-running Cirque du Soleil show on the Strip.

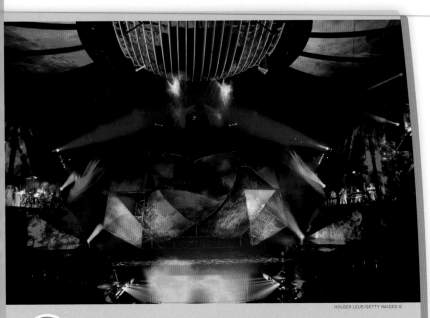

HOLGER LEUE/GETTY IMAGES ©

⭐ Don't Miss
Treasure Island's Best

Anchors aweigh! Landlubbers approach the property via a wood-bottomed bridge with hemp-rope-supported sides that spans artificial Sirens Cove, set beside a vague replica of an 18th-century sea village. Floating in the water are two mock sailing ships – a Spanish privateer and a British frigate – that, sadly, no longer shoot off fireworks nightly.

Entertainment-wise, the true highlight is Cirque du Soleil's classic production **Mystère** (p152), an oddball celebration of life that begins with a pair of babies making their way in a world. During the 90-minute show, a misguided clown's humorous antics are interspersed with the agile feats of acrobats, aerialists and dancers.

Although the sailors' rations at Treasure Island's (TI) restaurants are meager and pricey, there's no excuse for dying of thirst on this Caribbean island, not with **Señor Frog's** (p151), a rowdy Mexican cantina overlooking Sirens Cove; **Gilley's Saloon & Dance Hall** (p151), a country-and-western bar and two-steppin' nightclub; and island-themed **Kahunaville** (p152), a poolside party bar where flair bartenders make boozy rum cocktails.

Reserved for hotel guests only, TI's pool complex offers VIP cabana and daybed rentals, a huge party-friendly hot tub that can fit up to 25 people and a DJ spinning a bumpin' soundtrack on hot summer weekends. You can also unwind with a Russian *banya* (bath) ritual or a rejuvenating facial and massage in TI's compact **Oleksandra Spa** (p153).

NEED TO KNOW
📞702-894-7111; www.treasureisland.com; 3300 Las Vegas Blvd S; 🕐24hr

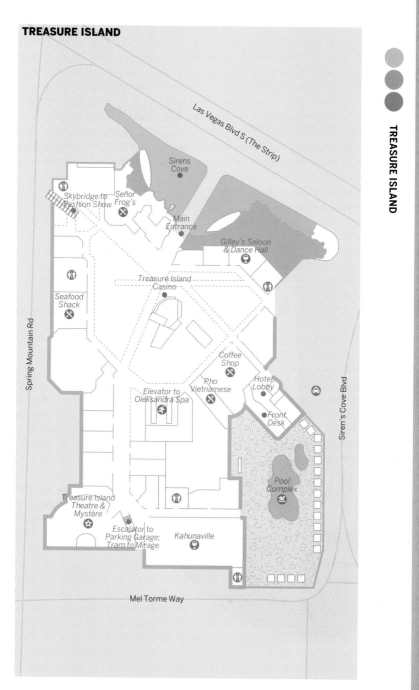

Las Vegas Blvd S (The Strip)

Sirens
Cove

Skybridge to
Fashion Show

Señor
Frog's

Main
Entrance

Gilley's Saloon
& Dance Hall

Seafood
Shack

Treasure Island
Casino

Spring Mountain Rd

Coffee
Shop

Pho
Vietnamese

Hotel
Lobby

Siren's Cove Blvd

Elevator to
Oleksandra Spa

Front
Desk

Pool
Complex

Treasure Island
Theatre &
Mystère

Escalator to
Parking Garage;
Tram to Mirage

Kahunaville

Mel Torme Way

Discover
Treasure Island

🔄 Getting There & Away

○ **Tram** A free tram glides over to the Mirage every 15 minutes or so between 7am and 2am daily.

○ **Monorail** Walk across Las Vegas Blvd to board the monorail at the back of Harrah's casino hotel, about a 15-minute walk from Treasure Island. Trains run daily until at least midnight.

○ **Bus** The 24-hour Deuce bus line, with service along the entire Strip and to downtown, stops outside Treasure Island (southbound) and the Venetian/Palazzo (northbound) every 15 to 20 minutes. Faster SDX buses (9:30am to midnight daily) stop outside the Fashion Show (southbound) and Wynn/Encore (northbound) every 15 minutes.

○ **Taxi** A taxi is your best bet if you're heading downtown. Expect to pay at least $17.50 (plus tip) one way.

👁 Sights

Treasure Island   Casino
Map p48 (🕐24hr) TI's extra-large, always busy casino is less wholesome than it once was: one-armed Playboy bandits await where playful pirates, plastic doubloons and chests full 'o' booty once reigned. Slot machines and gaming tables are tightly grouped, but no one seems to mind – the place is relentlessly packed.

🍴 Eating

TI is short on fine-dining establishments but features a handful of casual restaurants, some open late to accommodate the party crowd. For reservations, visit www.treasure-island.com/restaurants or call 📞866-286-3809. Otherwise, walk across the pedestrian skybridge to the **Fashion Show** (p59) mall for a bigger selection of value-priced, family-friendly eateries, as well as a fast-food court.

Coffee Shop & Pho Vietnamese
American, Vietnamese **$$**
Map p149 (mains $9-22; 🕐coffee shop 24hr, Pho Vietnamese 11am-11:30pm Sun-Thu, to 2:30am Fri & Sat; 👪) TI's standard-issue casino coffee shop does comfort food around the clock, from the 'Tower of French Toast' to giant overstuffed baked potatoes. Close to the casino's edge in the same space, Pho Vietnamese dishes up toned-down versions of southeast Asian

Spend the Night

Though the public spaces and amenities at **Treasure Island** (Map p149; 📞 800-944-7444, 702-894-7111; www.treasureisland.com; r weekday/weekend from $50/99; P❄️📶@♿) aren't anything special, its earth-toned hotel rooms are pretty good value for such a busy spot on the Strip. Floor-to-ceiling windows make smaller-than-average rooms seem bigger than they are, but watch out for those balconies – they're just props. Contemporary design and divine pillowtop beds add appeal, as do the panoramic views, whirlpool tubs and minifridges available in more spacious and expensive 'petite suites.'

The mandatory nightly resort fee ($25 plus tax) covers in-room wi-fi, fitness center access and sometimes a $20 credit toward a future hotel stay.

dishes like crab-stuffed spring rolls, pork *banh mi* sandwiches and, of course, *phở* noodle soup. Both are overpriced, but convenient late at night.

Señor Frog's
Mexican, American $$

Map p149 (📞 702-894-7777; www.senorfrogs lv.com; mains $12-28; 🕐 11am-10pm) It's a far cry from authentic Mexican – any place that promotes both burgers *and* fajitas probably isn't overly concerned with using the correct chili peppers – but this rollicking bar and grill, where the motto is 'if we're open, it's happy hour,' is mindless TI–style fun. You usually don't need a reservation, unless you want a Strip-view table fronting Sirens Cove.

Seafood Shack
Seafood $$$

Map p149 (📞 702-894-7223; mains $15-35; 🕐 5-10pm; 👶) Who wouldn't have a sudden craving for seafood in the desert? Hmmm. Beer-battered fish and chips sprinkled with Old Bay spice mix or jumbo-sized pan roasts of shrimp, scallops, clams, mussels and Maine lobster with your pick of regional American sauces are good bets here. Don't risk disappointment by ordering anything too fancy or that's not fried. Reservations helpful.

🍷 Drinking & Nightlife

Gilley's Saloon & Dance Hall
Bar, Nightclub

Map p149 (www.gilleyslasvegas.com; 🕐 11am-2am Sun-Thu, to 4am Fri & Sat) Yee-haw! Bring on the line-dancing cowboys and bikini-clad, mechanical-bull-riding cowgirls at this country-and-western theme bar and nightclub with live music and DJs. It bills itself as 'the only real honky-tonk saloon on the Strip,' but many of the acts are cover bands and it's a touristy crowd, unlike the original Gilley's at the New Frontier casino (RIP).

Heads up: the dance hall doesn't open till dusk (between 6pm and 8pm). Tuesday and Wednesday nights are usually given over to 'Dancing Karaoke,' when you can grab the mic and strut on stage like Shania Twain.

Señor Frog's
Bar

Map p149 (www.senorfrogslv.com; 🕐 11am-4am) The party continues after the kitchen closes at this rowdy Mexican cantina with DJs, live music, karaoke, silly contests and, naturally, busty cocktail servers pouring shots into the gaping mouths of frat boys. Check online for special events such as 'Margarita

Mondays' and Latin-band-backed salsa, merengue, cumbia and *bachata* dancing on Saturday nights.

Kahunaville   Bar
Map p149 (www.kahunaville.com; ⏱11am-2am Sun-Thu, to 3am Fri & Sat) The scantily clad young women handing out tickets for free shots are your first clue: this is yet another one of TI's riotous party bars. Sip a mai tai under a fake palm tree and watch the flair bartenders work the crowd while you soak up the beachy atmosphere – enhanced by a poolside patio in summer.

⭐ Entertainment

Mystère   Theater
Map p149 (☎800-392-1999, 702-894-7722; www.cirquedusoleil.com; tickets $69-119; ⏱7pm & 9:30pm Sat-Wed; 👪) What Dalí did for painting, this Cirque du Soleil production aims to do for the stage.

Although it doesn't have the wow factor of the aquatic *O* or musical *Beatles LOVE*, *Mystère* is a crowd-pleasing classic that's been running for decades. It's also the cheapest Cirque du Soleil ticket in town, especially for families.

Discounts are available for children under 13 years old. All children who are at least one year old must have their own ticket, even if they'll be sitting in someone's lap during the show. Some special effects may frighten younger kids.

Treasure Island Theater   Comedy
Map p149 (☎800-392-1999, 702-894-7722; www.treasureisland.com/shows/event-head liners; tickets from $35) A-list funny men and women such as Whoopi Goldberg, Bill Cosby, Tracy Morgan and Adam Carolla take on limited engagements at Treasure Island's casino theater. Check the website for an updated lineup. Buy tickets in advance.

Left: Ship's figurehead, Treasure Island Casino (p150); **Below:** Treasure Island hotel (p151)

(LEFT) LONELY PLANET/GETTY IMAGES ©; (BELOW) RICHARD I'ANSON/GETTY IMAGES ©

🔒 Shopping

A collection of small shops and boutiques are scattered throughout the casino hotel and on the upper levels of a Strip-facing mini-mall. But it's more vital to know that Treasure Island is connected to **Fashion Show** (p59), the Strip's largest shopping mall, by a pedestrian skybridge.

the surprisingly small 'O Spa & Salon' offers a standard menu of treatments, from massages to vitamin facials. More intriguing is the Russian-style *banya* ritual, with a bracing scrub-down followed by a steam with essential oils. Hotel guests can access the fitness center for 'free' (included in the mandatory resort fee).

🏃 Spas & Activities

Oleksandra Spa   Spa

Map p149 (☎ 800-944-7444, 702-894-7474; day pass $27; ⏰ spa 8:30am-7pm, fitness center 6am-7pm) Branded by Ukrainian beauty queen Oleksandra Nikolayenko,

Venetian & Palazzo

Impresario Sheldon Adelson broke ground with his replica of *La Repubblica Serenissima* (Most Serene Republic) – reputed to be the home of the world's first casino – shortly after the controversial implosion of the vintage Sands casino hotel in 1996.

On this hallowed ground, the Rat Pack had filmed the original movie version of *Ocean's Eleven* and hobnobbed with movie stars, senators and showgirls during Vegas' 'Fabulous Fifties.' When the Sands came tumbling down, a piece of history was lost – and new royalty was born. Inspired by the splendor of Italy's most romantic city, this luxury megaresort boasts reproductions of Venetian landmarks. A grandiose sequel resort, the Palazzo, threw open its doors to a sophisticated crowd in 2008. No gondoliers necessary – you can walk from Vegas' Venice to its offshore island in just a few minutes.

VENETIAN & PALAZZO – GROUND FLOOR

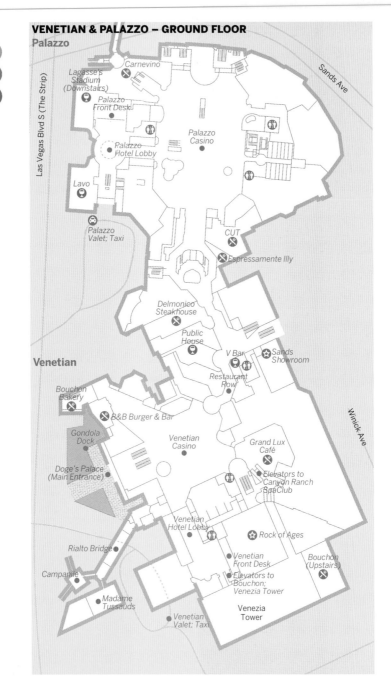

Palazzo

Carnevino

Lagasse's Stadium (Downstairs)

Palazzo Front Desk

Palazzo Casino

Palazzo Hotel Lobby

Lavo

Palazzo Valet; Taxi

CUT

Espressamente Illy

Delmonico Steakhouse

Public House

V Bar

Sands Showroom

Restaurant Row

Venetian

Bouchon Bakery

B&B Burger & Bar

Gondola Dock

Venetian Casino

Grand Lux Café

Doge's Palace (Main Entrance)

Elevators to Canyon Ranch SpaClub

Venetian Hotel Lobby

Rock of Ages

Rialto Bridge

Venetian Front Desk

Bouchon (Upstairs)

Campanile

Elevators to Bouchon; Venezia Tower

Madame Tussauds

Venezia Tower

Venetian Valet; Taxi

Las Vegas Blvd S (The Strip)

Sands Ave

Winick Ave

Palazzo

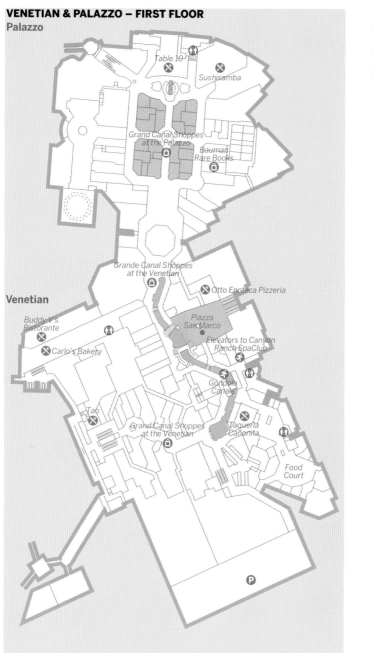

Table 10

Sushisamba

Grand Canal Shoppes
at the Palazzo

Bauman
Rare Books

Grande Canal Shoppes
at the Venetian

Otto Enoteca Pizzeria

Venetian

Buddy V's
Ristorante

Piazza
San Marco

Carlo's Bakery

Elevators to Canyon
Ranch SpaClub

Gondola
Canals

Tao

Grand Canal Shoppes
at the Venetian

Taqueria
Canonita

Food
Court

Discover
Venetian & Palazzo

Getting There & Away

o **Monorail** The closest monorail station is next door to the Venetian, at the far back of Harrah's casino hotel. The monorail connects selected casinos along the east side of the Strip with the city's convention center. Trains run until at least midnight daily.

o **Bus** The 24-hour Deuce bus line, with service along the entire Strip and to downtown, stops outside the Venetian (northbound) and Treasure Island (southbound) every 15 to 20 minutes. Faster SDX express buses (9:30am to midnight daily) pick up outside Wynn/Encore (northbound) and the Fashion Show mall (southbound) every 15 minutes.

o **Taxi** A taxi is your best bet if you're heading downtown. Expect to pay at least $16 plus tip one way.

Sights

Venetian
Casino

Map p48 (702-414-1000; www.venetian.com; 3355 Las Vegas Blvd S; ⊙24hr) The Venetian's regal 120,000-sq-ft casino has marble floors, hand-painted ceiling frescoes and 120 table games, including a high-limit lounge and an elegant no-smoking poker room, where women are especially welcome (unlike at many other poker rooms in town).

Palazzo
Casino

Map p156 (702-607-7777; www.palazzo.com; 3325 Las Vegas Blvd S; ⊙24hr) Slightly smaller than the Venetian, but equally lavish, this casino has the usual spread of high-limit table games and slot machines.

Madame Tussauds
Museum

Map p156 (866-841-3739, 702-862-7800; www.madametussauds.com/lasvegas; Venetian; adult/child 4-12yr $30/20; ⊙usually 10am-9pm;) Outside the Venetian next to the mock Rialto Bridge is this interactive version of the wax museum many love to loathe. Strike a pose with Elvis, pretend to marry George Clooney, go '4D' with Marvel Super Heroes or don Playboy Bunny ears and sit on Hugh Hefner's lap (be sure to touch him, because Hef's made of silicone – how appropriate!) Buy tickets ahead online for deep discounts or you may leave feeling ripped off.

Marilyn Monroe at Madame Tussauds, Venetian
RICHARD CUMMINS/GETTY IMAGES ©

RICHARD CUMMINS/GETTY IMAGES ©

⭐ Don't Miss
Venetian & Palazzo's Best

Even if you've had the good fortune to stroll the cobblestones and navigate the romantic canals of the world-famous Italian port city, you won't want to miss the Vegas version: in a city filled with spectacles, the **Venetian** (p158) is one of the most magnificent. Graceful bridges, flowing canals and vibrant piazzas faithfully imitate the Venetian spirit.

In the ongoing contest for Vegas' best copycat architecture, the Venetian wins the prize for elegant design, just edging ahead of Bellagio, its Italianate rival down the Strip. View the stunning exterior while approaching it over a pedestrian skybridge. Notice the scaled-down replicas of the Palazzo Ducale, the towering campanile (bell tower), the mini Rialto Bridge (anachronistically equipped with escalators) and a crowded cobblestone piazza where tourists gaze down at couples canoodling in gondolas steered by striped-shirted boatiers. Inside the Grand Canal Shoppes, colorfully dressed minstrels and operatic sopranos stroll past patrons sipping wine at faux-outdoor cafes in a miniaturized Piazza San Marco.

Next door, the sophisticated **Palazzo** (p158) lacks a theme, following the Strip's trend toward ever more refined luxury. Forget fun-loving circus acts and exploding volcanoes: the Palazzo is a luxe casino resort best known for its haute cuisine, cool pool club and high-end shopping. Meanwhile, the Venetian very much holds its own with hot nightlife, headliner entertainment and Broadway shows, a summer pool club and just as many celebrity chefs' dining rooms.

NEED TO KNOW

Venetian: ☎702-414-1000; www.venetian.com; 3355 Las Vegas Blvd S; ⊘24hr; Palazzo: ☎702-607-7777; www.palazzo.com; 3325 Las Vegas Blvd S; ⊘24hr

✖ Eating

Vegas' 'Little Italy' is a full-blown dining scene, with a stellar lineup of celebrity-chef-driven and internationally flavored restaurants. Online reservations are available via www.venetian.com/restaurants or call ☎702-414-1000.

Espressamente Illy
Cafe $

Map p156 (Grand Canal Shoppes at the Palazzo; snacks & drinks $3-8; ⏱6am-midnight Sun-Thu, to 1am Fri & Sat) Grab a cappuccino or gelato at this authentic Italian espresso shop. Beware of the 75¢ surcharge per person for dining in, rather than getting it to go.

B&B Burger & Beer
Burgers $$

Map p156 (☎702-414-2220; Venetian; mains $9-21; ⏱11am-2am) A brainchild of chef Mario Batali and his winemaking partner Joe Bastianich, this casual burger pub delivers a sunny Stripside patio and a sports-bar interior with a rockin' soundtrack. Chase down a 'Morning After' beef burger, topped by truffle aioli and a sunnyside-up egg, or an over-stuffed eggplant-parmigiano sandwich with a candied Nutella milkshake.

Grand Lux Café
American, International $$

Map p156 (www.grandluxcafe.com; Venetian; mains $8-24; ⏱24hr; ☙ ♿) The crowd-pleasing Grand Lux features ornate Italianate decor and decent renditions of American comfort food plus dishes from around the globe. Family faves include the Asian nachos and warm sticky-bun bread pudding. Call ahead for take-out orders.

Bouchon
French $$$

Map p156 (☎702-414-6200; www.bouchon bistro.com; Venezia Tower, Venetian; mains breakfast & brunch $12-26, dinner $19-51; ⏱7-10:30am Mon-Fri, 8am-2pm Sat & Sun, 5-10pm daily) Napa Valley wunderkind Thomas Keller's rendition of a Lyonnaise bistro features a seasonal menu of French clas-sics. The poolside setting complements the **Oyster Bar** (⏱3-10:30pm daily) and an extensive raw seafood selection. Deca-dent breakfasts and brunches, imported cheeses, caviar, foie gras and a superb French and Californian wine list all make appearances. Reservations essential.

The Venetian's trio of **Bouchon Bakery** locations (⏱6am-8 or 9pm daily), are a sweet spot for macaroons, petit fours, hot chocolate and espresso to go.

CUT
Steakhouse $$$

Map p156 (☎702-607-6300; www.wolfgang puck.com; Grand Canal Shoppes at the Palazzo; mains $39-119; ⏱5:30-10pm Sun-Thu, to 11pm Fri & Sat, lounge from 5pm daily) Peripatetic chef Wolfgang Puck strikes again and this time he's on fire – or 1200°F (650°C) in the broiler, to be exact. Modern earth-toned furnishings with stainless-steel accents and dried-flower arrangements complement a surprisingly smart menu, which dares to infuse Indian spices into Kobe beef and accompany Nebraska corn-fed steaks with Argentinean chimi-churri sauce or Point Reyes blue cheese.

Make reservations or have an impromptu dinner in the lounge.

Sushisamba
Fusion $$$

Map p48 (☎702-607-0700; www.sushisamba. com; Grand Canal Shoppes at the Palazzo; shared plates $3-28, mains $26-57; ⏱11:30am-1am Sun-Wed, to 2am Thu-Sat) Done up with the colors of Rio and martial-arts flicks digitally projected onto the walls, Sushisamba is a chic integration of Pe-ruvian, Brazilian and Japanese culinary traditions. Savor flawlessly grilled *robata* and churrasco meats, ceviche spiked with citrus and chilies, and delicate tempura with dipping sauces. Order caipirinhas during happy hour (4pm to 7pm and 11pm until closing daily, except Saturday).

Delmonico Steakhouse
Steakhouse $$$

Map p156 (☎702-414-3737; www.emerils restaurants.com; Venetian; lunch mains $14-21, dinner $36-55; ⏱11:30am-2pm daily, 5-10pm Sun-Thu, 5-10:30pm Fri & Sat) Designed by Emeril Legasse, Delmonico Steakhouse is a reliable classic on the Venetian's

Spend the Night

As the **Venetian** (Map p156; ☎866-659-9643, 702-414-1000; www.venetian.com; ste weekday/weekend from $149/289; P ❄ 🛜 @ 🏊 🛅) and **Palazzo** (Map p156; ☎866-263-3001, 702-607-7777; www.palazzo.com; ste weekday/weekend from $199/349; P ❄ 🛜 @ 🏊) advertise, 'our standard is suite.' Fronted by graceful canals and pedestrian plazas, these five-star 'standard' suites are anything but – in fact, they rank among the Strip's largest and most luxurious.

There are almost a dozen designs to choose from and every suite has a sunken living-room salon. The Venetian's high-flying Venezia Tower boasts a private pool, while at the Palazzo there's almost no limit to the perks for Prestige Suite guests, from having someone unpack your suitcases while you have afternoon tea in the lounge, to preparation of specialty baths and delivery of your personalized choice of pillows.

The mandatory nightly resort fee ($25 plus tax) includes in-room wi-fi and access to the fitness center at the Canyon Ranch SpaClub in the Grand Canal Shoppes at the Venetian.

restaurant row. Big oak doors open into a vaulted ceiling space and Creole-inflected dishes include New Orleans gumbo and BBQ salmon with andouille sausage hash, although steaks are the real star. Cocktail and whiskey lists are for connoisseurs. Reservations essential.

Carnevino
Steakhouse, Italian $$$

Map p156 (☎702-789-4141; www.carnevino.com; Palazzo; mains $34-85, tasting menu $150; ⊙5-11pm, bar noon-midnight) At this casino steakhouse – a high-flying collaboration between chef Mario Batali and wine-maker Joe Bastianich – it's all about red meat and wine. The house-aged beef and Italian-inspired side dishes are rich and satisfying, while the extensive wine list is heavy on French, Italian and Californian vintages. If you forgot to make reservations, grab a barstool in the taverna instead.

Otto Enoteca Pizzeria
Pizza $$$

Map p157 (☎702-677-3390; www.ottopizzeria.com; Grand Canal Shoppes at the Venetian; mains $19-30; ⊙11am-11pm; 🚹🛅) Don't even pretend to be surprised: this casual Italian pizzeria is yet another venture by chef Mario Batali. Nab a table looking out onto the Venetian's Piazza San Marco and nosh on crispy pizza, sophisticated pasta dishes like tagliatelle with pro-sciutto and poppy seeds, and addictive appetizers such as fried gnocchi. The extensive Italian wine list is heady. Reservations recommended.

Buddy V's Ristorante
Italian $$$

Map p156 (☎702-607-2355; buddyvlasvegas.com; Grand Canal Shoppes at the Venetian; mains $21-44; ⊙11:30am-10pm Sun-Thu, to 11pm Fri & Sat; 🚹) Owned by TV's *Cake Boss* star Buddy Valastro, this unfussy Italian spot piles on the nostalgia with red-and-white checked napkins, New Jersey–style fried mozzarella and pasta bowls and chicken picatta almost just like Nonna used to make. Across the hall-way, **Carlo's Bakery** shows off the chef's over-the-top cakes and lets you peek at the busy kitchen.

Tao
Asian, Fusion $$$

Map p157 (☎702-388-8338; www.taolasvegas.com; Grand Canal Shoppes at the Venetian; mains $28-48; ⊙5pm-midnight Sun-Thu, to 1am Fri & Sat) Feng shui design pervades this over-the-top Asian bistro, where an enormous Buddha floats above an

161

infinity pool. Tableside dim-sum service uses traditional carts, or dine royally on lacquered roast pork and 'typhoon' lobster stir-fry. A full bar stocks premium sake labels. Dress to impress, as this is a launchpad for **Tao** (p162) nightclub. Reservations essential.

Table 10
American, Southern $$$

Map p157 (📞702-607-6363; www.emerils restaurants.com; Grand Canal Shoppes at the Palazzo; mains lunch $15-32, dinner $26-48; 🕐11am-10pm) Named after a prime spot at Emeril Legasse's flagship restaurant in 'N'awlins', Table 10 dishes New American takes on classics such as lobster mac 'n' cheese, beet salad and Colorado lamb and filet mignon. Thickly layered banana cream pie is the must-have dessert. Reservations essential.

Taqueria Cañonita
Mexican $$$

Map p157 (📞702-414-3773; www.canonita.net; Grand Canal Shoppes at the Venetian; mains $14-37; 🕐11:30am-10pm Sun-Thu, to 11pm Fri & Sat) Beside the Venetian's indoor canal, this vibrant eatery serves contemporary Mexican dishes out of an open kitchen –

try the fresh, colorful ceviche trio, home-made tortillas or a plate of pork *barbacoa* doused in chipotle BBQ sauce – along with icy carafes of white sangria. Sip margaritas during happy hour (3pm to 6pm, and 9pm until closing daily).

🍷 Drinking & Nightlife

The Venetian and Palazzo casinos are overstuffed with bars and lounges.

Tao
Club

Map p157 (📞702-388-8588; www.taolasvegas. com; Grand Canal Shoppes at the Venetian; cover $20-50; 🕐nightclub 10pm-5am Thu-Sat, lounge 5pm-1am daily) Like a Top 40 hit that's maxed out on radio play, Tao has reached a been-there, done-that saturation point. Newbies still gush at the decadent details and libidinous vibe, from a giant golden Buddha to nearly naked go-go dancers languidly caress-ing themselves in rose-petal-strewn bathtubs. On the crowded dance floor,

Table 10, Palazzo

Paris Hilton look-alikes bump and grind to hip-hop remixes.

The sultry daytime pool club **Tao Beach** is open daily in summer and some weekends during spring and fall.

Lavo
Lounge

Map p156 (702-791-1800; http://lavolv.com; Palazzo; cover free-$20; 6pm-1am Tue-Thu, to 2am Fri, 7pm-2am Sat) After nibbling on modern Italian bites and drinks on the spacious Stripside terrace, head upstairs to the plush library-esque lounge with a small dance floor, where DJs spin Top 40 hits some nights. Weekend party brunches (10am until 4pm every Saturday, except during summer) with unlimited champagne mimosas are an ultratrendy destination for the clubbing set.

Happy hour runs from 6pm to 8pm Tuesday through Saturday.

Public House
Bar

Map p156 (http://publichouselv.com; Venetian; 11am-11pm Sun-Thu, to midnight Fri & Sat) Beer geeks unite: this tech-forward bar has two dozen beers on tap (check out the futuristic dispensing system visible through clear glass overhead), seasonal craft beers in casks and a 'beer cicerone,' who is basically a sommelier of ales and lagers. There's also gourmet pub food and a top-shelf list of whiskeys, ryes, bourbons and scotches from the USA and abroad.

Lagasse's Stadium
Sports Bar

Map p156 (702-607-2665; www.emerils restaurants.com/lagasses-stadium; Palazzo; 11am-10pm) Hidden downstairs, this slick race and sports book boasts stadium seating and haute pub grub by TV chef Emeril Lagasse. Show up early on Sunday mornings to catch all the NFL games while snacking on baby-back BBQ ribs, beer-steamed mussels and po' boy sandwiches.

V Bar
Lounge

Map p156 (702-414-3200; www.vbarvegas.com; Venetian; cover after 9pm $10-20; 5pm-2am Sun-Wed, to 3am Thu-Sat) Celebrities,

agents and glamorous young things meet and greet in this beautifully chill lounge. The low-key house and old-skool music is a mere accoutrement, as the low lighting, secluded sitting areas and sturdy classic cocktails encourage canoodling.

⭐ Entertainment

Visit www.venetian.com/entertainment for the latest high-profile performing acts.

Rock of Ages
Theater

Map p156 (866-641-7469, 702-414-9000; www.rockofagesmusical.com; Venetian; tickets $69-169; 8pm Tue-Fri & Sun, 7pm & 10pm Sat) Relive the 1980s era of big-hair glam-rock bands with this smash-hit Broadway musical. Set in the wild party scene of LA's Sunset Strip, this big-city love story is a throwback to the hedonism of the days when guitar solos couldn't be too long and the height of pop fashion was symbolized by a jean jacket and mullet haircut.

After the show, keep rocking out until the wee hours at the Venetian's '80s-themed Bourbon Room lounge with live entertainment (no cover charge).

Sands Showroom
Comedy, Live Music

Map p156 (866-641-7469, 702-414-9000; www.venetian.com/entertainment; Venetian) A rotating list of A-list comedians such as David Spade, Joan Rivers and Tim Allen crack audiences up in the Venetian's showroom, where the Australian doo-wop band Human Nature does some fancy footwork while singing dead-on covers of Motown's soulful hits.

🔒 Shopping

Grand Canal Shoppes at the Venetian
Mall

Map p157 (www.grandcanalshoppes.com; Venetian; 10am-11pm Sun-Thu, to midnight Fri & Sat) Wandering, painted minstrels,

jugglers and laughable living statues perform in Piazza San Marco, while gondolas float past in the canals and mezzo-sopranos serenade shoppers. In this airy Italianate mall adorned with frescoes, cobblestone walkways strut past Burberry, Godiva, Sephora and 85 more luxury shops.

Grand Canal Shoppes at the Palazzo   Mall

Map p157 (www.grandcanalshoppes.com; Palazzo; ⏰10am-11pm Sun-Thu, to midnight Fri & Sat) Don't be surprised to find Hollywood celebrities inside this high-design shopping mall. Anchored by the three-story department store Barneys New York, the Palazzo's shops are dazzling: Canali for tailor-made Italian apparel, London fashion imports Chloe and Thomas Pink and luxury US trendsetters such as Diane von Furstenberg. Bauman

Rare Books carries rare, signed editions and antiquarian titles.

🏃 Spas & Activities

Gondola Ride   Boat Tour

Map p157 (Grand Canal Shoppes at the Venetian; shared ride per person $19, child under 3yr free, private 2-passenger ride $76; ⏰indoor 10am-10:45pm Sun-Thu, 10am-11:45pm Fri & Sat, outdoor rides noon-9:45pm, weather permitting) As in Venice itself, a gondola ride in Vegas is a touristy activity that nonetheless holds allure for visitors from all over the world. Choose between a moonlit outdoor cruise in the resort's miniature lake facing the Strip or float through winding indoor canals past shoppers and diners. The ticket booth is inside the Grand Canal Shoppes.

164

Left: Gondola, Venetian; **Below:** Ceiling, Venetian

Canyon Ranch SpaClub   Spa

Map p156 (☎877-220-2688; www.canyon
ranch.com/lasvegas; 4th fl, Grand Canal
Shoppes at the Venetian; ☼spa 6am-8pm, salon
9am-7pm) This modern, health-minded
spa from Arizona focuses on well-being.
Offering more than 100 different spa
and salon services and fitness activities,
it specializes in massage and couples'
side-by-side therapies. On the spa's
hydrotherapy circuit, you can move
lazily from an herbal laconium to the salt
grotto to a meditative wave room. The
spa cafe serves light cuisine and fresh
fruit smoothies.

To get here, take the private elevator
next to the spa's Living Essentials
boutique inside the Grand Canal
Shoppes at the Venetian.

Wynn & Encore

Instead of featuring an exploding volcano or an Eiffel Tower to lure people, casino impresario Steve Wynn's eponymous resort is all about exclusivity – step inside and scoff at the hoi polloi flooding the Strip, while you remain secure in your lavish retreat.

Wynn stands on the former site of the vintage Desert Inn, which was imploded in 2000 to make way for this curvaceous, copper-toned casino hotel. Elements of both of the casino mogul's former projects peek through: Wynn sports the decor of Bellagio but with more vibrant colors and inlaid flower mosaics, and its lush greenery and waterfalls recall the Mirage.

The slightly newer addition next door, Encore casino resort, feels like a slice of the French Riviera in Las Vegas. Filled with indoor flower gardens, a butterfly motif and a dramatic casino with scarlet chandeliers, it's an aromatic oasis of bright beauty.

Wynn

DOUBBLE TROUBBLE/GETTY IMAGES ©

⭐ Don't Miss
Wynn & Encore's Best

Steve Wynn's signature (literally – his name is written in script across the top of the Wynn) casino hotel exudes secrecy: the entrance is obscured from the Strip by an artificial mountain of greenery, which rises seven stories tall in places. Inside, the resort comes alive with vibrant colors, inlaid flower mosaics, natural-light windows, lush foliage and tumbling waterfalls.

The same penmanship labels the adjacent Encore resort, where jeweled peacocks grace the elegant baccarat room and high rollers throw back martinis in cushy casino bars. Sunning yourself at fashionable **Encore Beach Club** (p174) on blazing hot summer days, you might feel like you're an extra in a hip-hop superstar's music video. Back inside the resort, glam **XS** (p174) and **Surrender** (p174) nightclubs host world-renowned DJs and musicians. The extravagant **Spa at Encore** (p175) is the Strip's best for beautifying or, after a big night, detoxifying.

Created by ex–Cirque du Soleil director Franco Dragone, the dreamy, fanciful and occasionally nightmarish series of vignettes that make up **Le Rêve – The Dream** (p175) cost Steve Wynn many millions. So did almost a dozen platinum-caliber restaurants inside both the Wynn and Encore resorts. Swish shopping promenades lined with brag-worthy brand-name boutiques are just as exclusive as the golf course at **Wynn Country Club** (p175), which is reserved for members and resort guests only.

NEED TO KNOW

📞702-770-7000; www.wynnlasvegas.com; 3131 S Las Vegas Blvd; 🕓24hr

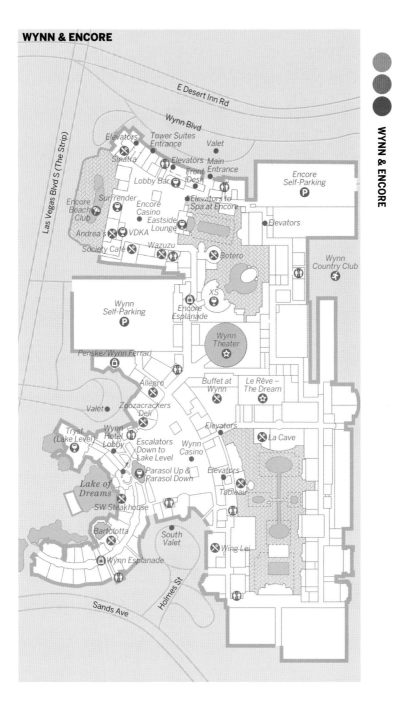

E Desert Inn Rd

Wynn Blvd

Las Vegas Blvd S (The Strip)

Elevators
Tower Suites Entrance
Valet
Sinatra
Elevators
Front Desk
Main Entrance
Lobby Bar
Encore Self-Parking
Encore Beach Club
Surrender
Encore Casino
Elevators to Spa at Encore
Elevators
Andrea's
VDKA
Eastside Lounge
Society Café
Wazuzu
Botero
Wynn Country Club
XS
Wynn Self-Parking
Encore Esplanade
Penske/Wynn Ferrari
Wynn Theater
Allegro
Buffet at Wynn
Le Rêve – The Dream
Valet
Zoozacrackers Deli
Wynn Hotel Lobby
Escalators Down to Lake Level
Wynn Casino
Elevators
La Cave
Tryst (Lake Level)
Lake of Dreams
Parasol Up & Parasol Down
Elevators
Tableau
SW Steakhouse
Bartolotta
South Valet
Wing Lei
Wynn Esplanade
Sands Ave
Holmes St

Discover
Wynn & Encore

Getting There & Away

o **Monorail** The closest monorail station is at the back of Harrah's casino hotel, south of the Venetian, about a 15-minute walk down the Strip. The monorail stops at selected casinos along the east side of the Strip, as well as at the city's convention center. Trains arrive every four to 12 minutes, operating until at least midnight daily.

o **Bus** The 24-hour Deuce and faster SDX (9:30am to midnight daily) bus lines, with service along the entire Strip and to downtown, stop outside Wynn/Encore (northbound) and the Fashion Show mall (southbound) every 15 to 20 minutes.

o **Taxi** If you're heading downtown, expect to pay at least $15 (plus tip) one way.

◉ Sights

Wynn & Encore   Casino
Map p48 (☎702-770-7000; www.wynnlas vegas.com; 3131 S Las Vegas Blvd; ☺24hr)
Inside the Wynn's elegant, sprawling casino is a popular poker room that lures pros around the clock. Not far away are slot machines from a penny up to $5000 per pull, a classy race and sports book, and a full spread of table games (mostly high minimum bets), including seasonal poolside blackjack by the cabana bar. Neighboring Encore's casino looks like a carbon copy of Wynn's, with outdoor casino tables standing ready in summer next to the resort's swimming pool.

✕ Eating

Of their first-rate dining scene, the Wynn offers the following smug statement: 'Saying you have award-winning chefs is one thing. Having them cook your dinner is another.' They're right: these eateries are less about name-dropping and more about haute cuisine, including an array of vegan and vegetarian options, with high prices to match the quality. Make reservations at www.wynnlasvegas.com/restaurants or by calling ☎888-352-3463.

Zoozacrackers
Deli   Deli $$
Map p169 (Wynn; items $7-16; ☺11:30am-10pm Mon-Fri, 8am-10pm Sat & Sun; ♿) Wynn's New York–style deli offers a standard array of sandwiches from triple-decker clubs to turkey burgers, Cobb salads and matzo

Botero (p172)

Spend the Night

It's no surprise that Sin City's most luxurious accommodations are at **Wynn** and **Encore** (Map p169; ☎877-321-9966, 702-770-7000, 702-770-7100; www.wynnlasvegas.com; r weekday/weekend from $189/249; ⓟ❄🕾@☒). Wynn's luxury resort rooms come with the works: floor-to-ceiling windows, huge flat-screen TVs, pillowtop beds covered in Egyptian cotton sheets and gigantic bathrooms with deep soaking tubs and high-end bath products. At Wynn's spacious Tower Suites, there's exclusive VIP check-in and complimentary breakfast or brunch daily. Encore's suites are even more lavish and large, and some have panoramic views.

The mandatory nightly resort fee ($25 plus tax) covers in-room wi-fi and fitness center access. The fee is waived for Tower, Salon and Parlor Suite guests.

ball soup. On weekend mornings, breakfast on the 'Zooza Benedict,' a potato latke topped with poached eggs, corned beef, pastrami and Russian dressing.

La Cave
Mediterranean $$
Map p169 (Wynn; shared plates $9-20; ⊙noon-10pm Mon-Thu, to 11pm Fri & Sat, 10:30am-10pm Sun) Flavorful seasonal tapas, brick-oven-fired flatbreads and Mediterranean-inspired plates, all meant for sharing, are the ticket at this laid-back hideaway. With romantic candlelight, Spanish-style archways and a pretty pool-view patio, La Cave is a secluded spot for a dinner date or a few glasses of tempranillo with an artisanal cheese or charcuterie board.

Andrea's
Asian, Fusion $$$
Map p169 (Encore; shared plates $10-55, mains $35-89; ⊙6-11pm Sun-Thu, to midnight Fri & Sat) Don't let that wall-sized painting of a woman's purple-shadowed eyes unnerve you. The Asian fusion platters are ideal for splitting among friends in the glamorous pre-clubbing crowd. Watch everyone's chopsticks snap up garlic-oil-seared sashimi, five-spice wok-fried squid or edamame tossed with spicy kim chi. Without reservations, you probably won't score a table at this ultra-trendy eatery.

While you wait to be seated, swill a martini from VDKA bar out front.

SW Steakhouse
Steakhouse $$$
Map p169 (Wynn; mains $35-65; ⊙5:30-10pm) Bearing Steve Wynn's own initials, this is not just any casino steakhouse: it's perched on the shore of the petite Lake of Dreams. A well-executed classic steakhouse menu hits all the right notes, from oysters on the half shell to chile-rubbed rib-eye steak and black-truffle creamed corn. Reservations are essential, especially for the coveted tables on the open-air terrace.

Bartolotta
Seafood, Italian $$$
Map p169 (Wynn; mains $30-60, tasting menus $150-180; ⊙5:30-10pm) Even in Vegas it doesn't get much posher than Bartolotta, where you can book a private cabana beside Wynn's Lake of Dreams and dine on fresh Mediterranean blue rock lobster under a fluttering white canopy. The upscale Italian-style seafood restaurant has a short, highly specialized menu – the whole fish served here are indigenous to Italy, and simply prepared.

What you're really paying for is the atmosphere, not the fresh seafood. Reservations essential.

Allegro
Italian $$$
Map p169 (Wynn; lunch mains $12-24, dinner mains $31-49, tasting menus $75-85; ⊙noon-3pm Sat & Sun, 5:30-10pm daily, late-night menu 10:30pm-6am daily) If you're not feeling flush enough for Wynn's high-end dining rooms, try this airy trattoria instead,

with tables overlooking the busy casino floor. Wood-fired pizza, meatball sandwiches and fettucini carbonara keep both the pre-theater and pre-clubbing crowds happy. Tiramisu, cannoli, pistachio cheesecake and house-baked biscotti tip the dessert scales. Reservations recommended.

Botero   Steakhouse, Seafood $$$

Map p169 (Encore; mains $35-75; ⏲6-10pm Sun-Thu, to 11:30pm Fri & Sat) Paintings and sculptures by Colombian artist Fernando Botero are the centerpiece of Encore's contempo steakhouse. The 'surf' side of the menu is on par with divine chophouse cuts, whether you're biting into grilled octopus with chorizo hash or olive-oil-poached wild salmon. Twice-baked potatoes and chimichurri and roasted red pepper sauces complement the juicy steaks. Reservations essential.

Society Café   Eclectic $$$

Map p169 (Encore; mains $15-39; ⏲7am-11pm Sun-Thu, to 11:30pm Fri & Sat) Black-and-white neo-Victorian decor with pops of fuchsia and lime green should tip you off that this modern American cafe is much more eclectic than any run-of-the-mill casino coffee shop. Creativity is poured into breakfasts of huckleberry souffle pancakes and pumpkin waffles. The late-afternoon menu (served 3pm to 5pm daily) can be a life-saver – try the steakhouse sliders. Reservations recommended.

Wing Lei   Chinese $$$

Map p169 (Wynn; mains $34-98; ⏲5:30-10pm) Gleaming gold and cool jade hues, ornate fabric-covered walls and thronelike chairs backed with gold lamé set off this Michelin-starred dining room. It feels like stepping into a Shanghai mansion, but with Cantonese and Szechuanese flavors also on the menu: most memorable is the Peking duck-carved tableside.

Reservations are usually needed, and you'll want to dress the part.

Left: Wynn and Encore; **Below:** Swimming pool, Wynn
(LEFT) JACOB KEPLER/BLOOMBERG/GETTY IMAGES ©; (BELOW) RICHARD BROADWELL/ALAMY ©

Buffet at Wynn
Buffet $$$

Map p169 (Wynn; per person $22-40; ⊙8am-3pm & 3:30-10pm; 🖟) Wynn's buffet is an upscale version of the average all-you-can-eat feed on the Strip. A color palette of butter yellow, sea green and dusty rose, with floral arrangements bursting out of vases everywhere, lend some dignity to the gluttony of 15 live-action cooking stations, piles of cracked crab legs and an unlimited dessert bar.

Wazuzu
Asian $$$

Map p169 (Encore; mains $16-38; ⊙11:30am-10:30pm Sun-Thu, to 1am Fri & Sat; 🖉) The flamboyant decor at this upscale yet casual Asian eatery includes blood-red walls, giant golden pears and, for good measure, a 27ft-long crystal dragon. It's not all show, though: the Food Network featured chef Chen Wai Chan's drunken noodles on the TV show *The Best Thing I Ever Ate*. Eclectic Chinese, Korean, Japanese, Singaporean and Thai dishes fill the menu.

Sinatra
Italian $$$

Map p169 (Encore; mains $27-58; ⊙5:30-10pm Sun-Thu, to 10:30pm Fri & Sat) Ol' Blue Eyes would've felt right at home in these classy surrounds, with chandeliers, cream-colored banquettes, classical statuary and garden views. The kitchen delivers a mix of heart-warming and sophisticated Italian-American classics, from lasagna Bolognese and pan-roasted black cod, to osso bucco 'My Way' and good ol' spaghetti and clams with red sauce. Reservations highly recommended.

Tableau
American $$$

Map p169 (Wynn; mains $16-32; ⊙7am-2:30pm; 🖉) Inside Wynn's all-suites tower, this sunny pool-view bistro is outfitted with fresh and funky floral prints and crisp white linens. Rave to your attentive servers about the lobster and shrimp frittata with salmon roe or a bowl of black-pepper pappardalle with duck confit. Reservations are helpful.

173

🍷 Drinking & Nightlife

XS
Club

Map p169 (☎702-770-0097; www.xslasvegas. com; Encore; cover $20-50; ⏰9:30pm-4am Fri & Sat, from 10:30pm Sun & Mon)** XS is *the* hottest nightclub in Vegas – at least for now. Its extravagantly gold-drenched decor and over-the-top design means you'll be waiting in line for cocktails at a bar towered over by ultra-curvaceous, larger-than-life golden statues of female torsos. Famous-name electronica DJs make the dance floor writhe, while high rollers opt for VIP bottle service at private poolside cabanas.

Fashionable nightlife attire required (ie no athletic wear, no baggy or torn jeans) except for Sunday night swim parties during summer.

Encore Beach Club
Pool Club

Map p169 (☎702-770-7300; www.encore beachclub.com; Encore; cover $30-40; ⏰hours vary by season)** Soak up sunshine on a larger-than-life 'lilypad,' bob around the pool to DJ-spun tunes, play high-stakes blackjack by the poolside or kick back in a private bungalow or a cabana with its own hot tub. The club features three tiered pools (one with an island platform for dancing), plus a gaming pavilion and top international DJs.

No 'European' (topless) sunbathing allowed. Follow the strict dress code to avoid being refused entry; check the website for details.

Tryst
Club

Map p169 (☎702-770-7300; www.trystlas vegas.com; Wynn; cover $20-50; ⏰10:30pm-4am Thu-Sat)** Groove the night away at this opulent subterranean dance club, situated on a faux lagoon under a waterfall. Let your sugar daddy treat you to over-the-top cocktails like the gold-sprinkled Ménage á Trois. Older men in suits often outnumber the glam young things on the dance floor. You'll have a better time on nights when superstar DJs spin.

Dress to impress: no athletic wear, jeans, shorts or baggy clothing.

Surrender
Club

Map p169 (☎702-770-7300; www.surrender nightclub.com; Encore; cover $20-40; ⏰10:30pm-4am Wed, Fri & Sat)** Even the club-averse admit that this is an audaciously gorgeous place to hang out, with its saffron-colored silk walls, mustard banquettes, bright yellow patent leather entrance and a shimmering wall-art snake coiled behind the bar. Play blackjack or just hang out by the pool after dark during summer. EDM and hip-hop DJs and musicians pull huge crowds.

Stylish nightlife attire required (no hats, baggy clothing, shorts, sandals or athletic shoes).

Parasol Up & Parasol Down
Cocktail Bar

Map p169 (Wynn; ⏰Parasol Up 11am-4am Sun-Thu, to 5am Fri & Sat, Parasol Down 11am-2am) Stepping into the whimsical jewel-hued Parasol Up feels something like walking into a glamorous version of *Alice in Wonderland,* complete with bright, almost psychedelic flowers. Cozy up on a plush ruby-red loveseat and gaze out at the glassy Lake of Dreams. Down the fairytale-like curved escalator, Parasol Down's seasonal outdoor patio is the perfect spot for cucumber and ginger-infused martinis.

Lobby Bar
Bar

Map p169 (Encore; ⏰6am-2am) This romantically illuminated, rouge-colored lobby bar, located on the Encore's ground level near the guest elevators, is an atmospheric spot round-the-clock, whether you're stopping in for morning coffee or evening cocktails and tapas-style appetizers. House specialty drinks, such as cranberry-infused mojitos, will cost you.

Eastside Lounge
Lounge

Map p169 (Encore; ⏰6pm-4am) Velvet chairs and classic cocktails make this lounge somewhat reminiscent of a country club. It's most popular with a mature set, who come for the dueling pianos after 9pm nightly (no cover, two-drink minimum).

★ Entertainment

Le Rêve – The Dream   Theater
Map p169 (☏ 888-320-7110, 702-770-9966; http://boxoffice.wynnlasvegas.com; Wynn; tickets $105-195; ⊙7pm & 9:30pm Fri-Tue)
Underwater acrobatic feats by scuba-certified performers are the centerpiece of this intimate 'aqua-in-the-round' theater, which holds a one-million-gallon swimming pool. Critics call it a less-inspiring version of Cirque's *O,* while devoted fans find the romantic underwater tango, thrilling high dives and visually spectacular adventures to be superior. Beware: the cheapest seats are in the 'splash zone.'

The 'VIP Indulgence Package' gives you behind-the-scenes peeks at the performers on a private video monitor, with champagne and chocolate-covered strawberries delivered to your table.

Children under five years old are not permitted inside the theater.

🔒 Shopping

Wynn & Encore Esplanades   Mall
Map p169 (☏ 702-770-7000; Wynn & Encore; ⊙10am-11pm) Steve Wynn's blockbuster resort has lured top-of-the-line retailers such as Chanel, Cartier, Dior, Oscar de la Renta, Manolo Blahnik and Louis Vuitton to the twin shopping arcades at Wynn and Encore. After you hit the jackpot, take a test drive at the Penske/Wynn Ferarri dealership, or pay $10 to get inside and gawk at the exotic sportscars on display.

🏃 Spas & Activities

Spa at Encore   Spa
Map p169 (☏ 702-770-4772; Encore; spa & fitness center day pass $40; ⊙6am-8pm)
Newer than the spa at Wynn, Encore's luxurious spa is splurge-worthy. Stroll down exotic, tranquil passageways lined with flickering Middle Eastern lamps and golden Buddha statues, then sink into hot or cold plunge pools under glowing Swarovski crystal chandeliers or recline on a heated chaise lounge before trying a Thai oil fusion massage or the Moroccan mud wrap.

The spa and fitness center entry fee is waived with a treatment of $75 or more.

Wynn Country Club   Golf
Map p169 (☏ 702-770-4653; Wynn; green fees $300-500; ⊙tee times by reservation only)
The only 18-hole golf course attached to a resort on the Strip is located directly behind Wynn. Considering it's in the middle of the desert, the lush greenery and rushing waterfalls of the par-70 course look impressive. Complimentary loaner clubs and shoes and, for an extra fee, caddies and beverage-stocked golf carts are available.

Use of the course is exclusive to members and hotel guests of the Wynn and Encore resorts.

Downtown & Fremont Street

When the Strip feels too frenzied, you can always go downtown.

The city's original quarter has long been preferred by serious gamblers who feel that faux volcanoes are beneath them. The smoky, low-ceilinged casinos have hardly changed over the years – but a 'downtown renaissance' kicked off by ex-mayor Oscar B Goodman is shifting the landscape.

Recent additions to the burgeoning neighborhood include the Mob Museum, the sustainably built Smith Center for the Performing Arts, the pop-up Container Park and diverse local eateries and craft cocktail bars. Of course, there's no shame in coming down just for the Fremont Street Experience, a vibrant, open-air pedestrian mall with nightly light shows that converted downtown from an eyesore into a tourist attraction in 1995. After all, if you don't experience downtown for yourself, you can't claim to know what Old Vegas is really all about: diehard gambling, cheap booze and lotsa free entertainment.

Fremont Street Experience (p185)

177

Downtown &
Fremont Street Highlights

Mob Museum (p182)

Las Vegas' old federal courthouse – site of one of the biggest hearings on organized crime in US history – was repurposed to house this cutting-edge collection of mob memorabilia, FBI tools, historical exhibits and multimedia displays that trace the development of organized crime in early America. This museum is the first of its kind to explore this controversial topic on such a large scale.

1 MOB'S GREATEST HITS

2 Neon Museum (p184)

The Neon Museum's vintage neon signs, dating from the 1930s onward, are some of the only remaining artifacts of the original Sin City. The museum has salvaged old-school Vegas icons from demolished or abandoned casinos, hotels, bars and wedding chapels around town. Admire them ablaze at night along the Fremont Street Experience or out of service in the museum's fascinating 'boneyard.'

COURTESY THE NEON MUSEUM ©

Golden Nugget (p190)

When it opened its doors in 1946, this glittering downtown gem was arguably the largest casino in the world. Unlike many of its downtown neighbors, the Nugget is keeping up with the times, thanks to a style overhaul by Vegas big-shot Steve Wynn. Star attractions include the Hand of Faith (the world's largest golden nugget) and a 200,000-gallon shark tank encircled by an outdoor swimming pool.

Fremont Street Experience (p185)

Fronting downtown's yesteryear casinos, this five-block-long pedestrian mall's canopy puts on a blazing sound-and-light show every hour after dusk. Get more thrills on Fremont St's new zipline: after leaping off the 12-story-high Slotzilla platform, zoom past inebriated tourists getting up to all sorts of shenanigans beneath your flying feet.

Arts Factory (p187)

On the tattered fringes of downtown, hidden among antiques shops and vintage-clothing stores, is the city's emerging 18b Arts District. Drive by on a weekday and you might not notice the pivotal Arts Factory. But on the First Friday of each month, these rundown streets take on a carnival atmosphere as art lovers, hipsters, indie musicians and hangers-on turn it into one giant block party.

Downtown Walk

Behold the ongoing revival of downtown by taking a stroll through Fremont Street, stopping off in old-time casinos, a world-class museum and hipster dive bars. Start walking around sunset as all the neon signs begin to glow.

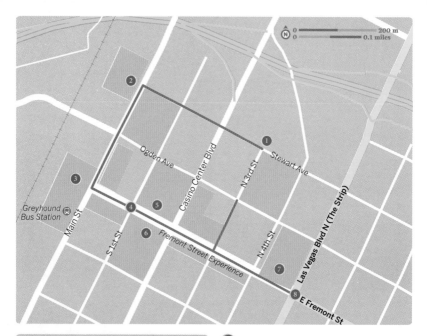

WALK FACTS

- **Start** Mob Museum
- **Finish** Fremont East
- **Distance** 0.9 miles
- **Duration** One to two hours

1 Mob Museum

Pop into this thought-provoking museum (p182) for an overview of organized crime in the USA from the turn of the 20th century to the present. If you're thirsty already, down a cocktail at the nearby Mob Bar (p191) inside the Downtown Grand (p186).

2 Main Street Station

Head west on Stewart Ave to Main Street Station (p185) for a self-guided tour of the eclectic antiques collection and a quick sample of the house microbrews at Triple 7 (p191). Continue south on Main St past the rail car once owned by Wild West showman Buffalo Bill Cody.

3 Plaza

Step into the revamped Plaza (p185), situated next to a now-defunct railway line, and imagine what pioneer life was like when the Union Pacific Railroad auctioned off dusty lots here in 1905, shortly after which the city was founded. Head upstairs to Oscar's (p191), the steakhouse and martini lounge dreamed up by the idiosyncratic ex-mayor Oscar Goodman, for flight-deck views over the Fremont Street Experience.

4 Fremont Street Experience

Walk east through the heart of Glitter Gulch, Vegas' original gambling quarter, reborn in 1995 as the Fremont Street Experience (p185). Adventure seekers whoosh overhead on the Slotzilla (p185) zipline. On your left is the Girls of Glitter Gulch strip club, atop which modern-day neon icon Vegas Vicky (aka Sassy Sally) kicks up her heels. Her pal, the 1950s-era neon cowboy Vegas Vic, stands tall on the opposite (south) side of Fremont St, at the corner of 1st St.

5 Binion's

Step inside historic Binion's (p185) to check out the action in the high-stakes poker room and watch real-life cowboys and cowgirls try their luck at blackjack.

6 Golden Nugget

Cross Fremont St to the classy Golden Nugget (p190). Ogle the gigantic Hand of Faith just off the casino floor, then slip outside onto the pool terrace to gawk at the enormous shark tank – be sure to walk around to the back side for the best views.

7 Neonopolis

Continue down to the Neon Museum – Urban Gallery (p185), an alfresco assemblage of vintage neon signs installed on the 3rd St cul-de-sac just north of Fremont St. More restored neon signs glow inside the Neonopolis, where you can take a tour and taste local craft beers at Banger Brewing (p189).

8 Fremont East

Keep going east toward the glowing neon martini glass standing at the entrance to the Fremont East Entertainment District, home to hipster watering holes such as Commonwealth (p191) and the indie shops and eateries of the Container Park (p193).

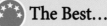

The Best…

PLACES TO EAT

Grotto Wood-oven-fired pizzas, Italian wines and a patio fronting the Nugget's shark tank. (p189)

Andiamo Steakhouse Classy Italian steakhouse with old-school manners. (p189)

Le Thai Vegan-friendly Thai fusion cooking in the heart of Fremont East. (p189)

Container Park Pop-up food vendors serving affordable, creative dishes. (p188)

PLACES TO DRINK

Commonwealth Prohibition-style saloon with a rooftop patio under the stars. (p191)

Downtown Cocktail Room Serious mixology at a speakeasy-esque cocktail lounge. (p189)

Beauty Bar A recycled beauty shop that's a tongue-in-cheek cocktail bar spotlighting live bands. (p191)

CASINOS

Golden Nugget Posh gambling den with a smart poker room. (p190)

El Cortez Vintage dive where all the low rollers go. (p186)

Don't Miss
Mob Museum

Opened to great fanfare on February 14, 2012 – the 83rd anniversary of the notorious St Valentine's Day Massacre in Chicago – this museum is officially known as the National Museum of Organized Crime & Law Enforcement. Even the museum's physical location is impressive, inside a historic US federal courthouse where mobsters sat for hearings in 1950–51. Parking in the adjacent lot costs $5.

Map p186

☎702-229-2734

www.themob
museum.org

300 Stewart Ave

adult/child 11-17yr
$20/14

🕙10am-7pm Sun-
Thu, to 8pm Fri &
Sat

🚌Deuce

SOMETHING
FOR NOTHING
BLACK MARKETS
BOOTLEG BOOZE
SEX DRUGS
INFLUENCE A
DEAL TOO GOOD
TO BE TRUE
SIN CITY JUICE
THE FIX
THE COVER-UP
PROTECTION
ACCESS
"VICTIMLESS"
CRIME
SHORTCUTS
KICK BACKS
POWER

GIVE THE PEOPLE
**WHAT THEY
WANT**

Sam Giancana

RIPPED
FROM THE
HEADLINES

Virginia Hill

FEBRUARY 14, 1929

AL CAPONE ON HIS WAY TO
PRISON OCTOBER 17, 1931

SIEGEL KILLED IN HOLLYWOOD
LOVE NEST JUNE 20, 1947

TO TOWN

MORE THAN 60 UNDERWORLD
BOSSES DETAINED IN SMALL
NY TOWN NOVEMBER 14, 1957

JFK ASSASSINATED ON
DALLAS STREET
NOVEMBER 22, 1963

JIMMY HOFFA MISSING:
POLICE HAVE NO CLUES
JULY 30, 1975

THE LAST DON, JOHN GOTTI,
DIES IN PRISON JUNE 10, 2002

127 BUSTED IN LARGEST
MAFIA ROUND UP IN FBI
HISTORY JANUARY 20, 2011

WHITEY BULGER ARRESTED:
MANHUNT ENDS ON TIP
JUNE 22, 2011

US LAUNCHES NEW PUSH ON
GLOBAL CRIME JULY 25, 2011

Exhibits

With a board of directors headed up by a former FBI Special Agent, this museum takes its sensationalistic subject seriously. The cutting-edge contemporary museum was designed by the same team behind Cleveland's Rock and Roll Hall of Fame and Museum and the International Spy Museum in Washington, DC. Thoughtfully curated exhibits tell the story of organized crime in America from the perspective of both gangsters and coppers. In addition to hands-on FBI equipment and mob-related artifacts, the museum boasts a series of multimedia exhibits featuring interviews with real-life Tony Sopranos.

Theater

Break up your journey through the museum's exhibits, which could easily take all morning or afternoon to see, with a visit to the small theater. Plonk yourself down in one of the plush seats to watch videos projected on the big screen. If you're looking for History Channel–style documentaries, just fuhgeddaboudit – the film clips being shown are mostly classic Hollywood gangster movies.

Gift Shop

Near the museum's front entrance, this gift shop is a trove of offbeat Sin City souvenirs, whether you're on the hunt for a gangster fedora, a spy pen that writes with ultraviolet ink, a wise guy's family cookbook or a coffee mug whose handle is made of brass knuckles. On a nerdy note, the shop fills its bookshelves with respectable tomes on the history of Sin City and the American mafia.

Special Events

The museum extends its educational mission by hosting special events, such as author readings and talks on everything from true-crime stories to casino cheating. Fascinating panel discussions take place inside the historic courtroom. If you're looking to get hitched in Vegas, the museum's weddings include a 'Made Man' ceremony, in which an actor offers you lifetime admission to 'the family.'

Local Knowledge

Don't Miss List

JONATHAN ULLMAN, EXECUTIVE
DIRECTOR AND CEO, MOB MUSEUM

. . . .

1 OLD FEDERAL COURTHOUSE
Dating from 1933, the former post office and US federal courthouse is one of the only surviving examples of Depression-era neoclassical architecture in Las Vegas. It's also the only building in the city that's considered historically significant on a national level – it was the site of one of the largest mob hearings in US history, one of the Kefauver Committee investigations that took place from 1950–51. Today the building is the home of the Mob Museum.

. . . .

2 INSIDE THE MUSEUM
The theme sounds very sexy and very 'Vegas,' but the museum puts into context the social conditions that allowed organized crime to develop in early America. Highlights include iconic artifacts such as the warehouse wall from the St Valentine's massacre in Chicago, filmed interviews with former mobsters, and interactive exhibits where visitors can use authentic FBI surveillance equipment tools and listen to real recorded wire taps.

. . . .

3 GETTING THERE
For years, people have been coming out to see the light show or ride the zipline at the wonderful Fremont Street Experience. But since the Mob Museum opened, we're seeing more pedestrian traffic along Stewart Ave as well. Walking from Fremont St to the Mob Museum, you'll see some of the **Neon Museum's** (p185) vintage signs in an outdoor gallery.

. . . .

4 THE MUSEUM'S NEIGHBORS
It's an organic and exciting time downtown. There's a revitalization – even a renaissance – going on here, from bars and restaurants to the development of the Neon Museum. The **Downtown Cocktail Room** (p189) is one of the coolest lounges ever. **Don't Tell Mama** (p192), a bar with live piano playing, is so much fun. I'd also recommend **Le Thai** (p189), a phenomenal Thai restaurant.

183

Discover Downtown & Fremont Street

Getting There & Away

Bus The 24-hour Deuce bus line, with service all along the Strip and to downtown, stops at the eastern entrance to the Fremont Street Experience every 15 to 20 minutes. Faster SDX express buses run about every 15 minutes from 9:30am until midnight daily; they make limited stops on the Strip and arrive downtown just off the Fremont Street Experience on Casino Center Blvd, then continue to Symphony Park and the Las Vegas Premium Outlets North.

Taxi Expect to pay around $15 to $25 one way (plus tip) to downtown from the Strip.

Sights

For tourists, the five-block Fremont Street Experience is the focal point of downtown. Further south, the **18b Arts District** (www.18b.org) revolves around the Arts Factory.

Golden Nugget   Casino
See p190.

Mob Museum   Museum
See p182.

**Neon Museum –
Neon Boneyard**   Museum
(📞702-387-6366; www.neonmuseum.org; 770 Las Vegas Blvd N; 1hr tour adult/child 7-17yr daytime $18/12, after dark $25/22; ⏱tours daily, schedules vary; 🚌113) This non-profit project is doing what almost no one else does: saving Las Vegas' history. Book ahead for a fascinating guided walking tour of the 'neon boneyard,' where irreplaceable vintage neon signs – Las Vegas' original art form – spend their retirement.

Start exploring at the visitor center inside the salvaged La Concha Motel lobby, a mid-century modern icon designed by African American architect Paul Revere Williams. Tours are usually given throughout the day, special events and weather permitting.

Make tour reservations at least a few days or a week in advance, as they book up quickly. Children under 12 years old aren't recommended on boneyard tours for safety reasons.

Neon Museum – Neon Boneyard
COURTESY THE NEON MUSEUM ©

Fremont Street Experience
Outdoors

Map p186 (www.vegasexperience.com; Fremont St, btwn Main St & Las Vegas Blvd; ⏲hourly dusk-midnight; 🚌Deuce, SDX) FREE A five-block pedestrian mall topped by an arched steel canopy and filled with computer-controlled lights, the Fremont Street Experience, between Main St and Las Vegas Blvd, has brought life back to downtown. Every evening, the canopy is transformed by hokey six-minute light-and-sound shows enhanced by 550,000 watts of wraparound sound and a larger-than-life screen lit up by 12.5 million synchronized LEDs. Soar through the air on ziplines strung underneath the canopy from **Slotzilla** (📞844-947-8342; rides from $20; ⏲noon-midnight Sun-Thu, to 2am Fri & Sat), a 12-story, slot-machine-themed platform.

Neon Museum – Urban Gallery
Outdoors

Map p186 (📞702-387-6366; www.neonmuseum. org; 450 E Fremont St, Neonopolis; ⏲24hr; 🚌Deuce, SDX) FREE Plaques tell the story of each restored vintage neon sign at these open-air galleries. Look for the flashy 40ft-tall cowboy on horseback, Aladdin's sparkling genie lamp, a glowing martini glass, a flaming steakhouse sign and more. The biggest assemblages are inside the **Neonopolis** and on the 3rd St cul-de-sac just north of the Fremont Street Experience.

Main Street Station
Casino

Map p186 (📞702-387-1896; www.mainstreet casino.com; 200 N Main St; ⏲24hr; 🚌SDX) This filigreed casino re-creates Victorian opulence with its unique design, detailed craftwork and an extensive antiques collection. Pick up a brochure at the hotel's front desk and take a self-guided tour of the *objets d'histoires*. Highlights include exquisite bronze chandeliers (originally from an 1890s Coca-Cola building in Austin, Texas), a graffiti-covered chunk of the Berlin Wall (now supporting a urinal in the men's restroom) and an art-nouveau chandelier from Paris' Figaro Opera House.

Outside on Main St stands the private rail car once used by Buffalo Bill Cody.

Golden Gate
Casino

Map p186 (📞702-385-1906; www.goldengate casino.com; 1 E Fremont St; ⏲24hr; 🚌Deuce, SDX) A gambling hall and hotel have stood on this corner since 1906, one year after the whistlestop railway town of Las Vegas was founded. It didn't become the Golden Gate until 1955, when a troupe of Italian Americans from San Francisco decamped and stayed on for four decades to manage what was previously known as the 'Sal Sagev' (the city's name spelled backwards). Today the Golden Gate's hypnotic sign is almost as irresistible as its famous shrimp cocktails.

Other than 24-hour **Du-Par's** diner, there's nothing much to draw you in besides lively craps tables and double-deck blackjack. Look for antique one-armed bandits by the hotel's front desk.

Binion's
Casino

Map p186 (📞702-382-1600; www.binions.com; 128 E Fremont St; ⏲24hr; 🚌Deuce, SDX) Binion's gambling hall and hotel was opened in 1951 by notorious Texan gambler Benny Binion, who wore gold coins for buttons on his cowboy shirts and spurred the transformation of Fremont St casino hotels from sawdust gambling halls to classy carpet joints. Benny was among the first to offer free drinks for slot-machine players and airport limo rides for high rollers. Today, what appeals most about this bedraggled downtown property is its genuine country-and-western flavor.

Watch cowboys and cowgirls dressed up in their finest duds win big in Binion's famous poker room.

Plaza
Casino

Map p186 (📞800-634-6575; www.plazahotel casino.com; 1 Main St; ⏲24hr; 🚌Deuce, SDX) Built on the site of a Union Pacific Railroad Depot, the Plaza opened in 1971. For decades it was a gaudy, cheap-looking hotel attracting package tourists and blue-haired, bingo-playing grandmothers. Although recently renovated with a

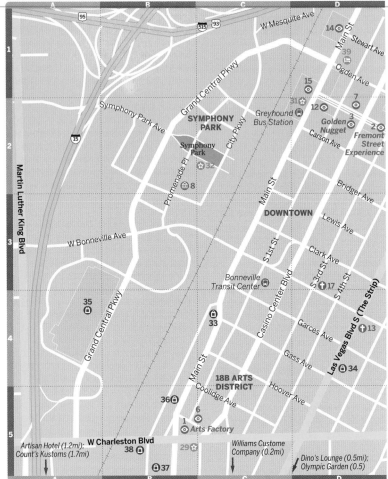

fresher, more contemporary appearance, the place is far from pretentious – it still packs in loyal gamblers with its rowdy $5 blackjack tables and cocktail waiters who call you 'hun.'

Downtown Grand
Casino

Map p186 (☎701-719-5100; www.downtown grand.com; 206 N 3rd St; ☺24hr; ☒Deuce, SDX) Reborn from the shell of the Lady Luck casino, the Downtown Grand is a shiny new player on the downtown gambling scene. Just north of Fremont St,

the urban-chic casino combines chandeliers with 'street dice' gamblers placing bets outdoors, weather permitting. The diminutive casino holds about 600 slot machines and 30 table games. A quirky bunch of bars and restaurants includes a rooftop pool bar serving food in picnic baskets.

El Cortez
Casino

Map p186 (☎702-385-5200; www.elcortez hotelcasino.com; 600 E Fremont St; ☺24hr; ☒Deuce) Head to the unabashedly retro El

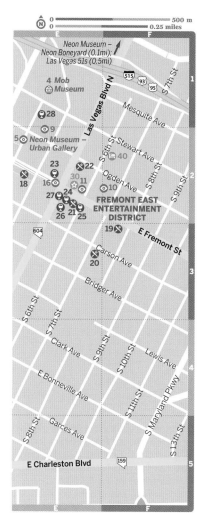
Neon Museum –
Neon Boneyard (0.1mi);
Las Vegas 51s (0.5mi)

4 Mob
Museum

Mesquite Ave

28
9

5 Neon Museum –
Urban Gallery

S Stewart Ave

23   22
18   16   30   11
27   24
26 21 25

FREMONT EAST
ENTERTAINMENT
DISTRICT

19

E Fremont St

Carson Ave
20

Bridger Ave

S 6th St
S 7th St

S Clark Ave

S 9th St
S 10th St
Lewis Ave

E Bonneville Ave

S 11th St
S Maryland Pkwy

Garces Ave

S 13th St

E Charleston Blvd

Cortez, Vegas' oldest continuously operating casino, on the National Register of Historic Places. Going strong since 1941, it's one of the only carpet joints left where the slot machines are the real thing. If you hit the jackpot, you'll enjoy the clatter of actual coins – none of that newfangled paper ticket nonsense.

Burlesque Hall of Fame   Museum
Map p186 (☎888-661-6465; www.burlesquehall.com; 520 E Fremont St; suggested donation $5; ☺usually noon-5pm Wed-Sun; ☐Deuce) Set amid the funky artist workshops, gallery spaces and yoga studios of the Emergency Arts complex, this tiny two-room museum pays homage to the history of burlesque performance in the USA. Gawk at fab sequined outfits and photographs of some of the genre's sultriest stars from yesteryear. Enter from the **Beat** (p191) coffee house.

Arts Factory   Arts Center
Map p186 (☎702-383-3133; www.theartsfactory.com; 107 E Charleston Blvd; ☺9am-6pm daily, to 10pm 1st Fri of month; ☐Deuce, SDX) Las Vegas' fractured art scene received an enormous boost in the late 1990s, when commercial photographer Wes Isbutt accidentally established this arts complex downtown. Today, the Arts Factory is the lynchpin for **First Friday** (p192) events, with as many as 10,000 people stepping inside the vibrant collective to see gallery exhibits on the first Friday evening of every month. Next door, **Art Square** (p192) has even more galleries, eclectic shops, experimental theater space and an arty bar.

Discovery Children's Museum   Museum
Map p186 (☎702-382-5437; www.discoverykidslv.org; 360 Promenade Pl, Symphony Park; admission $12; ☺9am-4pm Tue-Fri, 10am-5pm Sat, noon-5pm Sun early Sep-May, 10am-5pm Mon-Sat, noon-5pm Sun Jun-early Sep; ☖; ☐SDX) Designed for toddlers to pre-teens, the Discovery Children's Museum has undergone a major overhaul and reopened in a state-of-the-art building in Symphony Park. Highlights include 'The Summit,' a 12-story tower of interactive activities and play space, plus themed educational and entertaining exhibits such as Eco City, Water World, Toddler Town, Fantasy Festival, Patents Pending and Young at Art.

Eating

On first glance, you might think that hot dogs, deep-fried Oreos and yard-long margaritas are the extent of your eating options along the Fremont Street Experience. But downtown's dining scene is evolving: in addition to a few worthy restaurants inside casinos, trendy eateries are popping up in the city's historic core.

Once a month look for **Vegas Streats** (http://vegasstreats.com; ⊙ 2nd Sat of month), a multiblock party with food trucks, live music and local art and fashion on the Fremont Street Experience and in the Fremont East Entertainment District.

Container Park   Fast Food **$**
Map p186 (☏702-637-4244; http://downtown containerpark.com; 707 E Fremont St; most items $3-9; ⊙11am-11pm Sun-Thu, to 1am Fri & Sat) With food-truck-style menus, outdoor patio seating and late-night hours, food vendors inside the cutting-edge Container Park sell something to satisfy everyone's appetite. When we last stopped by, the ever-

changing line-up included **Pinche's Tacos** for Mexican flavors, **Pork & Beans** for piggy goodness, Southern-style **Big Ern's BBQ**, raw-food and healthy vegan cuisine from **Simply Pure** and **Bin 702** wine bar. After 9pm only over-21s are allowed.

Wild   Pizzeria, American **$$**
Map p186 (☏702-778-8800; http://eatdrinkwild. com; 150 Las Vegas Blvd N, Ogden; pizzas $9-26, brunch prix-fixe menu $18; ⊙7am-7pm Mon-Sat; ☑; ⊡Deuce) ⊘ At sidewalk level in a high-rise condo complex, this gluten-free pizzeria sources farm-fresh ingredients that are sustainably harvested. Up the feel-good factor with a fruit smoothie from the juice bar or with a side salad of kale and smoked tofu. Pizza flavors are rule-breaking, from white-truffle ricotta to chicken tikka masala. The unique beer and wine list encourages socializing.

eat.
Breakfast, American $$

Map p186 (☏702-534-1515; http://eatdtlv.com; 707 Carson Ave; mains $7-14; ⏲ 8am-3pm Mon-Fri, to 2pm Sat & Sun) Community spirit and creative cooking are more than enough reasons to venture off Fremont St to find this cafe. With a concrete floor and spare decor, it can get loud as folks chow down on truffled egg sandwiches, cinnamon biscuits with strawberry compote, shrimp po'boy sandwiches and bowls of New Mexican green chili chicken posole.

Le Thai
Thai, Fusion $$

Map p186 (☏702-778-0888; www.lethaivegas.com; 523 E Fremont St; mains $9-15; ⏲ 11am-11pm Mon-Thu, to 2am Fri & Sat; ✎; 🚊 Deuce) Although tasting none too authentic, this unpretentious Thai eatery has a lot going for it: a prime location next door to the hipster bars of Fremont East, fantastic drunken noodles and vegan curries, a small patio and a full bar turning out Asian-inspired house cocktails. The small space is crowded most nights, so consider calling ahead.

Grotto
Italian, Pizzeria $$

Map p186 (☏702-385-7111; www.goldennugget.com; 129 E Fremont St, Golden Nugget; pizzas $14-17; ⏲ 11am-10:30pm Sun-Thu, to 11:30pm Fri & Sat, pizza bar until midnight Sun-Thu, 1am Fri & Sat; 🚊 Deuce, SDX) At this Italian trattoria covered in painted murals, you'll be drawn to the sunlight-filled patio next to the Nugget's shark-tank waterslide and swimming pool. Wood-oven-fired, thin-crust pizzas (the only thing on the menu we can recommend) are accompanied by a 200-bottle list of Italian wines. Happy hour runs 2pm to 6pm daily.

Andiamo Steakhouse
Steakhouse $$$

Map p186 (☏702-388-2220; www.thed.com; 301 E Fremont St, The D; mains $23-79; ⏲ 5-11pm; 🚊 Deuce, SDX) Of all the old-school steakhouses inside downtown's carpet joints, the current front-runner is Joe Vicari's Andiamo Steakhouse. Upstairs at the D casino hotel, richly upholstered half-moon booths and impeccably polite waiters set the tone for a classic Italian steakhouse feast of surf-and-turf platters and house-made pasta, followed by a rolling dessert cart. Extensive Californian and European wine list. Reservations recommended.

Bar + Bistro
Fusion $$$

Map p186 (☏702-202-6060; http://barbistroaf.com; 107 E Charleston Blvd, Arts Factory; mains breakfast & lunch $8-15, dinner $23-32; ⏲ 11am-3pm Mon-Sat, 5-10pm Mon-Thu, 5-11pm Fri & Sat, 11am-8pm Sun; ✎; 🚊 Deuce, SDX) ✔ An energetic Puerto Rican chef delivers eclectic flavors to the table from around the globe. The cuisine is technically Latin fusion, but freely adds elements from Europe and Asia. Savor the steak chimichurri Cobb salad and *pastelitos* (Cuban pastries) stuffed with plantains, Kobe beef and pancetta. Weekend brunch brings Bloody Marys and live bluegrass music until 4pm.

🍷 Drinking & Nightlife

Locals and in-the-know tourists make a beeline to the **Fremont East Entertainment District** (www.fremonteast.com), east of Las Vegas Blvd along Fremont St.

Downtown Cocktail Room
Lounge

Map p186 (☏702-880-3696; www.thedowntownlv.com; 111 Las Vegas Blvd S; ⏲ 4pm-2am Mon-Fri, 7pm-2am Sat; 🚊 Deuce) With a serious list of classic cocktails and house-made inventions, this low-lit speakeasy is undeniably romantic, and it feels decades ahead of downtown's old-school casinos. The entrance is ingeniously disguised: the door looks like just another part of the wall until you discover the sweet spot you have to push to get in. Happy hour runs 4pm to 8pm weekdays.

Banger Brewing
Brewery

Map p186 (☏702-456-2739; http://bangerbrewing.com; 450 E Fremont St, Neonopolis; ⏲ 5pm-midnight Sun-Thu, to 1am Fri & Sat; 🚊 Deuce, SDX) Stop by downtown's upstart microbrewery to sample unusual

MICHAEL DEFREITAS/GETTY IMAGES ©

★ Don't Miss
Golden Nugget's Best

Check out the polished brass and white leather seats in the casino: day or night, the Golden Nugget is downtown's poshest address. With classy eateries and a swimming pool famous for its shark tank, the Golden Nugget outshines the competition. This swank carpet joint rakes in a moneyed downtown crowd with a 38,000-sq-ft casino populated by table games and slot machines with the same odds as at Strip megaresorts. The nonsmoking poker room hosts daily tournaments.

Wunderkind entrepreneurs Tim Poster and Thomas Breitling bought this vintage Veges casino hotel, which was once owned by none other than casino impresario Steve Wynn, in 2003. The duo catapulted the Nugget into the national limelight on the Fox reality-TV series *Casino,* but then sold it off to Landry's Inc.

One of the Golden Nugget's claims to fame is the Tank, an outdoor pool featuring a three-story waterslide through a 200,000-gallon shark tank. Swimmers can press their faces against the glass to come face-to-face with six species of sharks, rays and tropical fish. If you want to get up close to the fish without getting wet (or being a hotel guest), take a behind-the-scenes tour ($30) or stop for a drink at **Chart House** (Map p186; ⏱11am-midnight Sun-Thu, to 1am Fri & Sat), a seafood restaurant where you can perch at the bar encircling a 75,000-gallon tropical aquarium.

Another of the Nugget's famous attractions is the Hand of Faith, the world's largest single gold nugget still in existence. Discovered in Australia and weighing a massive 61lb, it's on display under glass near the North Tower elevators. Taking photos is not permitted in most casinos for security reasons, but the Golden Nugget smiles benignly upon wide-eyed visitors who photograph the mighty rock.

NEED TO KNOW
Map p186; 📞702-385-7111; www.goldennugget.com; 129 E Fremont St; ⏱ 24hr; 🚌 Deuce, SDX

brews like jalapeño hefeweizen, super-hoppy black IPA and brown ale infused with apples and cinnamon. Free behind-the-scenes tours are usually given hourly from 6pm until 10pm daily (sign up in advance online).

Commonwealth — Bar

Map p186 (☎702-445-6200; www.commonwealthlv.com; 525 E Fremont St; ⊗6pm-2am Wed-Fri, 8pm-2am Sat & Sun; ⃞Deuce) It might be a little too cool for school but, whoa, that Prohibition-era interior is worth a look: plush booths, softly glowing chandeliers, Victorian-era bric-a-brac and a saloon bar. Imbibe your old-fashioned cocktails on the rooftop patio overlooking the Fremont East scene. They say there's a secret cocktail bar within the bar, but you didn't hear that from us.

Beauty Bar — Bar

Map p186 (☎702-598-3757; www.thebeautybar.com; 517 Fremont St; cover free-$10; ⊗10pm-4am; ⃞Deuce) Swill a cocktail or just chill with the cool kids inside the salvaged innards of a 1950s New Jersey beauty salon. DJs and live bands rotate nightly, spinning everything from tiki lounge tunes, disco and '80s hits to punk, metal, glam and indie rock. Check the website for special events like 'Karate Karaoke.' There's often no cover charge.

Griffin — Bar

Map p186 (☎702-382-0577; 511 E Fremont St; ⊗usually 7pm-2am; ⃞Deuce) Escape from the casinos' clutches and imbibe craft beers and cocktails at this darkly lit lounge, an arty twist on the dive bar. Glowing fireplaces, leather booths and an almost unbearably cool jukebox make it popular with hipster sweethearts and rebels alike.

Beat — Cafe

Map p186 (☎702-385-2328; www.thebeatlv.com; 520 E Fremont St, Emergency Arts; ⊗7am-midnight Mon-Fri, from 9am Sat, 9am-5pm Sun; ☏; ⃞Deuce) The chalkboard menu at this indie cafe – a bohemian little place

that doubles as a record shop – spells out a short list of locally roasted coffee, snacks, salads and sandwiches. The coffeehouse vibe shifts to an over-21 bar scene after 7pm, when craft beers and wine are served and acoustic acts sometimes serenade.

Triple 7 — Pub

Map p186 (www.mainstreetcasino.com; 200 N Main St, Main Street Station; ⊗11am-7am; ⃞SDX) This easygoing microbrewery inside Main Street Station's casino pours samplers of its craft beers, particularly hoppy IPAs, as well as red, amber and golden ales, smoky porter and fruity seasonal brews like blueberry wheat beer or dark cherry stout. Happy hour runs 3pm to 6pm weekdays.

Oscar's — Bar

Map p186 (www.oscarslv.com; 1 Main St, Plaza; ⊗lounge 4pm-late; ⃞SDX) Attached to a steakhouse upstairs at the Plaza, this watering hole belongs to Oscar B Goodman, the ex-mayor of Sin City. Here's a politician who has no trouble communicating exactly what he plans to deliver – the glittery sign declares 'Beef, Booze and Broads.' Enjoy a dry martini in the retro-glam interior offering stellar views down the Fremont Street Experience.

Mob Bar — Bar

Map p186 (☎702-719-5100; www.mobbarlv.com; 240 N 3rd St, Downtown Grand; ⊗4pm-midnight Sun-Thu, to 2am Fri & Sat; ⃞Deuce, SDX) Piggybacking on the gangster theme of the Mob Museum just up the street, this petite bar has a plush interior with wood-paneled walls, crystal chandeliers and blue-velvet couches. Sip martinis while listening to jazz piano or torch singers from Thursday to Sunday nights.

Dino's Lounge — Bar

(☎702-382-3894; www.dinoslv.com; 1516 Las Vegas Blvd S; ⊗24hr; ⃞Deuce) A true dive bar and proud of it, this spot (where you may end up doing shots with the owner) calls itself 'the last neighborhood bar

First Friday

On the first Friday evening of each month, downtown comes to life as art lovers, hipsters, foodies and musicians come out to play in the 18b Arts District and Fremont East Entertainment District. **First Friday** (Map p186; www.firstfridaylasvegas. com; ☾5-11pm) is like a giant block party, featuring art gallery openings, live music, performance art, children's activities and food trucks selling everything from snow cones to fried pickles.

The heart of the art-oriented festival is on Casino Center Blvd between Colorado and California Sts. Start further north at the **Arts Factory** (p187) and **Art Square** (Map p186; ☎702-483-8844; www.artsquarelv.com; 1025 S 1st St; ☾most galleries 1-7pm Wed-Fri, to 4pm Sat) complexes, peeking into galleries and workshops specializing in pin-up portraits, glasswork, edgy photography, metal sculpture and more. Later head up to Fremont St to catch some music at **Get Back Alley** behind the **Beauty Bar** (p191), on the same block as the **Emergency Arts** (Map p186; www.emergencyartslv.com; 520 E Fremont St) collective, which has more galleries.

First Friday hours vary, but the festival usually goes from 5pm to 11pm. Check the website for shuttle information to avoid traffic and paying for parking. Once the galleries close, after-parties (often featuring local bands) pop up at bars and clubs around the 18b Arts District and the Fremont East Entertainment District.

in Las Vegas.' Legendary karaoke with Danny G (starting after 10pm Thursday to Saturday nights), pool tables and First Friday after-parties keep things jumping.

⭐ Entertainment

Smith Center for the
Performing Arts Performing Arts
Map p186 (☎702-749-2000; www.thesmith center.com; 361 Symphony Park Ave, Symphony Park; tickets from $20; ☾schedule varies; ▣SDX) ✐ Brilliant acoustics and art-deco-inspired design are just part of the wow factor at this downtown performing arts complex. It's also sustainably built, making it the first performing arts center of its size to achieve Silver Leadership in Energy and Environmental Design (LEED) status. Cabaret jazz, Broadway shows, classical and contemporary music, dance troupes and comedians all perform here.

Insert Coin(s) Video Arcade
Map p186 (☎702-477-2525; www.insertcoinslv. com; 512 E Fremont St; ☾8pm-2am Wed-Sun; ▣Deuce) Relive the 1980s with classic arcade games such as Ms Pac-Man and Donkey Kong, or face off against your friends with the latest high-tech multiplayer video games at this Fremont East venue that feels almost like a geeks' nightclub, with a small dance floor, DJs and a meet-and-greet circular bar. There's usually no cover charge.

Don't Tell Mama Live Music
Map p186 (☎702-207-0788; 517 E Fremont St; ☾8pm-3am Tue-Sun; ▣Deuce) This friendly Fremont East piano bar is a hit with locals, who crowd the place on weekends to hear their favorite 'singing bartenders' belting out requests. Free-flowing cocktails keep the scene thumping into the wee hours. It only takes reservations if you plan to arrive before 9pm. No cover charge.

🔒 Shopping

Gold & Silver Pawn
Souvenirs, Antiques

Map p186 (📞702-385-7912; www.gspawn.com; 713 Las Vegas Blvd S; ⏰9am-9pm; 🚌Deuce) As seen on the reality-TV hit series *Pawn Stars,* this humble-looking storefront has untold treasures inside if you look hard, from Wild West shotguns to vintage Vegas casino memorabilia. Just don't expect to shake hands with the stars themselves – Rick, Corey, Chumlee and the old man – who are only in the shop signing autographs or filming some days.

Spin-off TV shows with shops that you can tour include **Rick's Restorations** (Map p186 📞702-366-7030; www.ricks restorations.com; 1112 S Commerce St; ⏰9am-5pm Mon-Fri, 10am-4pm Sat; 🚌Deuce, 108) and **Count's Kustoms** (📞702-733-6216; www.countskustoms.com; 2714 S Highland Dr, enter off Presidio Ave; ⏰9am-5pm Mon-Fri, from 10am Sat & Sun).

Gamblers General Store
Souvenirs

Map p186 (📞702-382-9903; www.gamblersgen-eralstore.com; 800 S Main St; ⏰9am-6pm Mon-Sat, to 5pm Sun; 🚌108, Deuce) This authentic gaming supply superstore has it all, starting with one of Nevada's largest inventories of vintage and new slot machines, as well as full-size roulette, poker, craps and blackjack tables. Less expensive gambling paraphernalia makes for perfect Sin City souvenirs, including customizable poker chips, rainbow-colored dice and collectible decks of cards actually used in Vegas casinos.

Nearby **Spinetti's Gaming Supplies** may have cheaper prices.

Container Park
Mall

(Map p186; 📞702-637-4244; http://downtown containerpark.com; 719 E Fremont St; ⏰10am-9pm Mon-Sat, to 8pm Sun) An incubator for up-and-coming fashion designers and local artisans, the edgy Container Park stacks pop-up shops on top of one another. Wander along the sidewalks and catwalks while searching out handmade jewelry, contemporary art and clothing at a half-dozen specialty boutiques. What you'll find on any given day is a whimsical toss-up.

Retro Vegas
Antiques, Vintage

Map p186 (📞702-384-2700; www.retro-vegas. com; 1131 S Main St; ⏰11am-6pm Mon-Sat, noon-5pm Sun; 🚌108, Deuce) Near downtown's 18b Arts District, this flamingo-pink-painted antiques shop is a primo place for picking up mid-20th-century modern and swingin' 1960s and '70s gems, from artwork to home decor, as well as vintage Vegas souvenirs such as casino-hotel ashtrays. Red Kat's second-hand clothing, handbags and accessories are also found here.

Smith Center for the Performing Arts
BRYAN STEFFY/GETTY IMAGES ©

Below: Fremont Street Experience (p185); **Right:** Mob Museum (p182)

Las Vegas Premium Outlets North
Mall

Map p186 (📞702-474-7500; www.premium outlets.com/vegasnorth; 875 S Grand Central Pkwy; ⊙9am-9pm Mon-Sat, to 8pm Sun; 🚻; 🚌SDX) Vegas' biggest-ticket outlet mall features 120 mostly high-end names such as Armani, Brooks Brothers, DianevVon Furstenberg, Elle Tahari, Kate Spade, Michael Kors, Theory and Tory Burch, alongside casual brands like Banana Republic and Diesel.

Rainbow Feather Dyeing Co
Souvenirs

Map p186 (📞702-598-0988; www.rainbowfeather co.com; 1036 S Main St; ⊙9am-4pm Mon-Fri, to 1pm Sat; 🚌108, Deuce) Where to satisfy that boa fetish? Need turkey, chicken, duck, goose, pheasant, ostrich or peacock quills? Rainbow stocks a positively fabulous selection of fine feathers and fans for Vegas showgirl costumes in every possible hue, from fire-engine red and hot pink to neon green and jet black.

Williams Costume Company

Clothing, Jewelry

(☏866-330-9824; www.williamscostumeco.
net; 1226 S 3rd St; ⊘10am-5:30pm Mon-Sat;
🚌Deuce) Friendly staff have supplied the
Strip's aspiring starlets with DIY costum-
ing goods since 1957. Check out the
headshots in the dressing rooms, then
pick up some rhinestones, sequins, feathers etc. Rentals are ideal for Halloween
masquerades, wacky themed weddings
or partying anytime on the Strip.

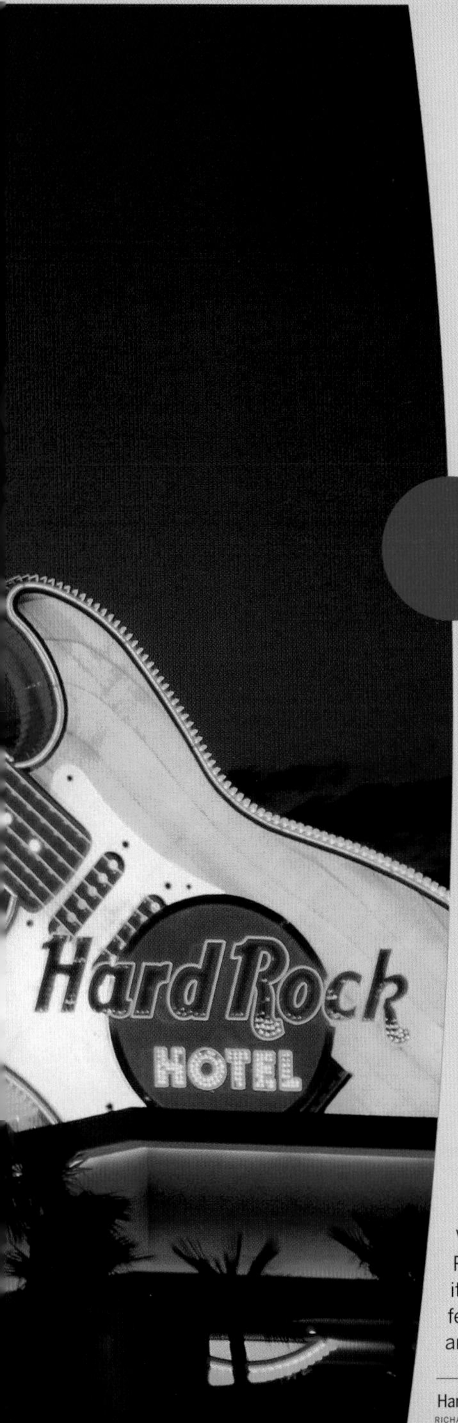

East of the Strip

Why venture off the Strip? Fair question. You won't find many powerhouse attractions east of Las Vegas Blvd, but there are a few draws.

Does an expansive collection of one-of-a-kind rock 'n' roll memorabilia tempt you? How about quirky museums paying homage to Vegas' atomic past and pinball games from yesteryear? Let's not forget value-priced eateries and bars popular with locals, funky shopping strips, a low-key university scene and a vibrant gay and lesbian nightlife district.

For tourists, the center of off-Strip gravity swings east toward Paradise Rd, where the dynamic Hard Rock casino resort anchors the after-dark action. The Fruit Loop, further south toward the airport, is the epicenter of Vegas' lesbigay community. Further north on Paradise Rd near the city's convention center, it's all business during the daytime but a different story at night, when business travelers and college students come out to play.

Hard Rock (p204)

RICHARD CUMMINS/CORBIS ©

Don't Miss
National Atomic Testing Museum

The fascinating multimedia exhibits at this museum focus on science, technology and the social history of the 'Atomic Age,' which lasted from WWII until atmospheric bomb testing was driven underground in 1961 and a worldwide ban on nuclear testing was declared in 1992. Examine southern Nevada's nuclear past, present and future, from Native American traditions to the environmental legacy of atomic testing today.

Map p202

📞 702-794-5151

www.nationalatomic
testingmuseum.org

755 E Flamingo Rd,
Desert Research
Institute

adult/child 7-17yr
$14/12

🕐 10am-5pm Mon-
Sat, noon-5pm Sun

🚌 202

Ticket Booth

Near the museum's front entrance, the ticket booth is a replica of a historical guard station from the Nevada Test Site, where atomic bomb testing began in 1951. Some of the museum volunteers who staff the ticket booth once worked at the test site.

Science & Technology Exhibits

As you make your way through the museum's permanent exhibits, take time to inspect at least a few of the 12,000 historical artifacts collected from the earliest days of atomic testing through to nuclear science today. Learn the history of how the first atomic bomb was developed, and also how atmospheric and underground testing differ. An eye-catching gallery of radiation trackers registers the sobering truth about the dangers of nuclear weapons testing, especially when the technology was brand new.

Cultural Exhibits

It's not only the science and technology of nuclear weapons that this Smithsonian-affiliated museum explores, but also the influence of atomic testing on society. Displays show what everyday life was like for Americans during the Cold War, when 'duck and cover' nuclear-bomb drills took place in elementary schools and Nevadans watched mushroom clouds bloom over the desert. Contemporary exhibits look at the environmental costs of atomic weapons, as well as Native American perspectives on land use and nuclear power.

Nevada Test Site

Usually every month, guided bus tours of the **Nevada National Security Site** (☎702-295-0944; www.nv.energy.gov/outreach/tours.aspx, **tours free**) depart from the museum. What's open at the site itself is subject to change, because it's still a working government facility. But you'll usually get to see surviving structures from the 1950s atomic testing era and moonlike craters that are many football fields wide. Apply online for tour reservations as far in advance as possible.

Local Knowledge

Don't Miss List

KAREN GREEN, CURATOR,
NATIONAL ATOMIC TESTING
MUSEUM

1 **GROUND ZERO THEATER**
Our museum's bunkerlike theater simulates what it was like to observe a real-life atmospheric atomic weapons test. After a countdown, you'll feel what someone stationed approximately 7 miles from ground zero would have felt, including shaking and seeing the dust cloud coming across the desert with the detonation's shock wave.

2 **PERMANENT EXHIBITS**
Highlights that visitors can see include a B53 bomb, once the largest in the USA's nuclear arsenal; a portable tactical bomb, called a 'backpack nuke'; and a gigantic diagnostic rack, which gives you some perspective on just how much larger than life many of the things used in nuclear testing were. Especially on weekdays, you'll often get to meet and talk with a museum docent who worked at the Nevada Test Site.

3 **ART AT THE MUSEUM**
Our continuing series of art shows features contemporary artists working in a variety of media. Exhibits change on an ongoing basis. In the past, we've displayed original paintings by a US soldier who witnessed atmospheric tests firsthand. Art is a way to show a different side of nuclear weapons testing, as seen through other people's eyes.

4 **SPECIAL MUSEUM EVENTS**
We offer public lectures on topics related to atomic testing and to special temporary exhibits at the museum, for example, 'Area 51: Myth or Reality?' We host a National Day of Remembrance for those who worked in US nuclear weapons programs. On 'family fun' days, we schedule activities for children. We'll also be hosting special events to celebrate the museum's 10th anniversary in early 2015.

5 **GIFT SHOP**
We have everything from science and technology stuff to retro atomic-age souvenirs to one-of-a-kind artwork. The museum also publishes its own journal and educational DVDs.

199

Discover East of the Strip

🔄 Getting There & Away

o **Bus** Local buses run east–west and north–south on major streets including Paradise Rd and Swenson St (bus 108), Flamingo Rd (bus 202) and Tropicana Ave (bus 201). Connecting the Strip and downtown, SDX express buses stop at the city's convention center approximately every 15 minutes.

o **Monorail** The monorail connects selected casino hotels on the east side of the Strip with the city's convention center. Trains run every four to 12 minutes until at least midnight daily.

o **Shuttle** A free shuttle runs between the Hard Rock and the Strip, but it's reserved for hotel guests only.

o **Taxi** If you're heading downtown, expect to pay at least $20 (plus tip) one way; to the Strip usually costs less.

👁 Sights

Hard Rock Casino
See p204.

National Atomic Testing Museum Museum
See p198.

Pinball Hall of Fame Museum
Map p202 (www.pinballmuseum.org; 1610 E Tropicana Ave; per game 25¢-$1; ⏰11am-11pm Sun-Thu, to midnight Fri & Sat; 👪; 🚌201) You may have more fun at this no-frills arcade than playing slot machines back on the Strip. Tim Arnold shares his collection of 200-plus vintage pinball and video games with the public. Take time to read the handwritten curatorial cards explaining the unusual history behind these restored machines.

🍴 Eating

Most of the culinary action east of the Strip is found along Paradise Rd, fanning northward from the Hard Rock casino hotel to the city's convention center. Budget-priced eateries set up on Maryland Pkwy, bordering the University of Nevada, Las Vegas (UNLV) campus.

Firefly on Paradise Tapas $$
Map p202 (📞702-369-3971; www.fireflylv.com; 3824 Paradise Rd; shared plates $5-12, mains $15-20; ⏰11:30am-midnight; 🚌108) Firefly is always packed with a fashionable local crowd, who come for well-prepared

National Atomic Testing Museum (p198)
RICHARD CUMMINS/GETTY IMAGES ©

Spanish and Latin American tapas, such as *patatas bravas,* chorizo-stuffed empanadas and vegetarian bites like garbanzo beans seasoned with chili, lime and sea salt. A backlit bar dispenses the house specialty sangria – red, white or sparkling – and fruity mojitos. Reservations recommended.

Show up for happy hour from 3pm to 6pm Monday through Thursday (till 5pm on Friday).

Culinary Dropout
American, Fusion $$

Map p202 (☏702-522-8100; www.hardrock hotel.com; 4455 Paradise Rd, Hard Rock; mains brunch $8-14, lunch & dinner $14-32; ⏱11am-11pm Mon-Thu, 11am-midnight Fri, 10am-midnight Sat, 10am-11pm Sun; 🚌108) With a pool-view patio and live bands rocking on weekends, there's no funkier gastropub around. Dip warm pretzels in provolone fondue or homemade potato chips in onion dip, then bite into fried chicken and honey biscuits. Weekend brunch (9am to 3pm on Saturday and Sunday) gives you the hair of the dog with bacon Bloody Marys. Reservations essential on weekends.

Lotus of Siam
Thai $$

Map p202 (☏702-735-3033; www.saipin chutima.com; 953 E Sahara Ave; mains $9-30; ⏱11:30am-2:30pm Mon-Fri, 5:30-10pm daily; 🅿; 🚌SX) Saipin Chutima's authentic northern Thai cooking has won almost as many awards as her distinguished European and New World wine cellar. Renowned food critic Jonathan Gold once called it 'the single best Thai restaurant in North America.' Although the strip-mall hole-in-the-wall may not look like much, foodies flock here. Reservations essential.

Lindo Michoacan
Mexican $$

(☏702-735-6828; www.lindomichoacan.com; 2655 E Desert Inn Rd; mains $13-21; ⏱10:30am-11pm Mon-Thu, 10:30am-12:30am Fri, 9am-12:30am Sat, 9am-11:30pm Sun; 🚻; 🚌203) Handmade ceramics and faux adobe

walls make this hideout feel far away from the Strip. Family recipes fill the gigantic and satisfying menu of Mexican classics, including seafood, *nopalito* (cactus) salad, beef lengua (tongue) and menudo (tripe and hominy soup). Call ahead for free shuttle service to/from the convention center's monorail station.

Envy
Steakhouse $$$

Map p202 (☏702-784-5700; www.envysteak house.com; 3400 Paradise Rd, Renaissance Las Vegas; mains $29-56; ⏱5-10pm; 🅿; monorail Convention Center) A dramatic entrance leads inside where power brokers recline against high-backed chairs amid boldly colored paints and theatrical curtains. The signature steaks and wine cellar get unfailingly high marks, with gourmet side dishes like bourbon creamed corn. It's next door to the city's convention center. Reservations recommended.

East of the Strip Highlights

The perennial wild party-animal spot is **Hard Rock** (p204), with live music and a rock-star casino.

At the **National Atomic Testing Museum** (p198), delve into Sin City's atomic past, when mushroom clouds arose on the horizon.

Tapas plates sate a crowd of good-looking locals and savvy out-of-towners at **Firefly on Paradise**, see opposite.

Fire off your best shot at the indoor shooting range **Gun Store** (p205) – novices welcome.

There are retro arcade treasures from decades past at **Pinball Hall of Fame,** see opposite, all restored by hand.

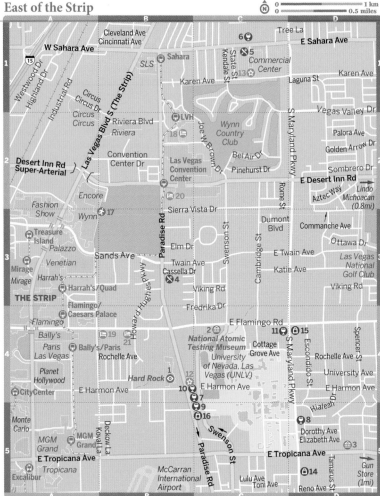

🍷 Drinking & Nightlife

South of the Hard Rock along Paradise Rd, the 'Fruit Loop' district is the after-dark home of Vegas' lesbigay community (see p248).

Double Down Saloon   Bar

Map p202 (www.doubledownsaloon.com; 4640 Paradise Rd; ⏱24hr; 🚌108) This dark, psychedelic gin joint appeals to the lunatic fringe. It never closes, there's never a cover charge, the house drink is called 'ass juice' and it claims to be the birthplace of the bacon martini. When live bands aren't terrorizing the crowd, the jukebox vibrates with New Orleans jazz, British punk, Chicago blues and surf-guitar king Dick Dale.

Hofbräuhaus   Bar

Map p202 (www.hofbrauhauslasvegas.com; 4510 Paradise Rd; ⏱11am-11pm Sun-Thu, to midnight Fri & Sat; 🚌108) This Bavarian beer hall

East of the Strip

and garden is a replica of the original in Munich. Celebrate Oktoberfest year-round with premium imported suds, fair *fräuleins* and live oompah bands nightly.

Freakin' Frog   Bar
Map p202 (📞702-217-6794; www.freakinfrog.com; 4700 S Maryland Pkwy; ⏰2pm-4am; 🚌WAX) College students adore this zany bar because it's a short stroll from the UNLV campus. Beer geeks love it for Nevada's biggest list of bottled beers (more than 1100) and more than a dozen brews on tap – ask your 'beertender' which ones to try tonight.

Hookah Lounge   Lounge
Map p202 (📞702-731-6030; www.hookah lounge.com; 4147 S Maryland Pkwy; ⏰5pm-1am; 🚌109, 202) Recline languorously with a water pipe stuffed with your pick of 20-plus premium flavored Egyptian tobaccos and exotic cocktails like lychee martinis. The ambience is worthy of a pasha.

✪ Entertainment

Joint   Music, Comedy
Map p202 (📞888-929-7849; www.hardrock hotel.com; 4455 Paradise Rd, Hard Rock; most

tickets $40-200; 🚌108) Concerts at the Hard Rock's scaled-down music venue, holding just 4000 people, feel like private shows, even when rock royalty like the Red Hot Chili Peppers and David Bowie are in town. Intimate acoustic shows happen inside **Vinyl** lounge (cover charge varies, from nothing up to $40), off the main casino floor.

🛍 Shopping

Bargain-priced bookstores, boutiques and music shops patronized by college students line S Maryland Pkwy.

Alternate Reality Comics   Books
Map p202 (📞702-736-3673; www.alternate realitycomics.net; 4110 S Maryland Pkwy; ⏰11am-6pm Sun-Tue, 10am-7pm Wed-Sat; 🚌109, 202) This indie comics shop for adults fills its shelves with the hippest graphic novels, such as *Blue Pills* and *Exit Wounds,* plus Japanese manga, collectible comics and zines.

Buffalo Exchange   Clothing
Map p202 (www.buffaloexchange.com; 4110 S Maryland Pkwy; ⏰10am-8pm Mon-Sat, 11am-7pm Sun; 🚌109, 202) Trade in your nearly

⭐ Don't Miss
Hard Rock's Best

The world's original rock 'n' roll casino houses what may be the most impressive collection of rock-star memorabilia ever assembled under one roof. Priceless items being watched over by security guards suited up like bouncers include concert attire worn by Elvis, Britney Spears and Prince; a display case filled with Beatles mementos; Jim Morrison's handwritten lyrics to one of The Doors' greatest hits; and dozens of leather jackets and guitars formerly owned by everyone from the Ramones to U2.

The Hard Rock's sexy, see-and-be-seen scene is perfect for rock stars and entourage wannabes alike. Especially favored by Southern Californians, this party hotel opens on to a circular casino with a competitive spread of table games, a state-of-the-art race and sports book, a busy poker room and the glowing Peacock high-limit gaming salon.

Trendy restaurants include the rule-breaking **Culinary Dropout** (p201) and Fú for pan-Asian plates, plus contemporary classics such as Nobu sushi bar and Mr Lucky's diner. Raucous bars and music venues range from an intimate lounge space called Vinyl and the floating poolside Palapa Bar, to the renowned **Joint** (p203) concert theater and glamorous Body English, a cavernous subterranean nightclub.

There's seasonal swim-up blackjack at the Nirvana Pool, and rollicking Rehab pool parties on summer weekends at Paradise Beach. For hip hangover cures, head to the hotel's **Reliquary Spa & Salon** (p205). To act like a real rock star, get a spontaneous tattoo at Hart & Huntington Tattoo and pick up naughty bedroom toys at Love Jones before retreating to a plush HRH Tower suite outfitted in silver-studded velvet and cool leather.

NEED TO KNOW

Map p202; ☎800-473-7625, 702-693-5000; www.hardrockhotel.com; 4455 Paradise Rd; ⏱24hr; 🖵108

new garb for cash or credit at this savvy secondhand clothing chain dealing in 1950s to '90s vintage fashions, clubwear, costume goodies and designer duds.

🤸 Spas & Activities

Reliquary Spa & Salon   Spa
Map p202 (🖉 salon 702-693-5522, spa 702-693-5520; www.hardrockhotel.com; 4455 Paradise Rd, Hard Rock; spa & fitness center day pass hotel guests/nonguests $25/50; 🕑 spa 8am-8pm, salon 10am-7pm Tue-Sat, 10am-5pm Sun & Mon; 🚌 108) Retreat to the Hard Rock's aquatic sanctuary, where you can let that pesky hangover melt away as you bliss out with a Thai fusion massage or a 'Cloud Nine' facial while sipping on a freshly squeezed concoction from the juice bar. Rock-star makeovers happen in the salon.

KISS Monster Mini Golf   Golf
(🖉 702-588-6256; www.monster minigolf.com/kiss; 4503 Paradise Rd; per game $12; 🕑 10am-midnight; 🚌 108) Opposite the Hard Rock, this indoor minigolf course is a blacklight fantasia inspired by the rock band KISS. Sink your putt underneath a giant neon-colored guitar or shoot straight up Gene Simmon's catlike tongue. Diehard fans head for the gift shop and 'Hotter than Hell' wedding chapel. It's all nonsmoking, and you can buy beer.

Gun Store   Shooting Range
(🖉 702-454-1110; http://thegunstorelasvegas.com; 2900 E Tropicana Ave; packages from $90; 🕑 9am-6:30pm; 🚌 201) Gun enthusiasts can fire off a genuine Uzi or AK47 at this high-powered indoor shooting range. Handgun rentals let you feel the heft of a Beretta, Colt or Glock in your hand. Women usually get $40 off the basic shooter's package, which includes a souvenir T-shirt. Book ahead for one-on-one VIP instruction.

West of the Strip

Between the Strip and the desert mountains, a few big attractions beckon.

Two major casino resorts, the Palms and the Rio, each located less than a mile off the Strip down Flamingo Rd, lure a party-hearty crowd. The Palms, equal parts sexy and downright sleazy, attracts notorious celebrities and gossip standbys, as well as a younger, mostly local crowd of gamblers and nightlife lovers. The less-glamorous Rio with its Mardi Gras–style atmosphere boasts a brand-new rooftop zipline and an unpretentious nightclub with a breezy patio looking out at the Strip.

Throw in a detour to the eco-minded Springs Preserve, the city's most family-friendly diversion and home to the revamped Nevada State Museum, and add the multi-ethnic dining options spreading outward from Chinatown Plaza – certainly some of the best-value food options in the city – and you suddenly have reasons to head west.

Palms (p215)

Don't Miss
Springs Preserve

Planted on 180 acres atop the site of the original springs and las vegas *(the meadows), where southern Paiute peoples and old Spanish Trail traders once pitched their camps and, later, Mormon missionaries and Western pioneers settled in the valley, this $250-million educational complex is an incredible trip through historical, cultural and biological time. It's also a thought-provoking place to consider the future of the city's neon jungle amid this fragile desert environment.*

Map p211

☎ 702-822-7700

www.springs
preserve.org

333 S Valley View
Blvd

adult/child 5-17yr
$19/11

🕙 10am-6pm

🚼

🚌 104

Origen Museum

Visitors who want to dig beneath the surface of this desert oasis should start at the Origen Museum. The Natural Mojave gallery simulates flash floods and shows the variety of wildlife in the desert. The People of the Springs exhibit narrates Las Vegas' history, from Native American dwellings to the arrival of rail and construction of the Hoover Dam. The New Frontier rooms are full of interactive games and kid-friendly activities about conservation, the environment and life in the modern-day city.

Desert Living Center

Nevada's first platinum-certified LEED (Leadership in Energy and Environmental Design) buildings have been constructed of recycled materials and rammed-earth walls, with passive cooling, renewable heating, reclaimed water and solar-electricity panels, all harvesting clean energy and exemplifying the green future of sustainable design. Inside are classrooms, learning labs and family-oriented exhibits such as the Compost Crawl and Garbage Truck Theater.

Nevada State Museum

Inside the state's natural and cultural **history museum** (Map p211; ☏702-486-5205; http://museums.nevadaculture.org; 333 S Valley View Blvd; adult/child $19/free, with Springs Preserve admission free; ⊘10am-6pm Thu-Mon; [👶]), explore more educational exhibits including prehistoric skeletons such as Nevada's state fossil (ichthyosaur *Shonisaurus popularis*), a replica of a stalactite cave, an atomic explosion display and exhibits covering Sin City's glamorous bygone days.

DesertSol, Gardens & Trails

Outside the main buildings, where desert gardens with more than 30,000 plants flourish, step inside DesertSol, an ultra-efficient, solar-powered model home. Almost 4 miles of nature trails are signposted with interpretive displays piecing together Nevada's legacy, from Native Americans to Western pioneers. Take a train ride or rent a bike on weekends to explore them.

Local Knowledge

Don't Miss List

AARON MICALLEF, CURATOR OF EXHIBITS, SPRINGS PRESERVE

1 ORIGEN MUSEUM
This museum has galleries focused on natural history, history from the Native Americans to the present, a rotating gallery for traveling exhibits, live animal exhibits and an art gallery. Be sure to check out the flash flood exhibit where thousands of gallons of water come rushing at you.

2 BOTANIC GARDENS
Acres and acres of gardens feature desert-adapted plants from around the world. Something is in bloom year round. Springtime features art in the gardens, for example, sculptures from found objects made by a local artist.

3 TRAIL SYSTEM
We have a few miles of walking trails in our natural areas; it's not uncommon to see migratory and resident waterfowl, foxes, antelope, ground squirrels and many species of lizards. Also on the trails you will find archaeological evidence of Native Americans and early pioneers, along with interpretive stations. We recently expanded our trail system with our longest trail yet, and opened exhibits detailing historic railroad cottages and the water delivery process from the Colorado River.

4 SUSTAINABILITY GALLERY
The first section has exhibits for families about water and energy use, alternative energies and recycling. In the second section of the gallery we've created the interior of a sustainable home, along with information on the products used, to showcase more environmentally friendly construction options.

5 FAMILY-FRIENDLY ATTRACTIONS
We have animal shows on weekends, animal feedings, bike rides along trails and a 'compost crawl' for little ones. The Nature Exchange trading post in the Desert Living Center is a must-visit for all budding naturalists.

Discover West of the Strip

Getting There & Away

○ **Shuttle** A free shuttle bus runs between the Rio and Harrah's and Bally's/Paris Las Vegas casino hotels on the Strip approximately every 30 minutes from 10am to 1am daily. Another free shuttle bus connects the Orleans and Gold Coast with the Strip every 30 to 45 minutes between 9am and 12:30am daily.

○ **Bus** Local buses run east–west and north–south on major streets, including Tropicana Ave (bus 201), Flamingo Rd (bus 202), and through Chinatown on Spring Mountain Rd (bus 203).

○ **Taxi** One-way taxi fares to the Strip average $10 to $20 (plus tip), to downtown $20 to $25 (plus tip). Taxis are always available outside the Palms and Rio.

○ **Walking** Crossing the I-15 Fwy on foot can be dangerous, especially after dark.

◉ Sights

Palms   Casino
See p215.

Rio   Casino
See p216.

Springs Preserve   Museum, Park
See p208.

Orleans   Casino
Map p211 (🖉702-365-7111; www.orleanscasino. com; 4500 W Tropicana Ave; ⊘24hr; 🛗; 🖵free Strip shuttle) This New Orleans–themed casino hotel does a so-so job of re-creating the Big Easy. On the casino floor stand more than 3000 slot and video poker machines and a bustling race and sports book. Bonuses for families include a multiscreen movie theater, bowling alley, video arcade and child-care center.

Gold Coast   Casino
Map p211 (🖉702-367-7111; www. goldcoastcasino.com; 4000 W Flamingo Rd; ⊘24hr; 🖵202) The neighborhood west of the Strip has several old-school casino hotels, such as Gold Coast – now as well known for its authentic Chinese cuisine as its gaming tables and slot machines that target locals, retirees and the package-tour crowd.

✕ Eating

There are only a few reasons to venture west of the Strip just to dine – mostly at the Palms and the pan-Asian kitchens of Chinatown.

Orleans
MATTHEW MAWSON/ALAMY ©

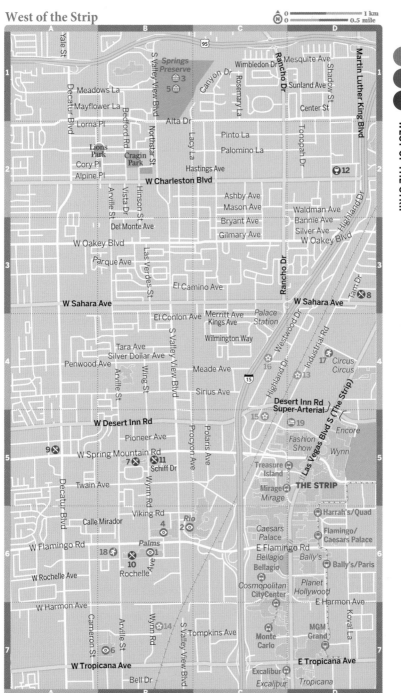

211

West of the Strip

Chinatown Plaza   Asian $

Map p211 (✆702-221-8448; www.lvchinatown. com; 4255 Spring Mountain Rd; most mains $6-18; ⊙hours vary; ♿; 🚌203) Head west from the Strip along Spring Mountain Rd and you'll find yourself in the heart of Las Vegas' strip-mall Chinatown. Slightly off the tourist radar, the district is a favorite with local foodies for its late-night Vietnamese noodle shops, Japanese sushi bars,

Korean barbecue grills and more. Start exploring at this plaza with an eye-catching Chinese gate.

Veggie Delight   Vegetarian $

Map p211 (✆702-310-6565; www.veggiedelight. biz; 3504 Wynn Rd; items $3-10; ⊙11am-9pm; ⊘; 🚌203) This Buddhist-owned, Vietnamese-flavored vegetarian and vegan kitchen mixes up chakra color-coded Chinese herbal tonics and makes *banh mi*–style sandwiches, hot pots and noodle soups.

Raku   Japanese $$

Map p211 (✆702-367-3511; www.raku-grill.com; 5030 W Spring Mountain Rd; shared dishes $2-12; ⊙6pm-3am Mon-Sat; 🚌203) At the place where LA chefs come to dine when they're in town, Japanese owner-chef Mitsuo Edo crafts small plates blossoming with exquisite flavors. You'll find yourself ordering just one more thing, again and again, from the menu of *robata*-grilled meats, homemade tofu and seasoned vegetables. Make reservations a few days in advance or angle for the tiny bar.

Also in the same Chinatown strip mall, try desserts-only **Sweets Raku**, Tokyo-style sushi bar **Kabuto** and casual, family-friendly **Monta Ramen**.

Ping Pang Pong   Chinese $$

Map p211 (✆702-367-7111; www.goldcoast casino.com; 4000 W Flamingo Rd, Gold Coast; most mains $8-20; ⊙10am-3am; 🚌202) Asian package tourists and Chinatown locals vote with their feet, and it's always crowded here. Designed by chef Kevin Wu, a wok-tossed menu ranges across the regions of China, from Beijing seafood stew to Shanghai noodles to Cantonese sausage fried rice. The dim sum carts roll until 3pm daily.

Noodle Exchange   Chinese $$

Map p211 (✆702-367-7111; www.goldcoast casino.com; 4000 W Flamingo Rd, Gold Coast; mains $9-16; ⊙noon-11pm; ♿; 🚌202) Another authentic Chinese dining option at the Gold Coast, Noodle Exchange banks on quick service, a casual atmosphere and unbeatable lunch specials. Savor the *dan*

dan noodles in sesame sauce, and Chinese hot pots filled with flavorful broth.

N9NE — Steakhouse $$$

Map p211 (☎702-933-9900; www.palms.com; 4321 W Flamingo Rd, Palms; mains $28-72; ⏰5:30-10pm Sun-Thu, to 11pm Fri & Sat; 🚌202) The Palms' dramatically lit steakhouse lets A-list celebs lounge inside a semi-private curtained dining space in the middle of a see-and-be-seen dining room. At edgy, mod tables and booths, the beautifully aged steaks and chops keep on coming, along with everything else from oysters Rockefeller to mushrooms stuffed with Alaska king crab and gruyere cheese. Reservations essential. Dress to impress.

Alizé — French $$$

Map p211 (☎702-951-7000; www.alizelv.com; 4321 W Flamingo Rd, 56th fl, Ivory Tower, Palms; mains $46-66, tasting menu without/with wine pairings $135/230; ⏰5:30-10pm; 🚌202) Las Vegas chef André Rochat's top-drawer gourmet room is named after a gentle Mediterranean trade wind. Enjoyed by nearly every table, panoramic floor-to-ceiling views of the glittering Strip are even more stunning than the haute French

cuisine and a remarkably deep wine cellar. Reservations essential. Upscale dress code.

Nove Italiano — Italian $$$

Map p211 (☎702-942-6800; www.palms.com; 4321 W Flamingo Rd, 51st fl, Fantasy Tower, Palms; mains $29-56; ⏰6-10pm Sun-Thu, to 11pm Fri & Sat; 🚌202) Sitting pretty and poised like a diva, this postmod Italian charmer attracts the preclubbing set with rococo furnishings and floor-to-ceiling neon light views. Just like the interior design, the menu is simultaneously classic (pizzas, pastas, salads) and globally minded (yellowtail crudo). Make reservations or drop in for happy-hour bar bites and cocktails.

Simon — American $$$

Map p211 (☎702-944-3292; www.palms.com; 4381 W Flamingo Rd, Palms Pl; mains lunch $12-24, dinner $24-32, Sun brunch buffet per person $40; ⏰7am-10pm; 🚌202) A hip crowd turns up at chef Kerry Simon's poolside kitchen. Most meals are hit-and-miss, but the Sunday brunch buffet offers gourmet comfort-food magic, from 'white trash' fried chicken and biscuits to marshmallow rice-krispie treats and cotton candy

Gold Coast (p210)

West of the Strip Highlights

Day and night, **Palms** (see opposite) is an off-Strip party spot, with pool parties, chic restaurants and sky-high nightclubs.

Educational and ecoconscious, the **Springs Preserve** (p208) museum complex with gardens is literally a breath of fresh air.

Detour to Chinatown's most popular kitchen, **Raku** (p212): a Japanese grill revered by chefs and foodies alike.

At **Rio** (p216), ride the new rooftop zipline, shake hands with Penn & Teller and play poker with pros.

Frankie's Tiki Room is a groovy tiki fantasia where the tropical cocktails are all knock-out punches.

(add all-you-can-drink champagne or Bloody Marys for an extra $21).

Carnival World & Village Seafood Buffets   Buffet $$$

Map p211 (702-777-7757; www.riolasvegas.com; 3700 W Flamingo Rd, Rio; per person $23-45; Carnival World 11am-10pm Mon-Fri, 10am-10pm Sat & Sun, Village Seafood 3:30-9:30pm daily; free Strip shuttle) Carnival World is an OK all-around buffet, with stir-fries, pizza, a taco bar and house-made gelato. Pricier Village Seafood is for those who can't get enough snow crab legs, lobster tails and freshly shucked oysters.

Golden Steer   Steakhouse $$$

Map p211 (702-384-4470; www.goldensteersteakhouselasvegas.com; 308 W Sahara Ave; mains $29-55; 5-11pm; SX) The Rat Pack, Marilyn Monroe and Elvis all dined at this fabulously retro steakhouse with the steer's head out front. Soak up the vintage Vegas vibes.

🍷 Drinking & Nightlife

The after-dark scene at the Palms is hot; the Rio trails behind.

Frankie's Tiki Room   Bar

Map p211 (702-385-3110; www.frankiestikiroom.com; 1712 W Charleston Blvd; 24hr; 206) At the only round-the-clock tiki bar in town, insanely inventive tropical cocktails are rated in strength by skulls on the menu. Renowned tiki designers, sculptors and painters have their work on display all around, and the souvenir tiki mugs are crazy cool. Walk in wearing a Hawaiian shirt on 'Aloha Friday' between 4pm and 8pm, and your first drink is half-off.

ghostbar   Lounge

Map p211 (702-942-6832; www.palms.com; 4321 W Flamingo Rd, 55th fl, Ivory Tower, Palms; cover $10-25; 8pm-4am; 202) A clubby crowd, often thick with pop-culture celebs and pro athletes, packs the Palms' sky-high watering hole. DJs spin hip hop and house while wannabe gangsters and Jersey girls sip pricey cocktails. The plush mansion decor and 360-degree panoramas are to die for. Dress to kill. Happy hour goes until 10pm nightly.

VooDoo Rooftop Nightclub   Club

(702-777-6875; www.riolasvegas.com; 3700 W Flamingo Rd, 51st fl, Masquerade Tower, Rio; cover $20-30; 9pm-3am Mon-Wed, to 4am Thu-Sun; free Strip shuttle) The distant views of the Strip's neon glow from the outdoor patio are fantastic, but the DayGlo decor and DJs inside are just for laughs. An unpretentious crowd dances to old-school, retro and techno tunes while swigging exotic, oversized cocktails steaming with dry ice. Retirees and buttoned-down conventioneers let loose here.

⭐ Entertainment

Pearl   Music, Comedy

Map p211 (702-944-3200; www.palms.com; 4321 W Flamingo Rd, Palms; most tickets

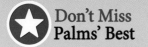

RETNA LTD/CORBIS ©

⭐ Don't Miss
Palms' Best

The ultramodern Palms casino hotel burns brightly with a mix of entertainment designed to seduce gen-Xers and -Yers. Infamous for its starring role on MTV's *Real World: Las Vegas* reality TV series, the Palms has a high-drama, neon-lit atmosphere that's equal parts sexy and sleazy – just like the pinup babes, the Palms Girls. With some of the best odds near the Strip, the casino ropes in plenty of tourists and locals too.

The Palm's enormous 95,000-sq-ft casino offers more than 2000 slot and full-pay video machines, table games, a poker room with low-limit to no-limit games, and a 120-seat race and sports book featuring interactive TV terminals and specialty wagers. But it's not just the ultracool casino that makes this detour from the Strip worthwhile: fashionable restaurants include **N9NE** (p213) steakhouse, romantic **Alizé** (p213) and **Nove Italiano** (p213), as well as poolside Sunday brunch at **Simon** (p213).

Topping off the Palms (literally) is ghostbar, see opposite, located on the roof of the 55-story Ivory Tower. It's a hip-hop and celebrity hangout with fantastic views of the Strip. Pop-music superstars like Gwen Stefani rock the Pearl, a state-of-the-art concert venue linked to an 8000-sq-ft recording studio. The Palms has also raised its star power with **Palms Place** (☎866-942-7772, 702-944-3257; www.palms.com; ⏰24hr), a hip, high-rise hotel, condo and spa complex connected to the main casino hotel by the 'SkyTube' moving walkway.

NEED TO KNOW

Map p211; ☎702-942-7777, 866-942-7770; www.palms.com; 4321 W Flamingo Rd; ⏰24hr; 🚌202

ETHAN MILLER/GETTY IMAGES ©

★ Don't Miss
Rio's Best

Despite its giddy Carnaval theme, the all-suites Rio casino hotel is often overshadowed by the action at the Palms casino hotel across the street. Occupying most of its corny two-story 'Masquerade Village' is a 100,000-sq-ft casino decked out with a colorful motif and more than 1200 slot machines, 80 table games, a full-service race and sports book with 100 TVs and a cut-throat poker room that's home to the **World Series of Poker** (www.worldseriesofpoker.com) finals.

An innovative new bar system guarantees you won't go thirsty: iPad-wielding 'Beverage Ambassadors' take your order, then 'BevErtainers' bring your drinks in between doing 90-second song-and-dance numbers back on the main floor. Ringed around the casino are run-of-the-mill retail shops and a pair of overhyped **buffets** (p214). The crowd-pleasing comedy and magic duo **Penn & Teller** (p217) draw in fans from far and wide, as do the flirty Chippendales dancers.

Fifty floors above the village, atop one of Rio's towers and reached by a glass elevator, is **VooDoo Rooftop Nightclub** (p214), a past-its-prime dance floor where revelers bop around to '80s music while drinking in the views – and some seriously gigantic cocktails. More thrilling is the new **VooDoo Zipline** (Map p211; ☏702-777-7776; www.voodoozipline.com; 3700 W Flamingo Blvd, day/night ride $25/37; ☉noon-midnight Mon-Thu, from 10am Fri-Sun, weather permitting), which slingshots tandem riders more than 30mph.

NEED TO KNOW

Map p211; ☏866-746-7671; 702-777-7777; www.riolasvegas.com; 3700 W Flamingo Rd; ☉24hr; 🚌free Strip shuttle

$50-100; 🖵202) A shining beacon for pop divas and rock bands, the Palms' 2500-seat concert hall has a sophisticated sound system. Comedy kingpins and modern rockers from Gwen Stefani to Morrissey have burned up this stage, with most seats only 120ft or less away from the performers. Live albums are minted at the state-of-the-art recording studio.

Penn & Teller   Comedy

Map p211 (📞855-234-7469, 702-777-2782; www.pennandteller.com; 3700 W Flamingo Rd, Rio; tickets from $75; 🕐9pm Sat-Wed; 🖵free Strip shuttle) This intellectual odd couple (one talks, the other doesn't) has been creating and destroying illusions for more than two decades, with dry wit, peppery profanity and some amazing stunts such as catching bullets in their teeth. The gimmick? They explain some (but not all) of their tricks to the audience. Stick around after the show for autographs and selfies.

Brenden Theatres
& IMAX   Cinema

Map p211 (📞702-507-4849; www.brendentheatres.com; 4321 W Flamingo Rd, Palms; adult/child 3-12yr $10.50/7, IMAX $17/14; 🖵202) Showing new Hollywood releases, as well as independent festival-circuit features and documentaries, the swankiest off-Strip movieplex is fitted with IMAX and Dolby 3D Digital Cinema and Dolby Atmos sound, plus rocker-chair stadium seating for superior sightlines. Matinee shows before 6pm are discounted for adults.

🏃 Spas & Activities

Drift Spa & Hammam   Spa

Map p211 (📞702-944-3219; www.palms.com; 4381 W Flamingo Rd, Palms Pl; day pass for hotel guests/nonguests $15/25; 🕐6am-7pm; 🖵202) Let your soul unwind at this glam spa. Bathe yourself in steam at the co-ed traditional Turkish hammam (sorry, *not* clothing-optional), dip into the hot-soaking and cold-plunge pools and get lost in the garden, where couples' treatment rooms are lit by aromatherapy candles after dark. Ayurvedic health remedies and detox body wraps are available on demand.

Pole Position Raceway   Racing

Map p211 (📞702-227-7223; www.polepositionraceway.com; 4175 S Arville St; 1-week membership $6, per race $22-26; 🕐11am-10pm Sun-Thu, to midnight Fri & Sat; 🖵202) Dreamed up by Nascar and Supercross champs and modeled on Formula 1 road courses, this European-style raceway boasts the USA's fastest indoor go-karts – up to 45mph! All drivers must be at least 48in tall and wear closed-toed shoes (rentals available for a fee).

Gold Coast Bowling Alley   Bowling

Map p211 (📞702-367-4700; www.goldcoastcasino.com; 4000 W Flamingo Rd, Gold Coast; per game $2-3.25, shoe rental $3; 🕐24hr; 🖵202) A 70-lane bowling alley with pool tables and video arcade games, this family-friendly place rocks out with cosmic bowling (think crazy lights, fog and disco balls) on weekend nights. 'Graveyard' bowling in the wee hours costs just a buck a game.

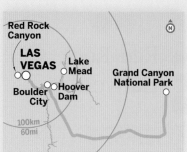

Day Trips

Red Rock Canyon (p220)

A quick escape from the Strip takes you out into the rugged Mojave Desert, where outdoor activities abound along a 13-mile scenic drive through a national conservation area.

Hoover Dam, Lake Mead & Boulder City (p221)

A marvel of engineering, Hoover Dam is a short drive from Las Vegas. Nearby Lake Mead features 700 miles of shoreline, while Boulder City remains Nevada's only casino-free town.

Grand Canyon National Park (p225)

Further afield, the USA's best-known natural attraction, the Grand Canyon, is more than a mile deep. It's an incredible spectacle of Technicolor rock strata.

South Rim, Grand Canyon (p227)
KELLY NIGRO/GETTY IMAGES ©

Red Rock Canyon

The startling contrast between Las Vegas' artificial neon glow and the awesome natural forces in this national conservation area can't be exaggerated. Created about 65 million years ago, the canyon is more like a valley, with a steep, rugged red rock escarpment rising 3000ft on its western edge, dramatic evidence of tectonic-plate collisions. Today this outdoor playground buzzes with rock climbers, hikers and wildlife watchers. Summer days are blazing hot in the Mojave Desert, so it's better to visit during spring and fall, when it's cooler.

Getting There & Away

Car From the Strip, take I-15 south, exit at Blue Diamond Rd (NV Hwy 160), and drive westward, veering right onto NV Hwy 159. For the return trip, keep driving east on Hwy 159, which becomes Charleston Blvd, continuing east to I-15 and Las Vegas Blvd.

Need to Know

o **Area code** 702
o **Location** 18 miles west of the Strip

Sights

Red Rock Canyon
Visitor Center   Visitor Center
(702-515-5350; www.redrockcanyonlv.org; 8:30am-4:30pm;) Stop here, near the start of the scenic loop drive, for natural-history exhibits and information on hiking trails, rock-climbing routes and 4WD routes. **Red Rock Canyon Interpretive Association** (702-515-5367; www.redrockcanyonlv.org) operates the nonprofit bookstore and organizes outdoor activities, including geology, birding and wildflower walks (advance reservations may be required).

Scenic Loop Drive   Scenic Drive
(entry per car/bicycle $7/3; 6am-8pm Apr-Sep, to 7pm Mar & Oct, to 5pm Nov-Feb) This 13-mile, one-way scenic drive passes some of the canyon's most striking features. From roadside parking areas, you can access hiking trails and rock-climbing routes, or simply be mesmerized by the vistas. Cyclists are allowed on the fully paved scenic drive – but watch out for dangerous potholes and distracted drivers! – and on paved spur roads.

Activities & Tours

Las Vegas Cyclery   Cycling
(702-596-2953; http://lasvegascyclery.com; 10575 Discovery Dr; bicycle rental per day $40-100; 10am-7pm Mon-Fri, 9am-6pm Sat, 10am-4pm Sun) Rent high-quality road and mountain bikes in suburban Summerlin, 10 miles west of the Strip. Ask about guided cycling and mountain-biking tours of Red Rock Canyon.

Safe Hiking

Hiking from the canyon's rim to the Colorado River and back in one day should *not* be attempted, especially during the hottest months of May through September – people have died trying. As a rule of thumb, it will take you twice as long to hike back uphill as it did to descend into the canyon.

Bring enough food (including salty snacks) and water for your entire hike, plus extra. For more hiking safety tips, check the park website or the free seasonal park newspaper, available at all park entrance stations and visitor centers.

Cowboy Trail Rides   Horseback Riding

(📞702-387-2457; www.cowboytrailrides.com; off Hwy 159; tours $69-329) To ride 'em cowboy, make reservations for a good ol' Western horseback ride along Fossil Ridge on the canyon rim or a sunset trip on the canyon floor followed by a BBQ cookout.

Scoot City Tours   Tour

(📞702-699-5700; www.scootcitytours.com; per 2 people $250; 🕗8am & 1pm daily Apr-Oct, 1pm Nov-Mar) An alternative to ho-hum bus and van tours, drive your own three-wheeled scooter-car around the canyon's scenic loop drive on a semi-guided group tour. It can be very cold in winter. Drivers must be at least 21 years old; no passengers under eight years old allowed.

Hoover Dam, Lake Mead & Boulder City

Even those who challenge, or at least question, the USA's commitment to damming the US West have to marvel at the engineering and architecture of the Hoover Dam. Set amid the almost unbearably dry Mojave Desert, the dam towers over Black Canyon and provides electricity for the entire region.

Hoover Dam created Lake Mead, while Davis Dam created the much smaller Lake Mohave, straddling the Arizona border. The stretch of the Colorado River through Black Canyon links the two lakes. All three bodies of water are protected inside Lake Mead National Recreation Area.

On your way to Hoover Dam or Lake Mead, stop for a stroll in the charming small town of Boulder City, where gambling is illegal. Originally erected during the Depression to house dam construction workers and their families, casinos were outlawed here so the workers would not be distracted from their monumental task.

Getting There & Away

Car From the Strip, take I-15 south to I-215 east, then continue on I-515/US 93 and 95 over Railroad Pass. Highway 93 continues past Boulder City to Hoover Dam, passing a turnoff to Lake Mead.

Parking Approaching the dam from Boulder City, there's a multilevel parking garage ($10) before you reach the visitor center. If you drive across the Arizona state line, you'll find another parking lot ($10) and limited free roadside parking.

Bus Guided bus tours from the Strip cost $30 to $90 per person.

Need to Know

o **Area code** 📞702

o **Location** 33 miles southeast of the Strip

o **Nevada Welcome Center** (📞702-294-1252; www.visitbouldercity.com; 100 Nevada Hwy, Boulder City; 🕗8am-4:30pm)

o **Alan Bible Visitor Center** (📞702-293-8990; www.nps.gov/lake; Lakeshore Scenic Dr, off US Hwy 93; 🕗9am-4:30pm Wed-Sun) In Lake Mead National Recreation Area.

◎ Sights

Hoover Dam   Historic Site

(📞866-730-9097, 702-494-2517; www.usbr.gov/lc/hooverdam; off Hwy 93; visitor center admission & 30min tour adult/child 4-16yr/under 4yr $15/12/free; admission & 1hr tour $30, child under 4yr free; 🕗9am-6pm Apr-Oct, to 5pm Nov-Mar; 👪) A statue of bronze winged figures stands atop Hoover Dam, memorializing those who built the massive 726ft-high concrete structure, once the world's tallest dam. Guided tours of this art-deco masterpiece of engineering begin at the modern visitor center, where a video features original construction footage. After the 10-minute

screening, you'll take an elevator ride more than 50 stories below to view the dam's massive power generators, each of which alone could power a city of 100,000 people.

Originally named Boulder Dam, this New Deal public works project, completed ahead of schedule and under budget in 1936, was the Colorado River's first major dam. Thousands of men and their families, eager for employment at the height of the country's Great Depression, came to Black Canyon and worked in excruciating conditions – dangling hundreds of feet above the canyon in 120°F (about 50°C) desert heat. Almost 100 died.

Note, the last visitor center admission is 45 minutes before closing, with tour ticket sales ending another 30 minutes earlier. One-hour guided-tour tickets, which are sold on a first-come, first-served basis, may sell out several hours before closing, so arrive early.

Mike O'Callaghan–Pat Tillman Memorial Bridge   Bridge

(Hwy 93) With a pedestrian walkway that captures perfect views upstream of Hoover Dam, this bridge is not recommended for anyone with vertigo. It's a short but steep climb up 70 stairs or along a wheelchair-accessible ramp from the free parking lot, located on your right past the security checkpoint as you approach the dam from Boulder City.

Boulder City/Hoover Dam Museum   Museum

(☏702-294-1988; www.bcmha.org; 1305 Arizona St, Boulder Dam Hotel, Boulder City; adult/child $2/1; ⏱10am-5pm Mon-Sat; 👪) You'll enjoy the dam tour more if you stop at this small but engagingly hands-on museum in Boulder City first. It's upstairs at the historic Boulder Dam Hotel, where Bette Davis, Will Rogers and Howard Hughes once slept. Through oral

Left: Hoover Dam and Lake Mead; **Below:** Mike O'Callaghan–Pat Tillman Memorial Bridge
(LEFT) DARRELL CRAIG HARRIS/GETTY IMAGES ©; (BELOW) DANITA DELIMONT/GETTY IMAGES ©

histories, photographs and historical artifacts, exhibits focus on Depression-era America and the tough living conditions endured by the people who came to build the dam. A 20-minute film features historic footage of the project.

🏃 Activities & Tours

Lake Mead National Recreation Area
Outdoors

(📞info desk 702-293-8906, visitor center 702-293-8990; www.nps.gov/lake; 7-day entry per vehicle $10; ⏰24hr; visitor center 9am-4:30pm Wed-Sun) It's less than an hour's drive from Las Vegas to the most visited part of this 1.5-million-acre national recreation area, a popular boating, swimming, hiking and weekend camping destination for many locals. Within this protected area of the almost unbearably dry Mojave Desert are Lake Mead, which extends 110 miles toward the Grand Canyon; 67-mile-long Lake Mohave, which runs along the Arizona–Nevada border; and miles of spectacular desert washes, mountains and canyons surrounding the lakes.

Lake Mead Cruises
Boat Tour

(📞702-293-6180; www.lakemeadcruises.com; Lakeshore Rd; 90min noon cruise per adult/child 2-11yr $26/13; ⏰noon & 2pm Apr-Oct, schedules vary Nov-Mar) Sail away on board triple-decker, Mississippi-style paddle wheelers, which are (most importantly) air-conditioned. Lunch and dinner cruises aren't worth the extra money. Cruises depart from Hemenway Harbor, near the lake's southern end.

Black Canyon River Adventures
Rafting

(📞800-455-3490, 702-294-1414; www.black canyonadventures.com; Hacienda Hotel &

223

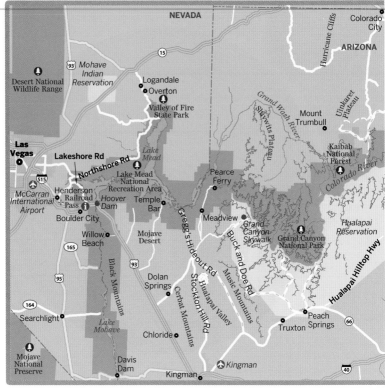

Casino, Hwy 93, Boulder City; 5hr tour adult/child 5-12yr $92/58) Motor-assisted Colorado River raft floats launch beneath Hoover Dam, with stops for swimming and lunch. Round-trip transportation from Las Vegas is available (surcharge $49), and 30-minute Hoover Dam 'postcard' float trips cost less (per person $35).

Desert Adventures   Kayaking

(☎702-293-5026; www.kayaklasvegas.com; 1647a Nevada Hwy, Boulder City; full-day Colorado River kayak $169; ⏰9am-6pm Apr-Oct, 10am-4pm Nov-Mar; @) With Lake Mead and the Black Canyon of the Colorado River just a short drive away, would-be river rats should check in here for guided kayaking and stand up pad-dling (SUP) tours. Experienced paddlers can rent canoes and kayaks for DIY trips.

All Mountain
Cyclery   Cycling, Kayaking

(☎702-453-2453; http://allmountaincyclery.com; 1404 Nevada Hwy, Boulder City; mountain-bike rentals per day $40-75, half-/full-day tour $180/200; ⏰11am-6pm Mon, 10am-6pm Tue-Fri, 9am-6pm Sat, 9am-4pm Sun) Bounce along single-track in Bootleg Canyon on a guided mountain-biking tour, or get a real workout with an all-day excursion that includes Lake Mead kayaking. Mountain-bike rentals and shuttle available.

Bootleg Canyon
Flightlines   Outdoors

(☎702-293-6885; www.flightlinezbootleg.com; 1512 Industrial Rd, Boulder City; 2hr tour

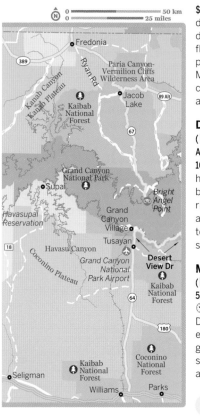

$6-10; ⏱6am-2pm; 🚹) At this classic downtown diner, lines snake outside the door just for a chance to fork into waffles with design-it-yourself fillings like peanut butter, coconut or bacon, or the Mexican pork chile-verde omelette with crispy hash browns. Breakfast served all day.

Dillinger   Burgers $$
(☎702-293-4001; www.thedillinger.com; 1224 Arizona St, Boulder City; mains $8-13; ⏱11am-10pm) After a day of mountain biking, hiking or kayaking, nothing sounds better than a burger and a cold beer, right? Head to this downtown 'drinkery' and order the namesake Dillinger burger topped with bacon and beef brisket, with sweet-potato fries on the side.

Milo's Cellar   Cafe $$
(☎702-293-9540; www.miloswinebar.com; 538 Nevada Hwy, Boulder City; mains $9-14; ⏱11am-10pm Sun-Thu, to 11pm Fri & Sat) Downtown, Milo's dependably delivers deli sandwiches, fresh salads and gourmet cheese and meat platters to sidewalk tables outside its lively wine and beer bar.

Grand Canyon National Park

Why do folks become giddy when describing the Grand Canyon? One peek over the edge makes it clear. The canyon captivates travelers because of its sheer immensity; it's a tableau that reveals the earth's history layer by dramatic layer. Mother Nature adds artistic details – rugged plateaus, crumbly spires, shadowed ridges – that flirt and catch your eye as the sun crosses the sky. Snaking along its floor are 277 miles of the Colorado River, which has carved out the canyon during the past six million years and exposed rocks up to two billion years old – half the age of the planet.

$159) This thrilling aerial adventure is like ziplining, but with a paragliding harness. Morning tours see the coolest temps, while late afternoon tours may catch sunset over the desert. Riders must weigh between 75lb and 250lb fully dressed and wear closed-toed shoes.

Eating

You'll find basic restaurants at the Hemenway Harbor, Callville Bay and Temple Bar marinas on Lake Mead. Other lakeshore marinas have convenience stores for snacks and drinks.

Coffee Cup   Diner $
(☎702-294-0517; www.worldfamouscoffee-cup.com; 512 Nevada Way, Boulder City; mains

The two rims of the Grand Canyon offer quite different experiences; they lie more than 200 miles apart by road and are rarely visited on the same trip. Most visitors choose the South Rim for its easy access, plentiful services and vistas that don't disappoint. The quieter North Rim has its own charms: at 8200ft elevation (1000ft higher than the South Rim), cooler temperatures bless wildflower meadows and tall, thick groves of aspen and spruce trees.

The park's most developed area is Grand Canyon Village, 6 miles north of the South Rim's South Entrance Station. The only entrance to the North Rim lies 30 miles south of Jacob Lake on Hwy 67. While the South Rim is open year-round, the North Rim shuts down between mid-October and mid-May. June is the driest month, July and August are the wettest. Summer temperatures inside the canyon regularly soar above 100°F (38°C), while daytime highs in winter hover just above freezing.

Getting There & Away

Car For the South Rim, take I-15 south from the Strip. Follow the signs for I-215 east, then merge onto US 93 south. In Kingman, take I-40 east, then follow AZ 64 north from Williams. The drive takes about 4½ hours one way.

Shuttle On the South Rim, free park shuttles operate seasonally around Grand Canyon Village, west to Hermits Rest and east to Yaki Point. Buses typically run every 15 to 30 minutes from before dawn until after sunset.

Air & bus Guided bus, plane and helicopter tours are all popular day-trip options from Las Vegas.

Need to Know

○ **Area code** ☏928

○ **Location** 280 miles east of the Strip

○ **Grand Canyon Visitor Center** (☏928-638-7888; www.nps.gov/grca; South Rim; ◷8am-5pm Mar-Nov, 9am-5pm Dec-Feb) By Mather Point.

○ **North Rim Visitor Center** (☏928-638-7864; www.nps.gov/grca; North Rim; ◷8am-6pm mid-May–Oct 15, 9am-4pm Oct 16-31) Next to Grand Canyon Lodge.

◉ Sights

The park entrance fee (per vehicle $25) is valid for seven days at both rims.

South Rim, Grand Canyon

South Rim

To escape the throngs on the South Rim, try visiting on a weekday during fall or winter. You'll also gain some solitude by walking a short distance away from the viewpoints on the Rim Trail or descending into the canyon itself.

Hermit Road   Scenic Drive

This scenic drive follows the canyon rim west of Grand Canyon Village for 7 miles to Hermits Rest. When the road is closed to private vehicles between March and November, it's well served by free shuttle buses, and cycling is encouraged. Roadside stops provide spectacular panoramas, with interpretive signs explaining the canyon's features.

Desert View Drive   Scenic Drive

Desert View Drive starts to the east of Grand Canyon Village and follows the canyon rim for 26 miles to Desert View, the park's eastern entrance. Roadside pullouts offer gape-worthy views while interpretive signs explain canyon geology, flora and fauna.

North Rim

Head here for blessed solitude in nature's embrace – only 10% of visitors make the trek to the North Rim. Meadows are thick with wildflowers and bordered by willowy aspens and aromatic pines, the air is often crisp and the skies are big and blue.

Facilities on the North Rim completely shut down between mid-October to mid-May. You can still drive into the park for day-use activities until the first snow falls or December 1, whichever comes first.

Bright Angel Point   Lookout

Walking out to Bright Angel Point is a North Rim must. Beginning from the back porch of Grand Canyon Lodge or the log shelter in the visitor center parking area, an easy, paved trail (just 0.5 miles round-trip) leads to a narrow finger of an overlook with fabulous canyon views.

🏃 Activities & Tours

South Rim

Rim Trail   Hiking

Passing right through Grand Canyon Village, the mostly paved Rim Trail is the most popular, and easiest, walk in the park. Stretching 13 miles from Hermits Rest to the South Kaibab Trailhead, the trail dips in and out of scrubby pines and connects canyon vista points and historical sights. Every viewpoint is accessible by free seasonal park shuttle buses.

The 'Trail of Time' exhibit borders the Rim Trail, starting outside the Yavapai Museum of Geology.

South Kaibab   Hiking

One of the park's prettiest hikes, this steep, rough and wholly exposed trail reveals stunning scenery and unobstructed 360-degree views with almost every step. Don't be fooled by how easy it seems to hike downhill – summertime ascents back uphill can be dangerously hot, and during this season, you should *not* hike beyond Cedar Ridge (3 miles round-trip).

In cooler weather, it's still a 6-mile, grueling round-trip from the trailhead to Skeleton Point, where you'll get your first glimpse of the Colorado River flowing far below.

Bright Angel Trail   Hiking

On this beautiful but steep 8-mile descent to the Colorado River, summer heat can be crippling, even fatal. Day hikers should either turn around at one of two rest houses (a 3- or 6-mile round-trip) or hit the trail by dawn to safely make the longer trek to Indian Garden (9 miles round-trip) or Plateau Point (12 miles round-trip). The trailhead is just west of Bright Angel Lodge.

Grand Canyon
Mule Rides   Guided Tour

(☎888-297-2757, 303-297-2757; www.grand canyonlodges.com; Grand Canyon Village; 3hr mule ride $120, 1-/2-night mule ride $520/730; ☺rides available year-round, hours vary) Rather than going below the rim, three-hour 'Canyon Vista' tours now take riders along the rim through ponderosa, piñon and juniper forest. Overnight and two-night trips follow the Bright Angel Trail all the way down to the Colorado River, where riders sleep at rustic Phantom Ranch. No previous riding experience is necessary, but strict height and weight limits apply.

If you arrive at the park without reservations (they are strongly recommended), ask about wait-list availability at the transportation desk inside Bright Angel Lodge.

Bright Angel Bicycles
Bicycle Rental

(☎928-638-3055; http://bikegrandcanyon. com; 10 South Entrance Rd, Visitor Center Plaza; bicycle rental full-day adult/child $40/30; ⊙usually Apr-Nov) Renting out 'comfort cruiser' bikes on the South Rim, the friendly folks here custom-fit each bike to the individual. Rates include helmet and bicycle-lock rental. Child trailers are also available, as are hourly and half-day rentals.

Papillon Grand Canyon Helicopters
Guided Tour

(☎888-635-7272, 702-736-7243; www.papillon. com; ground tours $150-355, air tours $219-569) This tour operator offers luxury tours of the Grand Canyon by helicopter or airplane, as well as less expensive (and admittedly less exciting) bus and van tours, with departures from Las Vegas and Boulder City, Nevada.

North Rim

North Kaibab Trail
Hiking

On the North Rim's only maintained rim-to-river trail, the first 4.7 miles are the steepest, dropping 3050ft below the canyon rim to Roaring Springs – a strenuous all-day hike that should *not* be attempted during summer. For a shorter day hike, walk just 0.75 miles down to Coconino Overlook or 2 miles to Supai Tunnel in the inner canyon.

The 28-mile round-trip to the Colorado River is a multiday backpacking trip (backcountry permit required).

Canyon Trail Rides
Guided Tour

(☎435-679-8665; www.canyonrides.com; North Rim; 1hr/half-day mule ride $40/80; ⊙schedules vary mid-May–mid-Oct) Unlike mule trips on the South Rim, you can often book a trip upon arrival at the Canyon Trail Rides desk (staffed from 7am to 5pm daily) inside the Grand Canyon Lodge's lobby. Mule rides don't descend into the canyon as far as the Colorado River, but a half-day trip will still give you a taste of life below the rim.

✖ Eating & Drinking

South Rim

Canyon Village Market & Deli
Supermarket $

(Market Plaza; ⊙7am-9pm Jun-Aug, 8am-9pm May, Sept & Oct, 8am-8pm Nov, Mar & Apr, 8am-7pm Dec-Jan) Stock up on groceries inside this combination supermarket, deli and outdoor equipment and supply store.

Bright Angel Bar
Lounge $

(www.grandcanyonlodges.com; Bright Angel Lodge, Grand Canyon Village; appetizers $5-10; ⊙11am-11pm) Perfect for those who want to unwind with a burger and a beer, this bar with live country-and-western and folk music is a fun place to relax at night when the lack of windows and dark decor aren't such a big deal. It's beside family-friendly Bright Angel Restaurant and near Canyon Coffee House for morning espresso and pastries.

El Tovar Dining Room & Lounge
Southwestern $$$

(☎928-638-2631, ext 6432; www.grandcanyon lodges.com; El Tovar, Grand Canyon Village; breakfast $9-13, lunch $11-16.25, dinner $17-34.25; ⊙restaurant 6:30-10:45am, 11:15am-2pm & 4:30-10pm, from 5pm Nov-Mar, lounge 11am-11pm) The memorable surroundings feature dark-wood tables set with china and white linen, and huge picture windows with views of the rim and canyon beyond. For breakfast, be tempted by the pancake trio (buttermilk, blue cornmeal and buckwheat pancakes with honey-pine-nut butter and prickly pear syrup) or blackened trout with two eggs. Lunch and dinner menus are equally savory.

To avoid lunchtime crowds, eat before the Grand Canyon Railway train arrives around noon. Reservations are required for dinner, when shorts and sandals are discouraged.

The adjacent El Tovar Lounge is busy for afternoon cocktails and after-dinner drinks.

Arizona Room   American $$$
(www.grandcanyonlodges.com; Bright Angel Lodge, Grand Canyon Village; lunch $8.25-12.25, dinner $8-29; ⏱4:30-10pm Mar-Dec & 11:30am-3pm Mar-Oct) 🖉 Antler chande-liers hang from the ceiling and picture windows overlook a small lawn, the rim walk and the canyon itself. Get on the waitlist when doors open at 4:30pm, because by 4:40pm you may have an hour's wait – reservations aren't ac-cepted. Hearty mains include steaks, BBQ ribs and roasted chicken, while appetizers like jalapeño shrimp pop-pers get more creative.

North Rim

Grand Canyon Lodge Dining Room   American $$
(📞Jan 1-Apr 15 928-645-6865, May 15-Oct 14 928-638-2611; www.grandcanyonlodgenorth. com; mains breakfast $6-13, lunch $10-15, dinner $13-33; ⏱6:30-10am, 11:30am-2:30pm, 4:45-9:45pm mid-May–mid-Oct; 🚻)
Although window seats are wonder-ful, canyon views from this rustic dining room are so expansive that it doesn't much matter where you sit. A solid menu offers bison-flank steaks, rainbow trout and limited vegetar-ian dishes, but don't expect culinary memories. Make reservations far in ad-vance to guarantee a spot for dinner; no reservations accepted for breakfast or lunch.

Local Knowledge

Don't Miss List

RECOMMENDATIONS FROM JUDY HELLMICH-BRYAN, CHIEF OF INTERPRETATION, GRAND CANYON NATIONAL PARK

1 VISITOR CENTER & PLAZA
The visitor center at South Rim, with its all-new interpretative exhibits, is really the place to start your visit. In the plaza area, a series of little medallions have a poem, like a Dr Seuss poem, so that you get a sense of discovery. A condor silhouette has been etched into the rock so you can see how big the condor is.

2 A JOURNEY OF WONDER
We've finished a high-definition park orientation film. It's 20 minutes long and screens every half hour. It takes visitors on a rim-to-river trip through the canyon, so you're learning about all the different aspects of the canyon, from geology to Native American history.

3 TRAIL OF TIME
The Trail of Time extends from the Yavapai Museum of Geology into Grand Canyon Village. Every meter represents a million years in the history of the earth. As you walk, there are samples of rocks from within the canyon that you can touch. Wayside exhibits explain the different processes that formed the canyon.

4 RIM TRAIL
The Rim Trail is the easy trail. On sections of it, you can get away from big crowds of people, especially if you walk between Mather Point and Grand Canyon Village. Another really nice section is west of Hermit interchange. The walk out to Hermits Rest is spectacular too.

5 TUSAYAN RUIN & MUSEUM
This is a wonderful exhibit on past and present Native American cultures that existed at the Grand Canyon and had ties to the canyon. It's an 800-year-old Ancestral Puebloan ruin, but people tend to drive right by it and not stop. It's on Desert View Dr, about 20 miles east of Grand Canyon Village.

Las Vegas
In Focus

Las Vegas Today

CityCenter p93

While the city embraces its risqué reputation, sex work is a charged issue

politics
(% of population)

41
Democrat

37
Republican

22
Other

if Las Vegas were 100 people

62 would be White
11 would be African American
6 would be Asian
21 would be Hispanic or other

population per sq mile

= 4300 people

Las Vegas   Los Angeles   New York City

Economy, Tourism & New Developments

You wouldn't guess it when you're pushing your way through the crowds on the Strip or vying for a hotel room on a weekend in July, but Las Vegas took a big hit during the economic recession. Between 2008 and 2010, tourist numbers were down, leaving Sin City with half-empty hotels, quiet casinos and a series of stalled housing developments and construction projects. The most notable of these were CityCenter and the Cosmopolitan – the former, originally conceived as a condominium complex, was caught up in a financial battle in 2009; while the latter, originally meant to be the Grand Hyatt Las Vegas, faced foreclosure in 2008. Today, both are lucrative hot spots on the Strip, and statistics show that almost 40 million visitors passed through Las Vegas in 2013, a 9% increase from 2009. The city's financial woes aren't exactly over – unemployment was measured at 8.9% (more than 35% higher than the national average)

MITCHELL FUNK/GETTY IMAGES ©

the city is often in violation of federal air-quality standards. On many days the sky harbors a dirty inversion layer, sometimes so thick that the mountains are barely visible. Vegas earns a failing 'F' grade for high ozone days in the American Lung Association's annual *State of the Air* report year after year. Local officials still haven't figured out how to keep air pollution at tolerable levels. Though the future looks smoggy, sustainably built new landmarks, notably the Gold Leadership in Energy and Environmental Design (LEED)–certified CityCenter, the Smith Center for the Performing Arts and the Desert Living Center at the Springs Preserve, are steps toward a more sustainable future.

at the start of 2014 – but lavish new construction projects such as the $550 million LINQ, a shopping, dining and entertainment district mid-Strip, and the rebirth of the shuttered Sahara as the luxury SLS casino resort are signs that things are on the upswing.

Environment

Economic good times come at a price. With its energy-draining megaresorts, neon lights burning brightly around the clock and millions of air conditioners that never turn off, this artificial desert metropolis is an environmentalist's nightmare. Water usage is the chief concern. Some scientists have projected that the Las Vegas Valley has a 50% chance of exhausting its entire water supply within the next decade.

Air pollution is an equally vexing topic: the valley is fringed by mountains that trap hazardous particles, and

Sex & the City

While the city embraces its risqué reputation ('What happens in Vegas, stays in Vegas'), sex work is a charged issue. Shared Hope International has targeted Vegas as one of the biggest hubs for sex trafficking in the US.

Prostitution is legal in many of Nevada's rural counties but, despite the racy 'Girls Girls Girls' ads or the promoters on the Strip passing out cards that promise women at your service, it has been illegal in Las Vegas since the 1940s. Oscar Goodman, the former mayor of Las Vegas, frequently went on record with his pro-prostitution stance, saying that legalizing prostitution would 'turn old motels into beautiful brothels.'

No matter how it's concealed, sanitized, slyly advertised or sanctioned by politicians, one thing's for sure – sex is everywhere in Vegas.

History

Welcome to Fabulous Las Vegas, Nevada sign (p46)

LEE PETTET/GETTY IMAGES

'What history?' you may ask. Native Americans inhabited this valley for almost two millennia before the Spanish Trail blazed through, and colorful characters have sought their fortunes in Sin City for more than a century. Contrary to Hollywood legends, there was more to this desert crossroads than ramshackle gambling dens and tumbleweeds before gangster 'Bugsy' Siegel opened the glamorous Flamingo casino in 1946.

Native Americans & Frontier Days

For many hundreds of years, Southern Paiute tribespeople lived a relatively peaceful if arduous existence in the desert around the present-day Las Vegas Valley. They were the descendants of Paiutes, one of the Native American tribes who lived near the Grand Canyon along the Colorado River. Their undoing as the dominant people of the region began with the arrival of Europeans.

300 BC

Southern Paiutes camp by a natural-springs oasis in what is now the Las Vegas Valley.

In 1829 Rafael Rivera, a scout for a Mexican trading expedition, was likely the first outsider to locate the natural springs in this valley, which Spanish colonists called *las vegas* (the meadows). Another traveler along the Old Spanish Trail, US Army officer John C Fremont, arrived in 1844 to explore and map the area. (Las Vegas' main downtown artery, Fremont St, bears his name today.)

Amid the legions of miners who arrived later in the mid-19th century was a group hell-bent on doing God's work. These Mormons were sent from Salt Lake City by church leader Brigham Young to colonize the state of Deseret, their spiritual homeland. In 1855 the Mormons built a fort near what is now downtown Las Vegas, but abandoned it less than two years later. After the US Civil War (1861–65), small farms and ranches flourished in the Las Vegas Valley.

On January 30, 1905, a railroad linking Salt Lake City with Los Angeles was completed in southern Nevada at a place called Jean, only 25 miles from Las Vegas. Later that year, during two days in mid-May, pioneers and real-estate speculators from LA bid for land in the newly established Las Vegas townsite, with some lots being auctioned off for up to 10 times their original asking price.

The Best...
Vintage Vegas Attractions

1 Welcome to Fabulous Las Vegas, Nevada Sign (p46)

2 Flamingo (p56)

3 Golden Gate (p185)

4 Neon Museum (p184)

5 Mob Museum (p182)

Sin City Booms, Not Busts

As the dust settled from the railroad and real-estate frenzy, the city of Las Vegas was officially founded. Sin quickly took root in a downtown red-light district known as Block 16. Home to gambling, booze and prostitution, this row of saloons, with their makeshift 'cribs' (brothels) out back, survived Nevada's several bans on gambling and the nation's supposedly 'dry' years of Prohibition.

The federally sponsored Boulder (later Hoover) Dam project and Nevada's legalization of gambling carried Las Vegas through the Great Depression that followed the Black Tuesday stock market crash on October 29, 1929. Lax divorce requirements, quickie weddings, legalized prostitution and championship boxing bouts proved money-making bets for local boosters. New Deal dollars kept flowing

1905
The railroad between Los Angeles and Salt Lake City is finished; the city of Las Vegas is founded.

1946
Backed by East Coast mob money, Benjamin 'Bugsy' Siegel opens the Flamingo casino hotel on the Strip.

1950
The federal Kefauver Committee holds investigative hearings on organized crime in downtown Las Vegas.

into southern Nevada's coffers right through WWII, which brought a huge air-force base to town, plus a paved highway to LA.

Betting Big on the Strip

More than anyone else, Los Angeles hotelier Thomas Hull deserves the credit for the Las Vegas of today. In 1941, Hull opened its first casino hotel, El Rancho Vegas, south of the city limits along the two-lane LA highway that eventually became Las Vegas Blvd, aka the Strip. Throughout the 1940s and '50s, the El Rancho attracted a new element to the desert – Hollywood movie stars, who enjoyed gambling and rubbing elbows with the other fascinating, sometimes shady folks that Sin City attracted.

One such character was mobster Benjamin 'Bugsy' Siegel, who had a dream of building an even more luxurious resort in the desert, which would draw high rollers from all over the world. Backed by East Coast mob money, Siegel took over LA-nightclub-owner and *Hollywood Reporter*–publisher Billy Wilkerson's bankrupt construction project and opened the $6-million Flamingo casino hotel on December 26, 1946. With its pastel paint job, tuxedo-clad janitors, Hollywood entertainers and flashing neon signs, the Flamingo became the visionary model for the glitzy, no-holds-barred Las Vegas high life to come.

The Fabulous Fifties

Along with the rest of the USA after WWII, Las Vegas felt like a boomtown. Casino hotels were erected at an increasingly fast pace, with everyone – gamblers and owners alike – trying to strike it rich.

In 1950 the lavish Desert Inn set the tone by throwing the city's biggest party yet for its grand opening. It was funded and primarily owned by Moe Dalitz, head of a Cleveland-based crime syndicate. That same year, a full-blown federal investigation led by US Senator Estes Kefauver made a disturbing trend crystal clear: the Vegas casino industry enjoyed ties to, and the hidden backing of, mobsters from across the nation.

And why not? The mob loved Las Vegas. It gave them a legitimacy and a glamorous cachet they had never experienced before, and by fixing the games, bribing local politicians and skimming profits both under and over the table, they were getting rich fast. And Las Vegans loved them back. Everyone from low-rolling 'grinds' to Tinseltown starlets flocked to the desert to soak up the extravagant spectacle – a gangster's vision of paradise – and the promise of instant wealth.

For many people, blue-eyed crooner Frank Sinatra (aka the Chairman) and his Rat Pack pals helped build this town. They weren't merely legendary headliners; they were also the darlings of gossip columns from LA to New York, and their all-night partying and tumultuous lives entertained millions. From the late 1950s into

1957
On the Strip, the Dunes and Stardust casino hotels cause scandals with their topless showgirls.

1959
Betty Willis' now iconic 'Welcome to Fabulous Las Vegas, Nevada' sign is installed on Las Vegas Blvd.

1967
Elvis Presley marries Priscilla Beaulieu at the Aladdin casino hotel (now Planet Hollywood).

Las Vegas in the Atomic Age

The 1950s ushered in the Cold War era with live nuclear-weapons testing at the Nevada Test Site, only 65 miles northwest of Las Vegas. During the next four decades, more than 900 atmospheric and underground nuclear explosions were initiated at the test site, which encompassed more than 1350 sq miles of desert and mountain wilderness.

Initially unconcerned about radiation fallout, Las Vegans took the atomic bomb blasts in stride. They celebrated the publicity and notoriety they brought, not to mention the tourism boost, by selling 'atomburgers,' crowning a Miss Atomic Bomb and even billing Elvis as the 'Atomic-Powered Singer.' Period photos show tourists partying and picnicking at 'Atomic City' casino hotels while mushroom clouds rise on the horizon in the distance.

At what is now called the Nevada National Security Site, nuclear-weapons testing was discontinued in 1992. Free all-day public tours (p199) are given monthly, departing by bus from the National Atomic Testing Museum (p198), east of the Strip. Tours fill up many months in advance, so preregister early.

the early '60s, the Rat Pack's antics at the Sands casino hotel on the Strip brought adoring fans, dames, movie stars and famous politicians to Las Vegas by the planeload.

Turning Away from Mobsters, to Megaresorts

Amid a slowdown in casino construction during the 1960s, federal and state regulators made an effort to clean up the gambling industry. Scandal after scandal plagued Las Vegas' casinos, as charges of corruption, racketeering, influence peddling and tax evasion were issued by federal agencies. All that bad publicity was hurting tourism too.

In 1966 eccentric billionaire Howard Hughes stepped into the picture. He arrived at the Desert Inn in the middle of the night on Thanksgiving in the back of an ambulance, and didn't set foot outside his hotel suite for four years. When he'd worn out his welcome, he simply bought the hotel for $13 million, then went on an unheralded Las Vegas buying spree that included the Sands, New Frontier, Landmark and Castaways casino hotels (none of which are still standing today).

Hughes lent the casino business a much-needed patina of legitimacy, a public relations boon for Nevada officials. If gambling was a dirty business, local papers

1980
A fire sweeps through the MGM Grand, killing 85 people. The hotel is rebuilt in just eight months.

1993
The Luxor's Egyptian pyramid and the pirate-themed Treasure Island casino hotel both open.

1995
The canopied Fremont Street Experience signals a revival of downtown's historical 'Glitter Gulch.'

blustered, then an industrialist like Hughes wouldn't be getting into it. After discovering that the mob was skimming a large part of his profits, and after the US Justice Department issued a monopoly lawsuit against him as Nevada's largest property owner, Hughes left town a poorer man in 1970.

High-roller Kirk Kerkorian upped the ante in 1973, when he built what was then the world's largest hotel, the MGM Grand. In 1989 casino impresario Steve Wynn built the even more miraculous Mirage. Financed mainly with junk bonds, the Mirage was forced to make a million dollars a day from the time it opened. The spectacular Polynesian-themed casino resort, with its faux volcano, tropical aquariums and waterfalls, pulled Las Vegas out of its construction slump, and sparked a rush of new Strip megaresorts with over-the-top themes, each more spectacular than the last.

Modernity for a New Millennium

Not to be outdone, Wynn dreamed up the $1.6 billion Bellagio, adorned with $300 million worth of art from his personal collection of masterpieces. Built on the ashes of the demolished 1950s-era Dunes, Bellagio was one of the world's most opulent casino hotels when it opened in 1998. It also brought a surprising touch of elegance to Sin City, which had become infamous for its down-and-dirty strip clubs and low-class culture.

Wynn sold the Mirage and Bellagio megaresorts to business rival MGM Grand in 2000. The newly minted MGM Mirage (now MGM Resorts International) corporation quickly expanded its empire to include Treasure Island, Circus Circus and nearly all of the southern Strip's casino hotels before embarking on the ambitious $9.2-billion CityCenter development, which transformed the Strip's skyline in 2009. Making Las Vegas Blvd look even more like a Monopoly game board, Harrah's (now Caesars) Entertainment company bought Caesars Palace, Bally's, Paris Las Vegas, the Flamingo and Imperial Palace (now the Quad) casino hotels in 2005, then tore up the middle of the Strip to create the LINQ open-air pedestrian district less than a decade later.

Meanwhile, Wynn imploded the vintage Desert Inn, then spent five years crafting his signature creation, Wynn Las Vegas. His eponymous casino resort opened in 2005, just as the city celebrated its centennial, and Wynn's sister resort, Encore, opened just three years later. Once again Steve Wynn set a new standard for the Strip, trending away from kitschily themed casino hotels to sophisticated and luxurious resorts, complete with classy casinos and plenty of attractions for nongamblers including powerhouse restaurants, international designers' shops and fantasy spas.

2005
The city of Las Vegas celebrates its centennial; Steve Wynn's eponymous megaresort opens to fanfare.

2009
Amid an economic recession, CityCenter opens and transforms the Strip's skyline with contemporary high-rises.

2014
High Roller, the world's tallest Ferris wheel, starts revolving over the now world-famous Strip.

Family Travel

Excalibur (p47)

KUMAR SRISKANDAN/ALAMY ©

Las Vegas half-heartedly sells itself as a family vacation destination. But because the legal gambling age is 21, many casino hotels would rather you left little ones at home. None of the megaresorts are truly child-appropriate; even at the best places, you'll still likely be exposing your kids to drunk people behaving badly. If you're in Vegas with children, here are our top survival tips.

Things to Do

If you look past the smoke and glitter – which is hard to do in this town – you'll notice a range of family-friendly attractions and activities. Most casinos have virtual-reality and video-game arcades. At New York–New York, a roller coaster shoots out of a fake Big Apple skyline, while Circus Circus has the Adventuredome theme park and free acrobat shows. Teens will get a thrill from the Stratosphere Tower and its adrenaline-pumping rides. Cirque du Soleil's show *Mystère* welcomes all-ages audiences, while *Ká, Zarkana, Michael Jackson ONE* and *Beatles LOVE* can be fun for children ages five and up.

For an educational experience, make time to head out to the Springs Preserve, also home of the Nevada State Museum, or the hands-on Lied Discovery Children's Museum in Symphony Park. Mandalay Bay's

Need to Know

○ **Baby food, formula and diapers (nappies)** Sold at supermarkets and pharmacies.

○ **Changing facilities** Available in many public restrooms, including at airports, restaurants, shopping malls and hotels.

○ **Childcare services** Hotel concierges can provide lists of licensed babysitters. A few hotels and resorts offer on-site childcare and activity day camps for kids.

○ **Cots/cribs** Some hotels provide cots and/or rollaway beds without a fee but most charge around $35 per night; always confirm availability ahead of time. If you need a crib, bring your own Pack 'n' Play.

○ **Highchairs** Usually only at family-friendly eateries, especially off the Strip.

○ **Kids' menus** Common at fast-food outlets and casual sit-down restaurants.

○ **Strollers** Not permitted inside some top-tier casino resorts.

walk-through Shark Reef Aquarium is entertaining, as is the Flamingo's free outdoor wildlife exhibit. Local families with young children like the outdoor children's park at Town Square shopping mall, south of the Strip.

Out-of-town excursions, especially to the Grand Canyon, make for more unforgettable family adventures.

Eating & Drinking

When traveling with kids, skip the Strip's lavish restaurants and look for casino and shopping-mall food courts. Some of the easiest budget-friendly family dining options include the Earl of Sandwich at Planet Hollywood, crepes at Paris Las Vegas and quick bites from New York–New York's ersatz Greenwich Village.

For sit-down meals, family-friendly faves include Carnegie Deli at the Mirage, Grand Lux Café at the Venetian and Serendipity 3 at Caesars Palace. All-you-can-eat buffets offer small discounts for children too. Don't forget to take the little ones past the world's biggest chocolate fountain at Bellagio – just be prepared to shell out for gelato afterwards.

Getting Around

Some upscale casino hotels, such as Bellagio and Wynn, prohibit strollers on their grounds. Otherwise the Strip is relatively stroller-friendly: protected pedestrian walkways and skybridges with elevators and escalators separate foot traffic from the crush of cars and buses. The monorail is great for families. Deuce and SDX buses are also useful, though the ease of getting on and off depends on the driver's friendliness.

In taxis, car seats are not legally required (and not provided) for babies or young children, so it's a good idea to bring your own and put it into the taxi. For rental cars, infant or child safety seats are mandated by law for children under seven years old who weigh less than 60lb (27kg); reserve these seats (daily rentals from $10) when booking your car or bring your own from home.

Dining in Las Vegas

Dining at Caesars Palace (p134)

ROBERT MORA/GETTY IMAGES ©

The Strip has been studded by celebrity chefs for years. All-you-can-eat buffets and $9.99 steaks still exist, but today's high-rolling visitors demand ever more sophisticated dining experiences, with meals designed – although not personally prepared – by famous tastemakers. Flash enough cash and you can taste the same cuisine served at revered restaurants from NYC to Paris to Shanghai.

Top Chefs Compete

Wolfgang Puck first upped the ante for Vegas casino restaurants when he imported his successful Spago restaurant from Beverly Hills to Caesars Palace's Forum Shops in 1992. Ever since, a vainglorious parade of celebrity chefs have set up eateries at nearly every megaresort on the Strip, with more famous names arriving every year. They don't always stick around, though.

Keep in mind that most celebrity chefs have almost nothing to do with the day-to-day operations of their namesake kitchens in Vegas. Bobby Flay, Mario Batali, Emeril Lagasse and Nobu Matsuhisa are just a few of the celebs seen on TV's Food Network who have proudly stamped their names on signature menus and over-the-top dining rooms at casinos on the Strip. Other kitchen geniuses who have leapt onto the Strip

Need to Know

○ **Price ranges** The symbols below indicate the average price of a main course in our Las Vegas reviews:

$ less than $10
$$ $10–20
$$$ more than $20

○ **Reservations** Always book ahead for upscale and popular casino restaurants, especially on weekends. Try www.opentable.com.

○ **Tipping** The standard tip is 18% to 20% of the bill. If a service charge has already been included (usually for groups of six or more), don't tip twice. At buffets, leave a couple of dollars per person on the table.

○ **Useful websites**
Eater Vegas (http://vegas.eater.com) has the scene covered: restaurant openings (and closings), chef interviews, gossipy rumors and 'heat maps' of where to eat right now.
Las Vegas Weekly (www.lasvegasweekly.com) digs up more budget-friendly and unusual finds, especially off-Strip.
Restaurant.com (www.restaurant.com) has discount dining certificates.

---

include Michael Mina, Joël Robuchon, Tom Colicchio, Susan Feniger, Rick Moonen, Françoise Payard, Gordon Ramsay, Giada de Laurentis, Thomas Keller and Daniel Boulud.

So what's the big attraction? Being bankrolled by a casino megaresort, for one. Then there's the fact that out-of-town visitors are looser with their wallets in a gambling capital such as Las Vegas, where paying $250 for a chef's tasting menu doesn't seem outrageously expensive after a big win at the poker table.

The Best...
Tables with a View

1 Top of the World (p53)

2 Todd English's Olives (p125)

3 Twist by Pierre Gagnaire (p100)

4 Eiffel Tower Restaurant (p118)

5 Alizé (p213)

Classic Casino Eats: Steaks, Buffets & More

Not into gastronomic name-dropping or see-and-be-seen dining? You can still get an old-school Vegas meal on or off the Strip. Get ready for a gluttonous trinity of Vegas casino classics – the coffee shop, the steakhouse and the buffet – and work up an appetite beforehand.

Sin City has scores of places to get a hunka burnin' red meat. If you want a quality cut, book a table at Gordon Ramsay Steak, which has a Himalayan salt room just for aging steaks, at Paris Las Vegas; Wolfgang Puck's Cut or Mario Batali's Carnevino, both classy places inside the Palazzo; Emeril Lagasse's reliable Delmonico Steakhouse at the Venetian; Joe Vicaro's Andiamo Steakhouse downtown at the D; or darkly seductive N9NE, where celebrities hide out at the Palms, west of the Strip.

Vegetarians will be happier with the fresh fruit (a rarity in this desert), design-your-own salads and the variety of international dishes at Vegas' all-you-can-eat buffets. Better casino buffets feature live-action stations for omelets, pasta, stir-fries etc. Among the starring dishes at opulent buffets inside the Strip's megaresorts are cracked crab, carved-to-order roast meats, house-made soups and breads, and pastry chefs' desserts. Show up early (eg before noon for Sunday brunch) to avoid the longest lines. The most popular buffets in town include Wicked Spoon at Cosmopolitan, Bacchanal at Caesars Palace, Le Village at Paris Las Vegas and the Buffet at Wynn, all conveniently on the Strip.

Eating off the Strip

There's no end to the eating options in Vegas, but almost every restaurant on the Strip and around downtown's Fremont Street Experience is inside a casino hotel, and they're almost universally overpriced. Since the party never ends, it's no surprise that every casino also has a 24-hour coffee shop and a fast-food court that's open late.

But where do you go when you tire of the ridiculously inflated casino prices? Venture to in-the-know places where locals drink and dine for far less than what dazed tourists are shelling out on the Strip. Not only will you get better gastronomic bang for your buck, you'll be able to take a little bite of everything from authentic Thai street snacks and Neapolitan pizzas to Asian-Mexican fusion tacos and crazy food-truck creations.

Scoring a Table

If you've got your heart set on dining at a particular restaurant, plan ahead, especially for weekends or during special events like huge conventions or holidays. Most restaurants take reservations for dinner and sometimes lunch, so call ahead if you can, even if it's just earlier on the same day.

Many restaurants in Vegas now offer online reservations, or try **OpenTable** (www.opentable.com), a free website and mobile-app booking service, which may show tables still available even when the restaurant says it's fully booked. If all else fails, ask your hotel concierge for help and be prepared to tip $10 for a primo table reservation.

The Best...
Late-Night Eats

1 Peppermill (p52)

2 Allegro (p171)

3 Earl of Sandwich (p108)

4 Hash House a Go Go (p53)

5 Raku (p212)

Drinking & Entertainment

Bargoers, Mandalay Bay (p61)

LONELY PLANET IMAGES/GETTY IMAGES ©

That sensory overload of blindingly bright neon lights means you've finally landed on Las Vegas Blvd. The infamous Strip has the lion's share of gigantic casino hotels, all flashily competing to lure you (and your wallet) inside, with larger-than-life production shows, celebrity-filled nightclubs and burlesque cabarets. Head off-Strip to find jukebox dive bars, arty cocktail lounges, strip clubs and more.

Where to Drink

In Vegas a lot of drinking takes place while blearily staring down slot machines and gaming tables. Yet the Strip's casinos, not to mention countless other nightspots around the city, offer diversity when it comes to drinking. With hundreds of places in which to imbibe and party around the clock, you'll never be left out to dry.

It's time to lay the cards on the table about one thing: the vast majority of Sin City's bars are smoke-filled. Antismoking laws banning cigarette, pipe and cigar smoking in bars that also prepare food are viewed with disgust, disdain and indignation by many locals. When in doubt, don't light up without asking the bartender if it's OK first.

Streets, Bars & Lounges

Vegas has an extremely liberal policy when it comes to drinking in public. On the Strip and

That's the Ticket!

Beware that most Vegas ticket outlets apply a surcharge for each ticket sold.

○ **Tix 4 Tonight** (☎ 877-849-4868; www.tix4tonight.com; ⏰ usually 10am-7pm or 8pm) All but the biggest-ticket shows are up for grabs at these same-day, discount ticket outlets, but you must show up in person (no online or phone sales). Get in line before 10am for the best selection of shows and seats. Check the website for convenient locations including at the Fashion Show, Hawaiian Marketplace, Showcase Mall and Bally's, Planet Hollywood and Circus Circus casinos on the Strip, and at the Four Queens casino on downtown's Fremont Street Experience.

○ **Vegas.com** (☎ 866-998-3427, 702-992-7990; www.vegas.com) Sells tickets to a variety of high-profile and low-budget shows, special events and touring exhibitions, as well as nightclub VIP and front-of-the-line passes.

○ **Ticketmaster** (Map p48; ☎ 800-745-3000; www.ticketmaster.com) A broker for mega-concerts and spectator sports.

at downtown's Fremont Street Experience, pedestrians can drink alcohol from open containers, although those containers must be made of plastic on busy holidays such as New Year's Eve.

Many bars stay open until the wee hours, and some never close. A lot offer two-for-one drinks and appetizers during happy hour (usually 4pm until 6pm, although times vary from one place to another). 'Graveyard' happy hours start around midnight. Tip bartenders at least $1 per drink or 15% per round.

The 'ultra lounge' fad lives on in Vegas. What's an ultra lounge, you ask? It's a bar with hoity-toity aspirations, often with DJs spinning, sexily dressed staff, expensive cocktails and sofas around a tiny dance floor. Ultra lounges are popular places to jumpstart your evening before moving on to da club. Turn up early for a seat.

Score Free Booze at Casinos

The key to getting free drinks in Vegas casinos lies in the answer to this question: 'Are you playing?' Even if you're just betting on the hot, hot penny slots, you *are* playing and have met the not-so-rigid requirements for free booze. If you're walking through a casino and ask a cocktail waiter for a drink, expect them to ask you where you're sitting. Replying that you're just wandering aimlessly around and would prefer to do it with a drink in hand isn't going to get you fistfuls of hooch. If you've holed yourself up with a slot machine that doesn't appear on the radar screen of a cocktail waiter, feel free to hunt one down and ask them to bring you a drink. In fact, feel free to order two. Unless you're falling-down drunk or being obnoxious, the casino couldn't care less.

Remember, the gears of Las Vegas are greased by tips. The short-skirted cocktail waitress who descended on you like an angel with free drinks might vanish forever if you don't favor her with a tip of at least a buck per drink.

Catch a Show

Las Vegas doesn't call itself an entertainment capital for nothing. Ticket prices to all shows at casinos both on and off the Strip are inflated (it helps to think of them in 'Vegas dollars'). You could go broke trying to see absolutely everything, or just let yourself be entertained for free on the Strip and downtown's Fremont Street Experience.

The Best...
Free Casino Entertainment

1 Circus Circus' Midway (p54)

2 Fountains of Bellagio (p124)

3 Mirage Volcano (p142)

4 Grand Canal Shoppes (p163), Venetian

5 'Dealertainers' at the Quad (p51)

6 Fremont Street Experience (p185)

The whirling Cirque du Soleil empire keeps expanding, most recently with the addition of two musical-themed spectaculars – *Beatles LOVE* and *Michael Jackson ONE* – and the fantastical variety show *Zarkana*. The much-ballyhooed invasion of the Strip by Broadway showstoppers has slowed, although big productions like *Jersey Boys* and *Mamma Mia!* still sweep through town for limited runs.

This is Vegas, so there's first-rate comedy, too, as well as heavyweight rock stars in constant rotation. Resident shows of late have included Celine Dion, Carlos Santana, Guns N' Roses and Britney Spears. Megaresort venues host a veritable who's-who of famous faces and voices throughout the year.

Old-school production shows at smaller casinos feature a variety of hokey song, dance and magic numbers that often don't follow a story line. Capitalizing on Sin City's reputation, there's also a grab-bag of erotically themed shows, from rock musicals to late-night pin-up revues, all featuring topless showgirls.

Sin City's new breed of bawdy, hilarious variety shows are staged cabaret-style in unusual venues, mostly on the Strip. Absinthe lights up a big-top circus tent outside Caesars Palace, while newer Vegas Nocturne at Rose.Rabbit.Lie dinner theater and nightclub confounds audience-participant expectations at Cosmopolitan.

Hit the Clubs

The Scene

No expense has been spared to bring nightclubs into the Strip's megaresorts on a par with LA and NYC. Wildly extravagant dance floors both on and off Las Vegas Blvd are like a Hollywood set designer's dream. Many clubs tend to play it safe, spinning mainstream grooves and mash-ups aimed to appeal to the masses. But every week the Strip's top-tier nightspots jet in famous DJs from North America, Europe and beyond.

Opening hours vary, though most nightclubs are closed early in the week. Typical cover charges are $50 on weekends and $20 on weeknights, with women usually paying less. VIP and front-of-the-line passes are sold on websites such as www.vegas.com, or try checking the club's website or calling directly to get on the guest list or make VIP bottle-service reservations (from $250 per person for groups of four or more).

It's not always necessary to pay the cover, especially if you're traveling without any guys. A group of women usually moves pretty quickly to the front of the line, and many clubs offer free entry and even free drinks or champagne for women who show up before midnight. Don't buy fake VIP or front-of-the-line passes from scam artists on Las Vegas Blvd.

Summer is when Vegas' pool party season gets into full swing, and daytime pool clubs are all the rage. Pool clubs operate a lot like nightclubs, with the same cover charges and long lines to get in, but with dancing outdoors in the sunshine. Expect killer DJs, bikini-clad cocktail servers and a scintillating dress code (how much do you dare to bare?). Call in advance for VIP cabana reservations for groups.

Vegas Clubbing 101

Brave the velvet rope – or skip it altogether – with these nightlife survival tips we culled from the inner circle of Vegas club bouncers, VIP hosts and concierges.

○ Dress to impress. The better you present yourself, the better your chances of moving into the club without an extended delay. Women and men can get away with smart jeans, but men need to look sharper to get into the top-tier nightlife venues – that means collared shirts, nice pants and leather shoes, not athletic wear.

○ Avoid waiting in that long line by booking ahead with a club promoter such as Chris Hornak of **Free Vegas Club Passes** (www.freevegasclubpasses.com).

○ Look for the club's own promoters, usually standing on the casino floor of the corresponding hotel or resort – they're giving out passes for expedited entry and free drinks, especially to well-dressed women.

○ Ask the concierge of your hotel for clubbing suggestions – he or she will almost always have free passes for clubs, or be able to make you table reservations (at the usual rates) with the club's VIP host.

○ At combo restaurant-nightclub complexes like Hakkasan and Tao, making a dinner reservation might not only get you on the guest list for the club, but also get the cover charge waived, a free drink ticket and possibly a VIP host to walk you directly into the club.

○ To see a different side of the scene, show up for 'industry nights' early in the week, when locals get in free. That's when clubs are less touristy and you may not always have to fight your way in past the bouncers.

○ If you've hit blackjack at the high-roller table or just want to splurge, think about bottle service. Yes, it's expensive, but it usually waives cover charges (and waiting in line) for your group, plus you get to chill at a table – invaluable 'real estate,' in club speak.

Sin City's Strip Clubs

Vegas is the original adult Disneyland. Prostitution may be illegal, but there are plenty of places offering the illusion of sex on demand. Unescorted women are not welcome at most 'gentleman's clubs,' especially not on busy nights. Bring cash for tips.

Most strip clubs sit in industrial areas west of the Strip and I-15 Fwy. Everything is larger than life at **Sapphire** (Map p211; ☏702-796-6000; www.sapphirelasvegas.com; 3025 Industrial Rd; cover $30-50; ⊕24hr), Vegas' largest strip club, with a stable of thousands of entertainers and VIP skyboxes overlooking a showroom cheesily dominated by a story-high martini glass. Beefy men strip upstairs on Friday and Saturday nights.

The glam factor is also high at **Spearmint Rhino** (Map p211; ☏702-796-3600; www.spearmintrhinolv.com; 3344 S Highland Dr; cover $30; ⊕24hr). The exotic-looking women are beautiful but the club is so popular that it's often standing-room only, so arrive early for the best seats. Nearby, **Treasures** (Map p211; ☏702-257-3030; www.treasureslasvegas.com; 2801 Westwood Dr; cover $30-35; ⊕4pm-6am Sun-Thu, to 9am Fri & Sat) gets more raves for its steakhouse and happy-hour buffet than its faux-Romanesque exterior and hard-hustling dancers.

Not even the FBI's 'Operation G-Sting' (aka 'Strippergate,' which concluded in 2006) could keep the doors of **Crazy Horse 3** (☏702-673-1700; www.crazyhorse3.com; 3525 W Russell Rd; cover $30; ⊕24hr; ⊟104) closed forever. This legendary gentleman's club, where porn star Jenna Jameson got started, has moved south to just off I-15. Opposite the Hard Rock casino east of the Strip, **Club Paradise** (Map p202; ☏702-734-7990; www.clubparadise.net; 4416 Paradise Rd; cover $10-30; ⊕6pm-6am; ⊟108) hires showgirls who look as if they've stepped out of a magazine's centerfold, but stripteases and specialty acts are pretty tame.

Vegas' Biggest Venues

Headliners often appear at these casino theaters and mega-event arenas:

Colosseum (p136) Elton John, Celine Dion and Shania Twain are among the pop-music divas who have burned up the stage at Caesars Palace's 4100-seat Colosseum.

Smith Center for the Performing Arts (p192) This architecturally beautiful multi-venue complex in downtown's Symphony Park has already drawn big names in jazz, rock, country and classical music, touring Broadway shows and dance troupes, and speakers like David Sedaris.

Mandalay Bay (p68) Championship fights and major musical acts from opera singers to country-and-western superstars regularly fill the 12,000-seat arena at the Mandalay Bay Events Center. Summer concerts at Mandalay Beach have seen anyone from Ziggy Marley to the Go-Gos play on the sand.

MGM Grand Garden Arena (p91) When pop stars such as U2, Cher and Miley Cyrus come to town, they play this 17,000-seat venue at the MGM Grand. Rowdy championship fight nights also fill the vast arena.

Cosmopolitan (p93) Concerts outdoors by the Boulevard Pool and indoors at the Chelsea bring the hottest big-name indie and pop acts to the Strip, from Bruno Mars to Fitz & the Tantrums. Up-and-coming bands set up on the casino's sports-book stage.

Hard Rock (p204) East of the Strip, hipster bands and singer-songwriters like Mayer Hawthorne make appearances at the casino's tiny acoustic showroom Vinyl, while rock 'n' roll and hip-hop legends and MMA fighters fill the 4000-seat Joint theater.

Pearl (p214) West of the Strip, the Palms casino resort's 2500-seat state-of-the-art concert theater gives you an intimate view of pop performers from Gwen Stefani to Morrissey – and comedy kingpins too.

Located on Las Vegas Blvd, just north of the Stratosphere Tower, **Olympic Garden** (702-386-9200; www.ogvegas.com; 1531 Las Vegas Blvd S; cover $30-40; 24hr; Deuce) is billed as 'the only strip club on the Strip.' More than 50 dancers work the rooms at any given time, so there's someone to please everyone. Studs strip upstairs for the ladies Wednesday through Sunday nights.

Gay & Lesbian Las Vegas

Nicknamed the Fruit Loop, the epicenter of Sin City's LGBTQ nightlife is about a mile east of the Strip, along Paradise Rd, south of Harmon Ave and the Hard Rock casino hotel. Most bars, clubs and drag showrooms found there are mainly for men, but some host women's nights.

Annual events include **Las Vegas Pride** (www.lasvegaspride.org), in September. To plug into the city's queer scene, **QVegas** (www.qvegas.com) offers online downloads of its monthly magazine, also freely available at **Get Booked** (Map p202; ☎702-737-7780; www. getbooked.com; 4640 Paradise Rd; ☺10am-midnight). Helpful community websites include www.gayvegastravel.com.

Megaclub **Krave** (Map p48; ☎702-677-1740; www.kravelasvegas.com; 3765 Las Vegas Blvd S; cover $20; ☺10:30pm-5am Fri & Sat) is the Strip's longest-running gay nightclub (although its location keeps changing). Victor Drai plans to open a new gay club at **Bally's** (p50) in summer 2014. The Mirage's **Revolution Lounge** (p144) goes gay every Sunday night. In summer, 'Temptation Sundays' at Luxor and 'Xposed' on Saturdays at the Tropicana (p47) are all-day gay pool parties with DJs.

Meanwhile, the alternative universe of the Fruit Loop orbits **Piranha** (Map p48; ☎702-791-0100; www.piranhavegas.com; 4633 Paradise Rd; cover free-$20; ☺10pm-6am; ▣108), a two-story lavishly designed club and ultra lounge that puts on outrageous theme parties and ladies-only and Latin nights. At the dive bar **Freezone** (Map p202; ☎702-794-2300; www. freezonelv.com; 610 E Naples Dr; ☺24hr; ▣108), some nights are saved for go-go girls, others go-go boys, drag cabaret or karaoke.

A more stealth scene revolves around the gay bathhouses and gyms of the Commercial Center, east of the Strip on Sahara Ave. Across the street, **Club Metro** (Map p202; ☎702-629-2368; www.clubmetrolv.com; 1000 E Sahara Ave; ☺2pm-5am) is a come-as-you-are bar with beer pong, cabaret nights and electronica DJs on weekends.

Elsewhere in an industrial area west of the Strip, **Share** (Map p211; ☎702-258-2861; www.sharenightclub.com; 4636 Wynn Rd; entry usually free; ☺usually 10pm-4am Thu-Sat; ▣201) nightclub draws a crowd to its ginormous dance floor ruled by go-go boys and *Vogue*-worthy hotties with attitude.

Cosmopolitan (p93)

Shopping

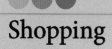

Crystals (p103)

RICHARD CUMMINS/GETTY IMAGES ©

Surprisingly, Vegas has evolved into a sophisticated shopping destination. International purveyors of haute couture on the Strip cater to cashed-up clientele, whether it's catwalk fashions fresh off this year's runways, diamond jewels once worn by royalty or imported sports cars. But Sin City is still the kind of place where porn-star-worthy bling, Elvis wigs and other tacky souvenirs just fly off the shelves.

Where to Shop

If all you want is a T-shirt, bumper sticker or shot glass announcing that you've been to 'Fabulous Las Vegas,' tacky souvenirs are everywhere. But if you're looking for something more unusual, the city's specialty shops are full of cool kitsch and priceless collectibles, from vintage casino memorabilia to showgirls' feather boas.

The Strip has the highest-octane shopping action, dominated by megamalls such as the Fashion Show, the Grand Canal Shoppes at the Venetian and Palazzo, the Forum Shops at Caesars Palace and Planet Hollywood's Miracle Mile Shops. More upscale boutiques await inside CityCenter's airy Crystals mall and luxe casino resorts like Wynn, Encore, Palazzo and Bellagio. Meanwhile, the hip Cosmopolitan casino resort collects the Strip's most eclectic indie and designer shops.

Downtown you'll find tacky souvenirs, but also cool vintage-clothing stores, antiques shops and art galleries, especially on Fremont St east of Las Vegas Blvd and in the 18b Arts District, radiating outward from the intersection of Main St and Charleston Blvd. Vegas' best discount outlet shopping mall is also downtown.

West of the Strip is where to go to uncover naughty adult toys, trashy lingerie, 'exotic' dance wear and go-go boots. East of the Strip near the University of Nevada, Las Vegas (UNLV), Maryland Pkwy is chock-a-block with cheapo shops. Trendy boutiques are scarce but they're popping up more and more in the 'burbs, where more everyday malls await.

Retail shopping hours are normally 10am to 9pm (to 6pm Sunday) but casino shops and megamalls typically stay open until 11pm (midnight on Friday and Saturday). Christmas is one of the few holidays when most shops close.

The Strip's Casino Megamalls

At Caesars Palace, the Forum Shops play fanciful homage to an ancient Roman marketplace, housing 160 designer emporia, including one-name catwalk wonders such as Armani and Fendi, a three-story H&M and specialty boutiques including Agent Provocateur for lingerie, Kiehl's old-world apothecary and modern MAC cosmetics.

Up the Strip at the Venetian's Italianate mall, the Grand Canal Shoppes, faux cobblestone passageways wind past more than 140 luxury shops, including Godiva, Jimmy Choo and Sephora. The mall extends into the Venetian's sister resort, the Palazzo, where you'll find designers like Diane von Furstenberg, Barneys New York department store and the museum-like Bauman Rare Books.

Backtrack down the Strip to Planet Hollywood, where the seemingly never-ending Miracle Mile Shops – the mall's corridors really are over a mile long – houses 170 contemporary retailers and more than a dozen bars and restaurants. If you love that 1950s pin-up look, make a beeline for Bettie Page clothing boutique.

Only-in-Vegas Shops

Quirky only-in-Vegas buys abound downtown and along Las Vegas Blvd between downtown and the north end of the Strip. For customizable poker chips and gambling accoutrements, head to the Gamblers General Store. If you can't take home your own showgirl-style feather boa from Rainbow Feather Dyeing Co, just rent a stage-worthy getup from decades past at Williams Costume Co.

Pick up your souvenir Vegas shot glass on downtown's Fremont Street Experience or at the pricier yet amusingly campy Bonanza Gifts, which bills itself as the 'world's largest gift shop,' located next door to the Stratosphere. Peruse more unusual and high-end collectibles at Gold & Silver Pawn Shop, made famous by the reality TV series *Pawn Stars*.

Outlet Malls off the Strip

Brand-name bargain hunters head to Vegas' jam-packed outlet malls. The best of the bunch is downtown's Las Vegas Premium Outlets North, which boasts designer names including Armani, DKNY, Dolce & Gabbana and Michael Kors, along with casual brands such as True Religion and Juicy Couture.

The Las Vegas Premium Outlets South mall isn't nearly as convenient for visitors and its line-up of stores is more humdrum, although if you've got children in tow, there's an indoor kiddie carousel for them to ride.

Way out in Primm, about a 45-minute drive from the Strip to the Nevada–California state line, the Fashion Outlets of Las Vegas mall offers more than 100 designer outlet stores but has little that you can't find at the outlet malls in town. A **Shopper's Shuttle** (702-874-1400; www.fashionoutletlasvegas.com; round-trip $15; schedules vary) runs between there and the Strip; book online (reservations required) for a small discount.

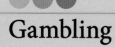

Gambling

Slot machines

You're on your third martini. You just won the last three hands. Adrenaline pumping, you double down and lose the down payment on your next car. For every game except poker, the house has a statistical winning edge over the gambler and for nearly every payout, the house 'holds' a small portion of the winnings. Have fun, but understand the games you're playing and stop when you're ahead.

Poker

The good news is that poker is a 'beatable' game. Most card rooms take only a small percentage of each pot – the rake – leaving the vast majority of the money to be won and lost by the players themselves. Luck still plays a major role in determining success, but a shrewd poker player who waits for the right opportunities can, over the long haul, be a winner. Psychology helps.

While it's not the only game in town, Texas hold'em is far and away the most common. The rules are simple. Each player is dealt two 'hole' cards, face down. After a round of betting, three shared community cards – called the 'flop' – are dealt face up in the middle of the table. After another round of betting, a fourth community card – the 'turn' – is dealt. After yet another round of betting, a fifth community card – the highly anticipated 'river' – is laid on the table. One last round of betting ensues. The player with the strongest five-card hand, combining his or her two hole cards with three out of the five community cards, wins the pot.

Blackjack

Players love blackjack for many reasons. It's fairly easy to master the basic strategies, and you can ask the dealer for help. The rules are fairly simple: you're going to get some cards, the dealer is going to get some cards, and each of you is going to add them up. 'Number' cards (2 through to 10) are worth their face value, 'face' cards (jacks, queens and kings) are worth 10, and the aces are worth 1 or 11, whichever works out to be more advantageous. The hand that comes closest to 21 – without going over – wins.

Slot Machines

The slots are wildly popular and the simplest games of all to play – you just put money in and pull the handle (or push a button). The player has no effect on the outcome. The probabilities are programmed into the machine, and the chances of winning (or, more likely, losing) are the same on every pull. Some machines pay back a higher proportion of the money deposited than others; those with larger-than-average returns (up to 98%) are called 'loose.' Never mind the odds, the melodiously hypnotic 'Ding! Ding! Ding!' of the slots and short-skirted cocktail waitresses serving free drinks tend to keep the casino seats filled with punters.

Poker Hands

You'll probably want to commit these rankings to memory before you sit down to play with the sharks:

Royal flush A straight, ace through 10, all of the same suit, eg A♣ K♣ Q♣ J♣ 10♣.

Straight flush Five consecutive cards of the same suit. The ace can be used for the high or the low end of the straight, eg A♠ 2♠ 3♠ 4♠ 5♠ but 'wrapping around' is *not* permitted, eg J♠ Q♠ K♠ A♠ 2♠.

Four of a kind Exactly what the name suggests, eg 7♣ 7♠ 7♥ 7♦ 9♣. Also called a 'case.'

Full house Three of a kind, plus a pair, eg 5♣ 5♦ 5♥ J♥ J♠. Also called a 'boat.'

Flush Any five cards of the same suit, eg A♥ Q♥ 8♥ 5♥ 3♥. If two or more players both have a flush, ties are broken by the highest flush card (or cards).

Straight Five consecutive cards of any suit, eg K♦ Q♣ J♦ 10♠ 9♠.

Three of a kind Eg 3♣ 3♦ 3♥ Q♥ 5♦. Also called 'trips,' or a 'set.'

Two pair If two or more players have the same two pair, the fifth card, or 'kicker,' is used to decide the winner; eg J♦ J♥ 5♣ 5♦ 7♣ beats J♣ J♠ 5♠ 5♥ 2♣.

One pair When your two hole cards match, you are said to have a pocket or wired pair; eg Q♥ Q♠ A♥ 10♠ 8♥.

High cards If no one has a pair or better, the player with the highest card(s) wins. Eg A♦ K♣ 7♦ 6♥ 2♠ beats A♦ 10♥ 7♣ 3♦ 2♦.

Blackjack Strategy

You	What the dealer is showing									
	2	3	4	5	6	7	8	9	10	A
17-21	S	S	S	S	S	S	S	S	S	S
16	S	S	S	S	S	H	H	SR	SR	SR
15	S	S	S	S	S	H	H	H	SR	H
14	S	S	S	S	S	H	H	H	H	H
13	S	S	S	S	S	H	H	H	H	H
12	H	H	S	S	S	H	H	H	H	H
11	DD	DD	DD	DD	DD	DD	DD	DD	DD	H
10	DD	DD	DD	DD	DD	DD	DD	DD	H	H
9	H	DD	DD	DD	DD	H	H	H	H	H
5-8	H	H	H	H	H	H	H	H	H	H
2,2	H	H	SP	SP	SP	SP	H	H	H	H
3,3	H	H	SP	SP	SP	SP	H	H	H	H
4,4	H	H	H	H	H	H	H	H	H	H
5,5	DD	DD	DD	DD	DD	DD	DD	DD	H	H
6,6	SP	SP	SP	SP	H	H	H	H	H	H
7,7	SP	SP	SP	SP	SP	SP	H	H	H	H
8,8	SP	SP	SP	SP	SP	SP	SP	SP	SP	SP
9,9	SP	SP	SP	SP	SP	S	SP	SP	S	S
10,10	S	S	S	S	S	S	S	S	S	S
A,A	SP	SP	SP	SP	SP	SP	SP	SP	SP	SP
A,2	H	H	H	DD	DD	H	H	H	H	H
A,3	H	H	H	DD	DD	H	H	H	H	H
A,4	H	H	DD	DD	DD	H	H	H	H	H
A,5	H	H	DD	DD	DD	H	H	H	H	H
A,6	H	DD	DD	DD	DD	H	H	H	H	H
A,7	S	DD	DD	DD	DD	S	S	H	H	H
A,8	S	S	S	S	S	S	S	S	S	S
A,9	S	S	S	S	S	S	S	S	S	S
A,10	Blackjack!									

H=Hit, S=Stand, SP=Split, DD=Double Down, SR=Surrender (if allowed, otherwise Hit)

Video Poker

Looking like slot machines and found in casinos, bars and even gas stations, video-poker machines deal five electronic cards. Typically you select the cards you want to hold, then draw again to complete a five-card hand. The 'payout' (or the amount you win) follows the same order of winning hands as at poker table games.

Quarter video-poker machines are common, though typical minimum bets vary from a nickel to $5. Before your hand is dealt you must have decided whether to bet the minimum (one coin) or the maximum (usually five coins). There is no real statistical advantage in betting two, three or four coins instead of just one so, unless you're prepared to wager the maximum every time, you should probably stick to playing just one coin per hand.

Gambling Terms

All in To bet everything you've got.

Ante A starting wager required to play table games.

Comps Freebies (eg buffet passes, show tickets, hotel rooms) given to players.

Cooler An unlucky gambler who makes everyone else lose.

Double down In blackjack, to double your bet after getting your first two cards.

Eye in the sky High-tech casino surveillance systems.

Fold To throw in your cards and stop betting.

High roller A gambler who bets big (aka 'whale').

Let it ride To roll over a winning wager into the next bet.

Low roller A small-time gambler (eg who likes penny slot machines).

Marker Credit-line debt owed to a casino.

One-armed bandit Old-fashioned nickname for a slot machine.

Pit boss A card dealer's supervisor on the casino floor.

Sucker bet A gamble on nearly impossible odds.

Toke A tip or gratuity.

Craps

A lively, fast-paced craps table has players shouting, crowds gathering around a sexy woman 'shooter' and everyone hoping for a 'hot' streak of the dice. The odds are exactly the same on every roll but that doesn't seem to stop people from betting on their 'hunches' and believing that certain numbers are 'due.'

Because the betting possibilities are complicated, and shift as play continues, it's important to spend some time studying a betting guide or take a free craps lesson at a casino that offers them (usually on weekday mornings). It's safer to begin playing with the simplest wager (on the pass/don't pass line) which, as it happens, is also one of the better bets in the casino.

Sports & Activities

Red Rock Canyon (p220)

HERMANN ERBER/GETTY IMAGES

Bodily indulgences abound in Las Vegas – but most are not of the healthy, life-affirming variety. If your idea of getting physical doesn't involve tattoos, lap dances or body shots, you can swing a golf club, pump iron or unwind in one of Sin City's sybaritic spas, then go hiking, rock climbing, mountain biking or kayaking just outside the city limits.

Golf & Tennis

Golf is in full swing from fall through spring, depending on temperatures (summers are just too darn hot). Morning tee times are cooler year-round but 'twilight' green fees are cheapest, and more so if you tee off during the sweltering midday heat. Tee-time reservations should preferably be made several weeks in advance. For discounts and last-minute availability, book through **Las Vegas Preferred Tee Times** (☎877-255-7277; www.lvptt.com).

There are dozens of golf courses in the Las Vegas Valley, most within 10 miles of the Strip. Favorites include Bali Hai, south of Mandalay Bay; Jack Nicklaus' Bear's Best; the Pete Dye–designed championship courses at Las Vegas Paiute Golf Resort, worth the long drive; Royal Links, mimicking famous holes from the British Open; PGA-tour-worthy TPC Las Vegas; and Badlands' challenging trio of nine-hole xeriscaped desert courses. Ask your hotel's concierge desk for more recommendations or for help with last-minute tee times. If you happen to be staying at the Wynn, you have access (for a fee) to Wynn Country Club, the only golf course on (or, technically, adjacent to) the Strip. Stay at any MGM Resorts International property and you'll get to play (again, for a fee, but this time including a comped limo ride) at Shadow Creek, designed by Tom Fazio.

Rather swing a racket than a club? On the Strip, Bally's and Cosmopolitan casino resorts have tennis courts. So does LVH casino hotel, which is off-Strip but on the monorail line.

Spas

Most day spas at casino hotels and megaresorts offer massage therapy, exotic body treatments, facials, mani-pedis and waxing and tanning services. Some spas are reserved for hotel guests on weekends, while others are for guests only, period. If you're not a hotel guest and you can get in, day-use passes cost $20 to $45 but this fee is often waived with a treatment of $75 or more. Expect to pay at least $120 for a 50-minute massage and from $75 for a 'quickie' facial or body scrub. Tip spa staff 15% to 20% of the total bill if a service charge hasn't already been included. Fresh fruit, juice and healthy snacks are usually gratis.

Fitness Centers & Gyms

Many casino hotels have small workout rooms or even fully fledged fitness facilities; access is given to hotel and spa guests or for the cost of a day pass (usually $15 to $30). Call ahead because some fitness centers are only open to hotel guests, particularly on weekends. Some of the best fitness centers include those at Caesars Palace and Aria, although the Flamingo and MGM Grand are more affordable. Off the Strip, LVH casino hotel offers 'twilight' and multiday discounts for its no-nonsense workout facilities.

Upscale hotels aimed at business travelers may have free but very limited fitness facilities (eg a cardio room with treadmills and a stationary bike, plus a small swimming pool). Getting into off-Strip gyms often requires being a local or paying for a membership, but a few gyms will let out-of-town visitors pay for a day pass ($10 to $25). Proper attire and nonstreet shoes are always required.

Pole Dancing School

Exotic dancers are Las Vegas icons, so Sin City is the perfect place to work sexy pole dancing into your exercise routine. Mimicking strippers' moves can be an amazing athletic workout, no joke. Marketed as 'pole dancing for housewives,' exotic dance classes (for women only) are taught by local fitness studios and are designed to help nervous Nellies bring out their inner blonde bombshells.

The original experience, **Stripper 101** (Map p48; ☎866-932-1818, 702-260-7200; www.stripper101.com; 3663 Las Vegas Blvd S, Miracle Mile Shops, V Theater; tickets from $40; ☼schedules vary), happens in a cabaret setting complete with strobe lights, cocktails and feather boas. It's popular with bachelorettes, who walk away with a certificate guaranteeing they're a 'genuine Las Vegas stripper.' Don't worry, though: no nudity is allowed. Bring comfy workout clothes and shoes, plus a pair of high heels to practice in.

Swimming Pools

Casino hotel and resort pools are generally reserved for guests only, except during summer pool-party club events. Keep in mind that most hotel pools are made for lounging, not getting exercise. One exception is Bally's, which has an Olympic-size swimming pool that's 12ft deep at one end. Otherwise, some off-Strip gyms have lap pools and aquatic exercise areas.

Outdoor Adventures

For active travelers needing their dose of endorphins, there are plenty of options outside the city limits that can be undertaken on a day trip. Red Rock Canyon National Conservation Area offers rock climbing and hiking, and there's good mountain biking outside Boulder City. Paddlers keen to get on the water can head to Lake Mead, where boating, fishing and watersports opportunities abound, or try paddling the Black Canyon, downstream from Hoover Dam on the Colorado River. Southern Nevada is ranching country, so joining a guided horseback ride is easy.

Many tour operators that arrange day trips out of town also sell guided activity trips around the region. **Pink Jeep Tours** (☎888-900-4480, 702-895-6777; http://pinkjeeptours.com) runs an all-day tour to Red Rock Canyon that includes a horseback ride and picnic lunch. For something a little more adventurous, opt for **Scoot City Tours** (p221), in which you'll drive your own scooter-car through Red Rock Canyon on a half-day tour.

To rent mountain bikes and/or take a single-track tour, head to **All Mountain Cyclery** (p224) in Boulder City. Out in suburban Summerlin, **Las Vegas Cyclery** (p221) rents road and mountain bikes and offers guided tours of Red Rock, Mt Charleston and beyond. To kayak Lake Mead or the Colorado River, talk to **Desert Adventures** (p224).

Spectator Sports

Although Vegas doesn't have any professional sports franchises, it's still a city of die-hard sports fans. You can wager on just about anything at race and sports books inside casinos, and nearly every watering hole runs Monday Night Football specials.

World-class championship boxing draws fans from all over the globe, and weekend 'fight nights' are huge on the Strip. Check www.boxinginlasvegas.com for the latest news, ringside pics and fight schedules. Auto racing at the **Las Vegas Motor Speedway** (☎800-644-4444; www.lvms.com; 7000 Las Vegas Blvd N, off I-15 Fwy) is enormously popular, especially during **NASCAR Weekend** (www.nascar.com) in March. The premier rodeo event of the year is the **National Finals Rodeo** (www.nfrexperience.com), held every December at the University of Nevada, Las Vegas' (UNLV) Thomas & Mack Center.

The **UNLV Runnin' Rebels** (☎866-388-3267, 702-739-3267; www.unlvtickets.com) college football and basketball teams enjoy a patriotic local following. With a googly-eyed alien mascot, the minor-league **Las Vegas 51s** (☎702-386-7200; www.lv51.com; 850 Las Vegas Blvd N, Cashman Field; ☒113) baseball team, a AAA franchise of the MLB Toronto Blue Jays, plays home games from late April through August. Affiliated with the NHL Phoenix Coyotes, the minor-league **Las Vegas Wranglers** (Map p186; ☎702-284-7777; www.lasvegaswranglers.com; 1 S Main St, Plaza) ice hockey team plays downtown from October to April.

Survival
Guide

The Strip (p39)
SYLVAIN SONNET/GETTY IMAGES ©

Sleeping

Accommodation Types

Vegas hits the jackpot, with more than 150,000 guest rooms. Even if a bankroll isn't burning a hole in your pocket, a little luxury can be had more cheaply here than almost anywhere else in the world. On your first trip to Las Vegas, almost any casino hotel on the Strip will dazzle, but don't go by name recognition alone.

The central Strip is where most of the magnificent megaresorts are and where the hottest action is, and you'll pay for it. The south Strip is a comfy compromise: you'll get the full Vegas experience but for less dough. Cheaper casino hotels on the north Strip have the most disappointing rooms and location. Downtown is for local gamblers and penny-pinchers who've tired of the Strip scene. Outlying hotels offer some deals for those willing to make the trip.

Don't be surprised if many of the hotel room amenities you're used to are missing in Vegas. Most casino hotel rooms do not have coffeemakers, refrigerators or individual climate controls. This is intended to drive you out of your room and back into the casino. Families and travelers who need more amenities will be better off at nongaming and off-Strip hotels or motels.

Though Vegas does have a few grungy backpacker hostels, they're located in a sketchy area between the Strip and downtown.

Casino Hotels & Resorts

Even so-called 'standard' rooms at casino hotels may have over-the-top marble bathrooms and high-tech bells and whistles such as flat-screen TVs and iPod docks. Room service 24/7, a concierge and expedited check-out are par for the course.

Some casino resorts offer all-suites accommodation with more amenities, such as jetted tubs and walk-in showers, separate lounge and working areas, and occasionally a kitchenette or a step-out balcony.

Whether you stay at a casino hotel or resort, expect to pay more for high floors and/or views – try asking politely at the front desk for an upgrade when you check in, preferably with a $20 tip in hand.

Check out the Spend the Night boxes in each casino chapter of this book for a closer look at the accommodations on offer at the major casino resorts.

Non-Casino Hotels & Motels

You'll trade convenience for peace and quiet (and probably a cheaper room rate) by staying off the Strip and/or at a nongaming hotel. Often offer-

Need to Know

PRICES

The following price ranges refer to a double room in high season. Taxes and nightly resort fees, which vary, are not included.

- **$** less than $100
- **$$** $100–200
- **$$$** more than $200

RESERVATIONS

Whatever you do, don't arrive in town without a reservation.

SMOKING

Most hotels offer nonsmoking rooms but that doesn't mean they'll be entirely smoke-free. If that worries you, make reservations at hotels that are *entirely* nonsmoking.

CHECK-IN & -OUT

Check-in time at casino hotels is 3pm or 4pm. Check-out is 11am or, if you're lucky, noon.

BREAKFAST

Breakfast is not usually included, although round-the-clock room service is available at most casino hotels.

ing swimming pools and extra amenities, these properties are more family-friendly or business-oriented – and won't necessarily deliver the wild Vegas experience most visitors are looking for. The same goes for chain motels just off the Strip, which are a good bargain on weekends when casino-hotel rates double or triple, but they're also dull. Avoid seedy downtown motels too far off the Fremont Street Experience or along the tattered stretch of Las Vegas Blvd from Charleston Blvd south to Sahara Ave.

Costs

During holidays and major events, all of the desirable rooms (and even the undesirable ones) will be booked out months in advance. Unless you're on a junket yourself, avoid visiting the city during huge conventions. Colossal crowds during major events and holidays such as New Year's Eve can be annoying, not to mention costly, as hotels jack up their rates and rooms become scarce.

Deals

It can pay to phone the hotel directly to ask for a better deal. Always ask whether the hotel will be undergoing renovations during your visit and whether or not the swimming pool will be open. Finally, don't try to book a hotel room on weekends. Wait until Sunday night or Monday morning instead, and you'll often see rates drop across the board.

Rebooking

It often pays to check with your hotel a few days or a week ahead of your stay to see if the rates you were quoted when you booked your room have changed. If they've fallen, you can keep the difference – simply by asking that your quoted rate be changed.

The savings can be substantial: let's say that on July 1 you booked a room at the MGM Grand for the first week of August at a cost of $139 per night. On July 21 you check the MGM Grand's online booking engine and learn that a room during the first week of August is now going for $89. If you phone the hotel directly and ask the reservations agent to make the adjustment, you'll be saving $40 per night.

Useful Websites

Lonely Planet
(www.lonelyplanet.com/hotels) Book hotels and other accommodations.

Travelzoo
(www.travelzoo.com) For discount hotel deals.

Priceline
(www.priceline.com) Lets you bid or 'express' buy your hotel room for less.

Travelworm
(www.travelworm.com) Comprehensive hotel listings and promo offers.

Where to Stay

NEIGHBORHOOD	FOR	AGAINST
THE STRIP	You're in the middle of the action – casino hotels and resorts offer easy access to dining, shopping and entertainment.	Some hotels and resorts are huge and impersonal, plus you'll pay an arm and a leg in 'resort fees' and other hidden costs.
DOWNTOWN	Vintage Vegas charm, cheaper nightly rates, fewer crowds and more affordable dining and drinking options.	Distance from the heart of the Strip action. Some areas off Fremont St aren't very safe after dark.
EAST OF THE STRIP	Proximity to the happening Hard Rock casino hotel, plus a vibrant local dining and nightlife scene.	Getting around isn't easy unless you have a car. It's not particularly convenient to return here late at night.
WEST OF THE STRIP	Close to the nightlife at the Palms casino resort, plus the pan-Asian eateries of Chinatown.	You will need a car unless you're patient with buses or willing to shell out extra cash for taxis.

Best Places to Stay

NAME		REVIEW
ENCORE $$$	The Strip	Newer than its sister resort Wynn, Encore offers similarly lavish yet even more spacious suites amid gorgeous surrounds.
PALAZZO $$$	The Strip	Enormous suites come with the Venetian's signature sunken living rooms and Roman tubs; Prestige Suites enjoy VIP check-in with complimentary champagne.
MANDARIN ORIENTAL $$$	The Strip	Business travelers and couples book the swanky Mandarin Oriental, with its staggering views and sumptuous design.
WYNN $$$	The Strip	It's luxury all the way: larger-than-life rooms and VIP Tower Suites, fabulous service, floor-to-ceiling windows and oversized Turkish towels.
VENETIAN $$	The Strip	Vegas' own 'Most Serene Republic' features huge suites with sunken living rooms and countless luxuries from deep soaking tubs to pillow menus.
COSMOPOLITAN $$$	The Strip	Frequented by style-conscious clientele, the arty, cool Cosmo wins the contest for the Strip's hippest hotel rooms.
MANDALAY BAY $$	The Strip	The upscale Mandalay Bay casino hotel, exclusive hotel Four Seasons and boutique Delano hotel offer variety at the Strip's southernmost resort.
BELLAGIO $$$	The Strip	Romantic and artistically designed, Bellagio is a lakeside monument to nouveau-riche opulence.
ARIA $$	The Strip	This sleek 4000-room casino hotel at CityCenter has no theme. Instead it's all about soothing design, spacious lodgings and deluxe amenities.
VDARA $$	The Strip	Cool sophistication, generously apportioned apartments and warm hospitality merge seamlessly at this nongaming, nonsmoking, all-suites hotel at CityCenter.
MGM GRAND $$	The Strip	Vegas' biggest hotel, with high-end Skylofts, apartment-style Signature suites and the Strip's most mammoth pool complex.
CAESARS PALACE $$	The Strip	Expect towers of oversized rooms with marble bathrooms, Nobu boutique hotel and the Garden of the Gods pool complex.
MIRAGE $$	The Strip	Remodeled rooms are delightfully contemporary, with bold color palettes, plush beds and geometrically patterned carpets.
TREASURE ISLAND $	The Strip	Breezily renovated rooms are comfortable enough, although on-site dining and amenities are only so-so. Good value for the location.

p171; Map p169; ☏877-321-9966, 702-770-7100; www.wynnlasvegas.com; 3131 Las Vegas Blvd S; weekday/weekend ste from $199/249; P✳@🛜≋

Moneyed nightclubbers

p161; Map p156; ☏866-263-3001, 702-607-7777; www.palazzo.com; 3325 Las Vegas Blvd S; weekday/weekend ste from $199/349; P✳@🛜≋

Honeymooners

p99; Map p97; ☏888-881-9578, 702-590-8888; www.mandarinoriental.com/lasvegas; 3752 Las Vegas Blvd S; r/ste from $225/435; P✳@🛜≋

Ornate Asian-style luxury

p171; Map p169; ☏877-321-9966, 702-770-7000; www.wynnlasvegas.com; 3131 Las Vegas Blvd S; weekday/weekend r from $189/249; P✳@🛜≋

Sophisticated splurge

p161; Map p156; ☏866-659-9643, 702-414-1000; www.venetian.com; 3355 Las Vegas Blvd S; weekday/weekend ste from $149/289; P✳@🛜≋👬

Sophisticated getaway

p99; Map p97; ☏855-435-0005, 702-698-7000; www.cosmopolitanlasvegas.com; 3708 Las Vegas Blvd S; r/ste from $160/220; P✳@🛜≋🐾

Trendy jetsetters (and dog owners)

p65; Map p63; ☏877-632-7800, 702-632-7777; www.mandalaybay.com; 3950 Las Vegas Blvd S; weekday/weekend r from $105/130; P✳@🛜≋👬

Faux-beach lovers

p125; Map p123; ☏888-987-6667, 702-693-7111; www.bellagio.com; 3600 Las Vegas Blvd S; weekday/weekend r from $169/239; P✳@🛜≋

European-style getaway

p99; Map p97; ☏866-359-7757, 702-590-7757; www.arialasvegas.com; 3730 Las Vegas Blvd S; r weekday/weekend from $129/189; P✳@🛜≋👬

Contempo look

p99; Map p97; ☏866-745-7767, 702-590-2111; www.vdara.com; 2600 W Harmon Ave; weekday/weekend ste from $119/179; P✳@🛜≋

Urban apartment living

p89; Map p87; ☏877-880-0880, 702-891-1111; www.mgmgrand.com; 3799 Las Vegas Blvd S; weekday/weekend r from $70/140; P✳@🛜≋👬

Poolside family fun

p135; Map p133; ☏866-227-5938, 702-731-7110; www.caesarspalace.com; 3570 Las Vegas Blvd S; weekday/weekend r from $90/125; P✳@🛜≋🐾

Original Vegas kitsch

p143; Map p141; ☏800-374-9000, 702-791-7111; www.mirage.com; 3400 Las Vegas Blvd S; weekday/weekend r from $95/130; P✳@🛜≋

Fantasy Vegas ambience

p151; Map p149; ☏800-944-7444, 702-894-7111; www.treasureisland.com; 3300 Las Vegas Blvd S; weekday/weekend r from $50/99; P✳@🛜≋

Lighthearted partiers

NAME		REVIEW
MONTE CARLO $$	The Strip	Literally the next best thing to CityCenter, this Euro-style hotel is more than just a poor man's Bellagio, and includes a lazy river ride.
PLANET HOLLYWOOD $	The Strip	Ultra-contemporary rooms contain black lacquer furnishings, club chairs and plush beds with leather headboards.
TROPICANA $$	The Strip	Keeping its tropical vibe going since the 1950s, the vintage Trop's multimillion-dollar renovation pays off with Miami-chic rooms painted in sunset hues.
NEW YORK–NEW YORK $	The Strip	A favorite of college students, these decent digs are rather tiny (just what one would expect in NYC).
PARIS LAS VEGAS $$	The Strip	Standard rooms are far from Parisian, but upgraded Red Luxury Rooms, some with lipstick-shaped sofas, evoke the Moulin Rouge.
FLAMINGO $	The Strip	Legendary gangster-era casino standing mid-Strip, next to the new LINQ complex. Waterslides and lagoons make it just barely family-friendly.
QUAD $$	The Strip	Unbeatable location next to the new LINQ complex with newly renovated but still reasonably priced rooms.
LUXOR $	The Strip	As long as you steer clear of the noisier Pyramid rooms, this less-expensive Strip resort is functional enough.
HARRAH'S $	The Strip	The Mardi Gras theme doesn't extend inside the average rooms at this always bustling casino hotel, next to the LINQ project.
BALLY'S $$	The Strip	Attracting an older crowd, this mid-Strip classic casino's reimagined Jubilee Tower rooms are popping with red.
JOCKEY CLUB $$	The Strip	Crammed between Bellagio and Cosmopolitan, this unpretentious hotel offers amazing value for its suites with kitchens.
STRATOSPHERE $	The Strip	The bland hotel rooms are not actually inside the tallest tower west of the Mississippi River but they're usually a bargain.
EXCALIBUR $	The Strip	A mock castle playing on its Arthurian theme, with throngs of stroller-pushing parents. Rooms are raggedy but the location is prime.
CIRCUS CIRCUS $	The Strip	It's a circus here, with rambunctious kiddos everywhere, well-worn high-rise tower accommodations, family-sized motel rooms and an RV park out back.
GOLDEN NUGGET $	Downtown	Pretend to relive the fabulous heyday of Vegas in the 1950s at this swank Fremont St address. Upgrade to a Rush Tower room.

PRACTICALITIES	BEST FOR
p47; Map p48; ☏ 800-311-8999, 702-730-7777; www.montecarlo. com; 3770 Las Vegas Blvd S; weekday/weekend r from $45/105; P ❄ @ 🛜 ♒	Quasi-elegance for less
p109; Map p107; ☏ 866-919-7472, 702-785-5555; www. planethollywoodresort.com; 3667 Las Vegas Blvd S; weekday/weekend r from $59/160; P ❄ @ 🛜 ♒ 🐾	Shopaholics and pop-culture fans
p47; Map p48; ☏ 800-462-8767, 702-739-2222; www.troplv.com; 3801 Las Vegas Blvd S; weekday/weekend r from $75/120; P ❄ @ 🛜 ♒	Old Vegas nostalgia
p81; Map p79; ☏ 866-815-4365, 702-740-6969; www. newyorknewyork.com; 3790 Las Vegas Blvd S; weekday/weekend r from $50/110; P ❄ @ 🛜 ♒	Fun-loving budget travelers
p117; Map p115; ☏ 877-796-2096, 702-946-7000; www.parislasvegas. com; 3655 Las Vegas Blvd S; weekday/weekend r from $60/135; P ❄ @ 🛜 ♒ 🐾	Francophiles
p56; Map p48; ☏ 702-733-3111, 800-732-2111; www. flamingolasvegas.com; 3555 Las Vegas Blvd S; weekday/weekend r from $30/85; P ❄ @ 🛜 ♒ 👫 🐾	History and a central location
p51; Map p48; ☏ 800-351-7400, 702-731-3311; www.thequadlv. com; 3535 Las Vegas Blvd S; weekday/weekend r from $80/160; P ❄ @ 🛜 ♒	Rock-bottom rates mid-Strip
p75; Map p73; ☏ 888-386-4658, 702-262-4000; www.luxor.com; 3900 Las Vegas Blvd S; weekday/weekend r from $45/85; P ❄ @ ♒ 👫	Money-saving Strip accommodations
p51; Map p48; ☏ 800-214-9110, 702-369-5000; www. harrahslasvegas.com; 3475 Las Vegas Blvd S; weekday/weekend r from $30/85; P ❄ @ 🛜 ♒	Fun-loving retiree gamblers
p50; Map p48; ☏ 877-603-4390, 702-967-4111; www.ballyslasvegas. com; 3645 Las Vegas Blvd S; weekday/weekend r from $75/170; P ❄ @ 🛜 ♒	Classic casino vibe
Map p48;48 ☏ 800-634-6649, 702-798-3500; www. jockeyclubvegas.com; 3700 Las Vegas Blvd S; ste from $100; P ❄ @ 🛜 ♒ 👫	DIY self-caterers
p58; Map p48; ☏ 800-998-6937, 702-380-7777; www. stratospherehotel.com; 2000 Las Vegas Blvd S; weekday/weekend r from $35/65; P ❄ @ 🛜 ♒ 👫	Unfussy business travelers
p47; Map p48; ☏ 800-879-1379, 702-597-777; www.excalibur.com; 3850 Las Vegas Blvd S; weekday/weekend r from $35/80; P ❄ @ ♒ 👫	Frugal families
p54; Map p48; ☏ 702-734-0410, 800-634-3450; www. circuscircus.com; 2880 Las Vegas Blvd S; weekday/weekend r $25/70; P ❄ @ 🛜 ♒ 👫	Energetic families and RVers
p190; Map p186; ☏ 800-634-3454, 702-385-7111; www.goldennugget. com; 129 E Fremont St; weekday/weekend r from $49/89; P ❄ @ 🛜 ♒	Classy downtown stay

NAME		REVIEW
DOWNTOWN GRAND $	Downtown	Colorful contemporary decor and pillowtop mattresses make this newbie a good bet, if you don't mind sleeping with earplugs.
MAIN STREET STATION $	Downtown	With tiled foyers, Victorian sconces and marble-trimmed hallways, the hotel has turn-of-the-century charm; bright, cheerful rooms have plantation shutters.
EL CORTEZ CABANA SUITES $	Downtown	Across the street from the 1940s casino, mod suites decked out in mint green hide fab retro tiled bathrooms with walk-in showers.
CALIFORNIA $	Downtown	Beloved by visitors from Hawaii, this exceptionally friendly hotel has tropical flair and basic rooms with plantation shutters and marble baths.
THE D $	Downtown	The D is just another Fremont St cheapie, albeit with spruced-up rooms (and a sky-high resort fee). Upgrades aren't worth paying for.
HARD ROCK $	East of the Strip	Sexy, oversized rooms and HRH suites at this shrine to rock 'n' roll pull in the SoCal party crowd. Free Strip shuttles for guests.
RUMOR $$	East of the Strip	Opposite the Hard Rock, a sultry, nightclub-cool atmosphere infuses mod suites, some with whirlpool tubs and white leather sofas.
PLATINUM HOTEL $$	East of the Strip	This nongaming and nonsmoking hotel near the Strip charms guests with a wellness spa and sanctuary-like suites with kitchens and whirlpool tubs.
RENAISSANCE LAS VEGAS $$	East of the Strip	Amenities at this nongaming business hotel include a 24-hour fitness club and minifridges and coffeemakers in each contemporary cookie-cutter room.
TUSCANY $	East of the Strip	Family-friendly Italianate casino hotel, tucked away from the hectic Strip, offering a curvy swimming pool and in-suite coffeemakers and minifridges.
M RESORT $$	East of the Strip	Elegant, earth-toned pads with marble baths beckon at this off-the-beaten-path casino resort offering free airport and Strip shuttles.
SOUTH POINT $	East of the Strip	Encompassing a cineplex, bowling alley and big rooms with comfy beds, this tidy casino hotel is flung south of the Strip, near an outlet mall.
CARRIAGE HOUSE $$	East of the Strip	A block east of the Strip, this timeshare complex rents small hotel rooms or double-sized suites with kitchenettes or full kitchens. With lit outdoor tennis courts.
LVH $	East of the Strip	Showing its age, the ex-Hilton offers rooftop tennis courts and some rooms with panoramic mountain views, minifridges and big bathtubs.

PRACTICALITIES	BEST FOR
p186; Map p186; ☎855-384-7263, 702-719-5100; www.downtowngrand.com; 206 N 3rd St; weekday/weekend r from $35/80; ⓟ❄@⬤⬤	Independent explorers
p185; Map p186; ☎702-387-1896, 800-713-8933; www.mainstreetcasino.com; 200 N Main St; weekday/weekend r from $35/70; ⓟ❄@⬤	Antiques buffs
p186; Map p186; ☎800-634-6703, 702-385-5200; http://elcortezhotelcasino.com; 651 E Ogden Ave; weekday/weekend r from $40/80; ⓟ❄@⬤	Quirky vintage weekend
Map p186; ☎800-634-6505, 702-385-1222; www.thecal.com; 12 E Ogden Ave; weekday/weekend r from $35/70; ⓟ❄@⬤⬤	Bargain-seeking islanders
Map p186; ☎800-274-5825, 702-388-2400; www.thed.com; 301 E Fremont St; weekday/weekend r from $25/59; ⓟ❄@⬤⬤	Insomniac low rollers
p204; Map p202; ☎800-473-7625, 702-693-5000; www.hardrockhotel.com; 4455 Paradise Rd; weekday/weekend r from $45/89; ⓟ❄@⬤⬤	Rock 'n' roll around the clock
Map p48; ☎877-997-8667, 702-369-5400; www.rumorvegas.com; 455 E Harmon Ave; weekday/weekend ste from $60/120; ⓟ❄@⬤⬤❂	Young bachelor/bachelorette parties
Map p202; ☎877-211-9211, 702-365-5000; www.theplatinumhotel.com; 211 E Flamingo Rd; weekday/weekend ste from $135/170; ⓟ❄@⬤⬤❂	Mellow off-Strip escapes
Map p202; ☎800-750-0980, 702-784-5700; www.renaissancelasvegas.com; 3400 Paradise Rd; r from $149; ⓟ❄@⬤⬤	Conventioneers
Map p202; ☎702-893-8933, 877-887-2261; www.tuscanylv.com; 255 E Flamingo Rd; weekday/weekend ste $39/89; ⓟ❄@⬤⬤⛶	Inexpensive family vacations
☎877-673-7678, 702-797-1000; www.themresort.com; 12300 Las Vegas Blvd S; r from $110; ⓟ❄@⬤⬤	Stylish off-Strip retreats
☎866-796-7111, 702-796-7111; www.southpointcasino.com; 9777 Las Vegas Blvd S; weekday/weekend r from $45/70; @⬤⬤⛶	Cowboys
Map p48; ☎800-221-2301, 702-798-1020; www.carriagehouselasvegas.com; 105 E Harmon Ave; ste $90-200; ⓟ❄@⬤⬤⛶	Laidback family reunions
Map p202; ☎702-732-5111, 888-732-7117; www.thelvh.com; 3000 Paradise Rd; weekday/weekend r from $25/50; ⓟ❄@⬤⬤⛶	Stepping back in time

NAME		REVIEW
WESTIN LAKE LAS VEGAS $$	East of the Strip	Although distant from the Strip, the lakeside setting of this low-key resort hotel may entice, especially if you have kids with boundless energy.
MOTEL 6 TROPICANA $	West of the Strip	Tiny rooms may be basic, but this all-American motel is within walking distance of the Strip. On weekends, you won't find cheaper rooms for miles.
TRUMP INTERNATIONAL HOTEL $$	West of the Strip	The Donald's nongaming and surprisingly affordable apartment-style high-rise hotel offers complimentary guest shuttles to the Forum Shops and Wynn casino resort.
PALMS & PALMS PLACE $	West of the Strip	Spacious rooms and outrageous party suites get easy access to the Palms' nightlife scene. Palms Place condos let you flaunt your VIP status.
RIO $	West of the Strip	Carnaval-themed all-suites hotel just off the Strip, which attracts families, poker players and bachelor/bachelorette parties. Free, frequent Strip shuttles and a rooftop zipline are bonuses.
ORLEANS $	West of the Strip	Tastefully appointed French-provincial rooms are good-value 'petite suites,' with fitness center access, on-site childcare, a movie theater and a bowling alley.
RED ROCK $$	West of the Strip	At this upscale casino hotel, forget about the faraway Strip and spend your time outdoors by the resort pool or at nearby Red Rock Canyon.
ELEMENT SUMMERLIN $$	West of the Strip	Ecominded, nonsmoking business hotel that's worth the drive for its modern suites with kitchens and complimentary full hot breakfasts.
GOLD COAST $	West of the Strip	Squeezed between the vibrant Palms and Rio casinos, this cheap crash-pad sports revamped rooms and free Strip shuttles, plus bowling.
ARTISAN HOTEL $	West of the Strip	Suites are themed around different artists' works at this weird Gothic baroque fantasy. Swingers and couples might appreciate the free in-room porn channel.

PRACTICALITIES	BEST FOR
☎866-716-8137, 702-567-6000; www.westinlakelasvegas.com; 101 Montelago Blvd, Henderson; r/ste from $130/170; P❄@🛜♨♿	Families with young kiddos
Map p48; ☎800-466-8356, 702-798-0728; www.motel6.com; 195 E Tropicana Ave; weekday/weekend r from $35/60; P❄@🛜♨♿	Cheapskates
Map p211; 211 ☎866-939-8786, 702-982-0000; www.trumphotelcollection.com/las-vegas; 2000 Fashion Show Dr; weekday/weekend ste from $99/159; P❄@🛜♨♿🐾	NYC–style glam
p215; Map p211; ☎702-942-7777, 866-942-7770; www.palms.com; 4321 W Flamingo Rd; weekday/weekend r from $59/99; P❄@🛜♨	Nightlife mavens
p216; Map p211; ☎866-746-7671, 702-252-7777; www.riolasvegas.com; 3700 W Flamingo Rd; weekday/weekend ste from $30/80; P❄@🛜♨♿🐾	Money-saving families and gruops
p210; Map p211; ☎702-365-7111, 800-675-3267; www.orleanscasino.com; 4500 W Tropicana Ave; weekday/weekend r from $45/95; P❄@🛜♨♿	Affordable family-sized accommodations
☎866-767-7773, 702-797-7777; www.redrock.sclv.com; 11011 W Charleston Blvd; weekday/weekend r from $95/140; P❄@🛜♨♿	Active families and outdoorsy folks
☎877-353-6368, 702-589-2000; www.starwoodhotels.com; 10555 Discovery Dr; ste incl breakfast from $100; P❄@🛜♨♿	On-the-go families and biusiness travelers
p210; Map p211; ☎888-402-6278, 702-367-7111; www.goldcoastcasino.com; 4000 W Flamingo Rd; weekday/weekend r from $30/75; P❄@🛜♨	Paying less near the Strip
off Map p186; ☎800-554-4092, 702-214-4000; www.artisanhotel.com; 1501 W Sahara Ave; weekend/weekday r from $35/90; P❄@🛜♨	After-hours partying and illicit affairs

Transport

Arriving in Las Vegas

Despite being in the middle of a desert, Las Vegas is a surprisingly easy city to reach. Most visitors arrive by driving or flying.

Las Vegas is a great road-trip destination, but in the desert, vehicles may overheat when outside temperatures top 90°F (32°C). If you're driving here on a hot day, watch your air-con usage to avoid overheating the engine. By car it's about a four-hour drive (265 miles) from Los Angeles, five hours (330 miles) from San Diego and 8½ hours (570 miles) from San Francisco. Expect long delays on weekends and holidays.

Landing in Las Vegas by plane is often easier, not to mention more scenic if you happen to have a window seat as you descend into the city past the neon-lit Strip. Vegas is served by McCarran International Airport, just a crapshoot from the south end of the Strip, and a couple of smaller general aviation facilities around the city.

Greyhound (☎ 800-231-2222; www.greyhound.com) runs long-distance buses to Las Vegas, including from LA ($9 to $68, five to eight hours, nine to 11 daily). Las Vegas' **Greyhound bus station** (☎ 702-384-9561; www.greyhound.com; 200 S Main St; ⊗ 24hr) is located just off Fremont St, a short walk from downtown casino hotels and the Deuce and SDX express bus lines south to the Strip.

Flights, cars and tours can be booked online at lonelyplanet.com.

McCarran International Airport

McCarran International Airport (LAS; www.mccarran.com; ☎ 702-261-5211; 5757 Wayne Newton Blvd) ranks among the USA's 10 busiest airports. Security lines are notoriously slow, but self-service check-in and luggage drop-off kiosks at the airport and off-airport locations, including the airport's rental-car center, the city's convention center and some Strip casino hotels, can ease headaches. For arriving passengers, the airport has advance check-in kiosks for a few Strip casino hotels, but skip them if lines are long.

Many domestic flights use Terminal 1 (A, B, C and satellite concourse D gates); international, charter and some domestic flights use Terminal 3 (E gates and satellite concourse D gates). A free, wheelchair-accessible tram links outlying gates, while free shuttle buses link Terminals 1 and 3. McCarran also offers free

wi-fi and gadget-recharging workstations; ATMs, a currency exchange booth and full-service bank; first-aid and police stations; a pharmacy and walk-in medical clinic for nonemergencies; a lost-and-found office; a post office; and tourist information desks.

The easiest and cheapest way to get to your hotel is by airport shuttle (one-way to Strip/downtown hotels from $7/9). As you exit baggage claim, look for shuttle bus kiosks lining the curb; prices and destinations are clearly marked. Taxis are another option – expect to pay at least $20 to the Strip, $25 to downtown, plus tip. If you're renting a car from the airport, catch a shuttle bus outside baggage claim to the McCarran Rent-a-Car Center.

Driving into Las Vegas

The main roads into and out of Las Vegas are the I-15 Fwy and US Hwy 95. US Hwy 93 connects downtown with Hoover Dam. I-215 goes by McCarran International Airport. Freeway traffic often crawls along, particularly during morning and afternoon rush hours and on weekend nights, especially near the Strip (Las Vegas Blvd).

When traffic is snarled on I-15 and Las Vegas Blvd, stick to surface routes, such as Paradise Rd, east of the Strip; Frank Sinatra Dr and Industrial Rd, west of the Strip; and the Desert Inn Rd superarterial, which flies east–west across the Strip and I-15. Tune into KXNT (100.5FM/840AM) for traffic and weather updates.

Getting Around Las Vegas

High rollers cruise the Strip in cherry-red convertibles and stretch limos, while low rollers plod along on foot or board public buses, the modern monorail and free trams (avoid those slow-moving trolleys). Gridlock along the Strip and the freeways around Las Vegas makes driving yourself a chore, although free self-parking and valet services are available almost everywhere. Taxis are plentiful too.

For pedestrians, the Strip has elevated skybridges across busy intersections. Remember that the Strip is more than 4 miles long – don't assume you can walk easily between casino hotels, even those that appear to be close together on the map. Don't jaywalk: more people are injured while crossing the street than in auto accidents.

Bus

Regional Transportation Commission of Southern Nevada (RTC; 800-228-3911, 702-228-7433; www.rtcsnv.com/transit; Deuce & SDX 2/24/72hr bus pass $6/8/20) buses operate from 5am to 2am daily, with popular Strip and downtown routes running 24/7 every 15 to 20 minutes. Double-decker Deuce buses to/from downtown stop every block or two along the Strip. Quicker SDX express buses stop outside some Strip casino hotels and at the Fashion Show, the city's convention center and a few off-Strip shopping malls. Have exact change or bills ready when boarding or buy a pass before boarding from ticket vending machines at bus stops.

Many off-Strip casino hotels offer limited shuttle buses to/from the Strip, usually reserved for hotel guests (sometimes free, but a surcharge may apply).

Car & Motorcycle

The only document that international short-term visitors legally need to rent or drive a car or motorcycle is a license from their home country. You may be required to show an international driving permit (IDP) if your license isn't written in English.

Driving on the Strip can be stressful. Other things to bear in mind while driving in Las Vegas:

● Drive on the right-hand side of the road.

● Obey posted speed limits, typically 25mph to 45mph around town, 55mph to 70mph on freeways.

● Buckle up: seat belts are mandatory for all passengers.

● Helmets are required for motorcyclists.

● Unless otherwise posted, U-turns are legal at intersections and right-hand turns at red lights are allowed after making a full stop.

● Pedestrians legally have the right of way at all times.

● Drivers must stop for pedestrians at crosswalks.

● Beware jaywalkers – many people are hit while crossing the street.

● If you are involved in an accident, dial 911 for emergency police, fire and ambulance assistance.

● The blood-alcohol limit over which you are considered legally drunk is 0.08%.

If you're not sober enough to drive, call **Designated Drivers** (702-456-7433; http://vegas.designateddrivers-inc.com; 24hr) to pick you up and drive your car back to your hotel; fees vary by mileage.

Climate Change & Travel

Every form of transportation that relies on carbon-based fuel generates CO_2, the main cause of human-induced climate change. Modern travel is dependent on airplanes, which might use less fuel per mile per person than most cars but travel much greater distances. The altitude at which aircraft emit gases (including CO_2) and particles also contributes to their climate change impact. Many websites offer 'carbon calculators' that allow people to estimate the carbon emissions generated by their journey and, for those who wish to do so, to offset the impact of the greenhouse gases emitted with contributions to portfolios of climate-friendly initiatives throughout the world. Lonely Planet offsets the carbon footprint of all staff and author travel.

Car Rental

Booking online through a car-rental agency or a discount travel website normally nets you the best rates. Economy car-rental rates start at $25/145 per day/week, though you might find a much cheaper deal by surfing the web ahead of time. Expect to pay extra for insurance (usually optional), taxes of over 10% and government surcharges of 10%. A facility charge (almost $4 per day) and 10% airport fee often apply as well.

Most companies require a major credit card, and some require that the driver be at least 25 years old. Car seats, which are legally required for infants and children six years and under who weigh less than 60lb, cost extra (from $10 per day); you'll need to reserve them in advance. Book cars at least two weeks in advance, especially for weekend rentals.

Agencies at McCarran Airport's Rent-a-Car Center include Advantage, Alamo, Avis, Budget, Dollar, Enterprise, E-Z, Hertz, National, Payless and Thrifty. Airport pick-ups are usually cheaper than having a rental car delivered to your hotel.

Advantage (🖉 800-777-5500; www.advantage.com)

Alamo (🖉 877-222-9075; www.alamo.com)

Avis (🖉 800-633-3469; www.avis.com)

Budget (🖉 888-922-0490; www.budgetvegas.com)

Dollar (🖉 800-800-4000; www.dollar.com)

Enterprise (🖉 800-261-7331; www.enterprise.com)

E-Z (🖉 800-277-5171; www.e-zrentacar.com)

Fox (🖉 800-225-4369; www.foxrentacar.com) Off-site location requires taking a second shuttle from McCarran Airport's Rent-a-Car Center.

Hertz (🖉 800-654-3131; www.hertz.com)

Las Vegas Exotic Car Rentals (🖉 866-871-1893, 702-736-2592; www.exoticcarrentalslasvegas.com) Book ahead – and be prepared to pay big bucks – for a glamorous sportscar.

Las Vegas Harley-Davidson (🖉 877-571-7174, 702-431-8500; www.lasvegasharleydavidson.com; 2605 S Eastern Ave; ⏲ 8am-7pm Mon-Fri, to 6pm Sat, 10am-5pm Sun) Rent Harley motorcycles from $100 to $225 per day, including helmets, rainsuits and limited mileage.

Payless (🖉 800-729-5377; www.paylesscar.com)

Thrifty (🖉 800-847-4389; www.thrifty.com)

Parking

There's free self-parking at Strip casino hotels and shopping malls. For valet parking, there's usually no charge either, but tip the attendant at least $2 when your keys are returned. Some downtown casino hotels offer free garage parking, although the maximum stay for non-guests is typically three to four hours. Before exiting the garage, nonguests usually need to validate their parking ticket at the cashiers' cage inside the casino (no purchase or gambling required).

Monorail

The **Las Vegas Monorail** (🖉 702-699-8299; www.lvmonorail.com; single-ride $5, 24/48/72hr pass $12/22/28; ⏲ 7am-midnight Mon, to 2am Tue-Thu, to 3am Fri-Sun) links some Strip casino resorts, zipping between the MGM Grand, Bally's/Paris, the Flamingo, Harrah's/Quad, the city's convention center, LVH and the former Sahara (now SLS). Although service is frequent (departing every four to 12 minutes), stations are only on the east side of the Strip, a long walk from Las Vegas Blvd at the far back of casino-hotel properties. On the plus side, air-conditioned trains are stroller- and wheelchair-friendly, and it takes just 13 minutes to travel the entire route.

Shuttle

Many off-Strip casino hotels offer limited free shuttle buses to and from the Strip, although some are reserved for hotel guests. Conveniently, free public shuttles connect the Rio with a couple of its sister casino-hotel properties on the Strip – Harrah's and Bally's/Paris Las Vegas – usually every 30 minutes from 10am until 1am daily.

Taxi & Limousine

It's illegal to hail a cab on the street. Instead taxi stands are found at almost every casino hotel and shopping mall. By law, the maximum number of passengers is five. All companies must have at least one wheelchair-accessible van, but you'll usually have to call ahead and then wait.

Vegas is surprisingly compact, so taxis can be reasonable on a per-trip basis. A lift from one end of the Strip to the other, or from mid-Strip to downtown, costs at least $20, depending on traffic. Tip the driver 10% to 15%, rounded up to the nearest dollar. Not all taxis accept credit cards (cash only) so ask when getting in.

For special occasions or stepping out in style, some parties will hire a limousine. Popular companies include **Presidential Limo** (📞 800-423-1320, 702-438-5466; www.presidentiallimolv. com). Hourly rates start at around $50 for a town car, and are up to $130 for a 14-passenger Super Stretch Hummer H2 Limo with a complimentary champagne bar.

Tram

Free air-conditioned trams that anyone can ride shuttle between some Strip casino hotels. One connects the Bellagio, CityCenter and the Monte Carlo. Another links Treasure Island and the Mirage. A third zips between Excalibur, Luxor and Mandalay Bay. Trams run all day and into the evening, usually stopping from late-night until the early-morning hours.

A-Z
Directory

Discounts

If you're willing to do your homework, there are plenty of ways to save cash in Vegas by planning ahead. Check **Smarter Vegas** (www.smartervegas.com) for promotional discount codes for sights, tours, shows and hotels.

A multiday **Las Vegas Power Pass** (📞 800-490-9330; www.visitticket.com; 1-/2-/3-/5-day pass per adult $85/110/135/195, per child 12yr & under $55/75/95/135) may be worthwhile only if you plan to visit *a lot* of big-ticket attractions and museums; it even lets you skip the lines at some of them. Don't bother buying MealTicket dining passes.

Electricity

120V/60Hz

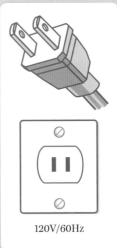

120V/60Hz

Emergency

Police, Fire, Ambulance (📞 911) For emergencies 24/7.

Police (☎ 311) For non-emergencies.

Rape Crisis Center (☎ 702-366-1640; www.rcclv.org) Free hotline counseling 24/7.

Internet Access

Most hotel business centers charge an arm and a leg for 24/7 internet access. High-speed wired/wireless internet access in hotel rooms typically costs $12 to $15 per 24 hours. You'll find free wi-fi at only a few casino hotels, restaurants and bars. Cheap internet cafes hide inside souvenir shops on the Strip and along Maryland Pkwy opposite the University of Nevada, Las Vegas (UNLV) campus.

Legal Matters

The legal drinking age of 21 is strictly enforced; always carry photo ID.

It is legal to purchase alcohol anytime, day or night.

It is legal to drink from an open container of alcohol on the street or while riding as a passenger in a taxi or limo.

Alcoholic beverages are not permitted on the monorail or public buses.

It's against the law to drink while driving or riding as the passenger of a private vehicle (eg car, motorcycle, RV).

The blood-alcohol limit over which you are considered legally drunk is 0.08%.

There is zero tolerance for any kind of illegal drug use. If police find any illegal substance on you, you'll be arrested and taken to jail.

Prostitution and brothels are legal in some of Nevada's rural counties, but not inside the Las Vegas city limits.

Smoking Laws in Las Vegas

Many tourists complain about the city's pervasive cigarette smoke. 'Smoke-free' and 'Las Vegas' are rarely mentioned in the same sentence: there are ashtrays at almost every telephone, elevator, swimming pool – even in toilets and taxis. A limited ban on smoking inside public buildings, including restaurants, shops and movie theaters, went into effect in 2006, but exceptions still permit smoking inside casinos, as well as at bars and clubs that don't serve prepared food. Most casino hotels claim to offer nonsmoking rooms but don't expect the air to be free of a whiff (or much more) of cancer sticks.

Medical Services

For minor ailments and injuries, it's usually less expensive to go to a walk-in clinic than to a hospital emergency room (ER).

Harmon Medical Center (☎ 702-796-1116; www.harmonmedicalcenter.com; 150 E Harmon Ave; ⏰ 8am-8pm Mon-Fri) Discounts for uninsured patients; limited translation services available.

Planned Parenthood (☎ 702-547-9888; www.plannedparenthood.org; 3300 E Flamingo Rd) Emergency contraception and HIV, STD and pregnancy-testing services.

Sunrise Hospital & Medical Center (☎ 702-731-8000; http://sunrisehospital.com; 3186 S Maryland Pkwy; ⏰ 24hr) Specialized children's trauma services available at a 24-hour emergency room.

University Medical Center (UMC; ☎ 702-383-2000; www.umcsn.com; 1800 W Charleston Blvd; ⏰ 24hr) Southern Nevada's most advanced trauma center has a 24-hour ER.

Walgreens (www.walgreens.com) The Strip (☎ 702-739-9645; 3765 Las Vegas Blvd S; ⏰ store 24hr, pharmacy 8am-10pm, clinic 9am-5:30pm Mon-Fri, 9:30am-5pm Sat & Sun); Downtown (☎ 702-385-1284; 495 E Fremont St; ⏰ store 24hr, pharmacy 9am-5pm) And multiple locations on the Strip.

Money

ATMs

Every casino, bank and shopping mall and most convenience stores have ATMs. Fees imposed by ATMs inside casinos (typically $4 to $5 per transaction) are much higher than at banks (usually around $3 per transaction).

Cash

Cold hard cash greases Sin City's wheels. You'll want to have bills of various sizes on hand, partly so you're ready to tip when necessary. Casinos have self-serve bill-breaking machines in their gaming areas.

Changing Money

Casinos charge ridiculous rates for currency exchange. Try **Travelex** (702-369-2219; www.travelex.com; 3200 Las Vegas Blvd S, Fashion Show; 10am-9pm Mon-Sat, 11am-7pm Sun) kiosks at the Fashion Show mall and inside McCarran International Airport to change your money at more competitive rates.

Credit Cards

Credit cards are widely accepted. All casinos will advance cash against plastic but fees are exorbitant – don't do it. To avoid surcharges, use your debit card to get cash back (usually maximum $40 on the Strip) when making purchases at noncasino businesses such as convenience stores and pharmacies.

Tipping

Keep small bills on hand. If you receive remarkably lousy service, you can leave a poor tip or, in exceptionally bad cases, none at all (but this is rare). Here's a thumbnail guide to tipping in Las Vegas:

Airport skycaps $2 per bag, $5 minimum per cart

Bartenders 15% per round, or at least $1 per drink

Bellhops and hotel porters $2 per bag, $5 minimum per cart

Cocktail waiters $1 per drink while gambling in a casino

Concierges Nothing for info, up to $10 for securing tickets to a sold-out show

Hotel maids $2 to $4 per night, left every day with the card or envelope provided

Limo drivers $5 per person, or 15% of the total fare, whichever is higher

Restaurants 18% to 20%; don't tip if a service charge (usually for groups of six or more) is already included on the bill

Room service 15%, minus any gratuity automatically charged on the bill

Taxis 10% to 15% of the metered fare, then round the total up to the next dollar

Valet parking attendants $2 to $5 per car, paid when the keys are handed back to you

Opening Hours

Open 24/7/365 is the rule at casino hotels.

Normal business hours are 9am to 5pm on weekdays. Some banks and post offices stay open later and on Saturday mornings. Retail shopping hours are 10am to 9pm (to 6pm Sunday); casino shops stay open until 11pm or later. Christmas is one of the few holidays on which most noncasino businesses close.

Public Holidays

Note that the only holiday that shops always close for is Christmas.

New Year's Day January 1

Martin Luther King Jr Day Third Monday in January

Presidents' Day Third Monday in February

Good Friday Friday before Easter in March/April

Memorial Day Last Monday in May

Independence Day July 4

Labor Day First Monday in September

Columbus Day Second Monday in October

Veterans Day November 11

Thanksgiving Day Fourth Thursday in November

Christmas Day December 25

Practicalities

○ **DVDs** Coded for regionDV 1 (USA and Canada) only

○ **Newspapers & Magazines** *Las Vegas Review Journal* (www.reviewjournal.com), *Las Vegas Weekly* (www.lasvegasweekly.com), *Las Vegas Life* (www.lvlife.com)

○ **Radio** National Public Radio (NPR), lower end of FM dial

○ **TV** PBS (public broadcasting); cable: CNN (news), ESPN (sports), HBO (movies), Weather Channel

○ **Weights & Measures** Imperial (except 1 US gallon = 0.83 imperial gallons)

Safe Travel

On the Strip and the Fremont Street Experience, police and private security officers are out in force, and surveillance cameras ('eyes in the sky') are omnipresent. Utilize in-room hotel safes and never leave valuables unattended, especially while gambling. Beware of pickpockets in crowds (eg on public transportation). If you wander downtown away from Fremont St, keep your wits about you, day and night. Likewise, the area between downtown and the Stratosphere can be sketchy.

Telephone

Cell Phones

You'll need a multiband GSM phone to make calls in the USA. Popping in a US prepaid rechargeable SIM card, which gives you a local phone number and voicemail, is usually cheaper than using your home network, on which international roaming charges may add up quickly.

On the Strip, some hotel business centers rent cell phones to guests. Using cell phones near casino race and sports books is illegal.

Phone Codes

Telephone area codes for Clark County, including Las Vegas, are 📞702 and 725; for the rest of Nevada, it's 📞775. When dialing a number outside the local area code, dial 1 first. International rates apply for calls to Canada, although the dialing code (1) is the same as for domestic long-distance calls. For other international direct-dial calls, dial 📞011 followed by the country code.

Phonecards

Sold at convenience stores and pharmacies, prepaid phonecards typically provide better rates than direct dialing from public payphones or hotel in-room phones. Beware of phonecards that advertise the cheapest per-minute rates; they may charge hefty connection fees for each call, especially for using the toll-free access number (at payphones, deposit 50¢ and dial the local access number instead). Avoid the hassle of bad connections by choosing a more expensive phonecard from a major long-distance carrier, such as AT&T.

Time

Nevada uses Pacific Standard Time (PST), the same as California. The Pacific time zone is one hour behind Mountain Standard Time (MST), used by the neighboring states of Arizona and Utah, and eight hours behind GMT/UTC.

Daylight Saving Time (DST), when the clocks move forward one hour, runs from the second Sunday in March to the first Sunday in November. Arizona (except for the Navajo Nation) does not observe DST.

Tourist Information

Many tour operators push unofficial 'visitor information' but there's only one official city tourism agency: the **Las Vegas Convention & Visitors Authority** (📞702-892-7575, 877-847-4858; www.lasvegas.com; 3150 Paradise Rd; ⊗8am-5:30pm Mon-Fri). The hotline provides up-to-date information about shows, attractions, activities and more, and staff may be able to help with finding last-minute accommodations.

●●●●
Travelers with Disabilities

Vegas has the most ADA-accessible guestrooms in the USA. Almost all attractions listed in this guide are wheelchair-accessible. Wheelchair seating is widely available and assisted listening devices are offered at most showrooms. Most public transportation and several hotel pools are lift-equipped. By law, all taxi companies must have a wheelchair-accessible van. If you're driving, bring your disabled-parking placard from home.

Guide dogs may be brought into restaurants, hotels and businesses. Some payphones are equipped for the hearing-impaired. Most banks offer ATMs with instructions in Braille and earphone jacks.

●●●●
Visas

Warning! All of the following information is highly subject to change. Double-check visa *and* passport requirements before coming to the USA at http://travel.state.gov (citizens of Canada and Mexico can consult www.getyouhome.gov). Temporary visitors from Canada do not normally need a visa for stays of up to 181 days, but they must bring their Canadian passport.

Visas aren't required for citizens of the 37 Visa Waiver Program (VWP) countries, who may enter the USA for up to 90 days visa-free. However, citizens of these countries must still apply for travel authorization online (see https://esta.cbp.dhs.gov) at least 72 hours before traveling; once approved, this registration ($14) is usually valid for two years or until their passport expires, whichever comes first. Their passport must meet current US standards and they must be in possession of a round-trip ticket covering onward travel to another country.

All other foreign citizens must wrangle a non-immigrant visa in advance from a US embassy or consulate. Best done in your home country, the process involves a nonrefundable fee (minimum $160), a personal interview and can take several weeks, so apply early.

Behind the Scenes

Acknowledgments

Climate map data adapted from Peel MC, Finlayson BL & McMahon TA (2007) 'Updated World Map of the Köppen-Geiger Climate Classification', Hydrology and Earth System Sciences, 11, 1633¬44.

Deuce on the Strip and SDX Map courtesy of Regional Transportation Commission of Southern Nevada © 2014. Las Vegas Monorail Map courtesy of Las Vegas Monorail © 2014.

Cover photographs: Front: Fountains of Bellagio, Maurizio Rellini/4Corners ©; Back: Vegas Vicky (aka Sassy Sally), the neon cowgirl, Jon Hicks/Corbis ©

This Book

This 2nd edition of Lonely Planet's *Discover Las Vegas* guidebook was researched and written by Sara Benson. The previous edition was written by Bridget Gleeson. This guidebook was commissioned in Lonely Planet's US office, and produced by the following:

Commissioning Editor Suki Gear

Coordinating Editor Kirsten Rawlings

Product Editor Amanda Williamson

Senior Cartographer Alison Lyall

Book Designer Mazzy Prinsep

Senior Editors Karyn Noble

Assisting Editors Kate Evans, Kate Mathews, Katie O'Connell

Assisting Cartographer Julie Sheridan

Assisting Book Designer Jessica Rose

Cover Researcher Naomi Parker

Thanks to Ryan Evans, Larissa Frost, Jouve India, Wayne Murphy, Amine Qourzal

SEND US YOUR FEEDBACK

Things change – prices go up, schedules change, good places go bad and bad places go bankrupt. So if you find things better or worse, recently opened or long since closed, or you just want to tell us what you loved or loathed about this book, please get in touch and help make the next edition even more accurate and useful. We love to hear from travelers – your comments keep us on our toes and our well-traveled team reads every word. Although we can't reply individually to postal submissions, we always guarantee that your feedback goes straight to the appropriate authors, in time for the next edition. Each person who sends us information is thanked in the next edition – the most useful submissions are rewarded with a selection of digital PDF chapters.

Visit lonelyplanet.com/contact to submit your updates and suggestions or to ask for help. Our award-winning website also features inspirational travel stories, news and discussions.

Note: We may edit, reproduce and incorporate your comments in Lonely Planet products such as guidebooks, websites and digital products, so let us know if you don't want your comments reproduced or your name acknowledged. For a copy of our privacy policy visit lonelyplanet.com/privacy.

Index

See also separate subindexes for:

🍷 Drinking & Nightlife p283

🍴 Eating p284

⭐ Entertainment p285

🔒 Shopping p286

🏃 Spas & Activities p286

279

Sights 000
Map pages 000

⭐ Entertainment

🔒 Shopping

🧭 Spas & Activities

Sights 000
Map pages 000